THE COMPLETE IDIOT'S GUIDE® TO

Islam

D1089270

ALPHA

A member of Penguin Group (USA) Inc.

Dedicated to my son for the joy of faith he brings to my heart.

ALPHA BOOKS

Published by the Penguin Group

Penguin Group (USA) Inc., 375 Hudson Street, New York, New York 10014, USA

Penguin Group (Canada), 90 Eglinton Avenue East, Suite 700, Toronto, Ontario M4P 2Y3, Canada (a division of Pearson Penguin Canada Inc.)

Penguin Books Ltd., 80 Strand, London WC2R 0RL, England

Penguin Ireland, 25 St. Stephen's Green, Dublin 2, Ireland (a division of Penguin Books Ltd.)

Penguin Group (Australia), 250 Camberwell Road, Camberwell, Victoria 3124, Australia (a division of Pearson Australia Group Pty. Ltd.)

Penguin Books India Pvt. Ltd., 11 Community Centre, Panchsheel Park, New Delhi—110 017, India

Penguin Group (NZ), 67 Apollo Drive, Rosedale, North Shore, Auckland 1311, New Zealand (a division of Pearson New Zealand Ltd.)

Penguin Books (South Africa) (Pty.) Ltd., 24 Sturdee Avenue, Rosebank, Johannesburg 2196, South Africa

Penguin Books Ltd., Registered Offices: 80 Strand, London WC2R 0RL, England

Copyright © 2011 by Yahiya Emerick

International Standard Book Number: 978-1-61564-129-1
Library of Congress Catalog Card Number: 2011905825

13   12   11   8   7   6   5   4   3   2   1

Interpretation of the printing code: The rightmost number of the first series of numbers is the year of the book's printing; the rightmost number of the second series of numbers is the number of the book's printing. For example, a printing code of 11-1 shows that the first printing occurred in 2011.

Printed in the United States of America

Note: This publication contains the opinions and ideas of its author. It is intended to provide helpful and informative material on the subject matter covered. It is sold with the understanding that the author and publisher are not engaged in rendering professional services in the book. If the reader requires personal assistance or advice, a competent professional should be consulted.

The author and publisher specifically disclaim any responsibility for any liability, loss, or risk, personal or otherwise, which is incurred as a consequence, directly or indirectly, of the use and application of any of the contents of this book.

Most Alpha books are available at special quantity discounts for bulk purchases for sales promotions, premiums, fund-raising, or educational use. Special books, or book excerpts, can also be created to fit specific needs.

For details, write: Special Markets, Alpha Books, 375 Hudson Street, New York, NY 10014.

Publisher: *Marie Butler-Knight*

Associate Publisher: *Mike Sanders*

Executive Managing Editor: *Billy Fields*

Executive Editor: *Lori Cates Hand*

Development Editor: *Megan Douglass*

Senior Production Editor: *Janette Lynn*

Copy Editor: *Cate Schwenk*

Cover Designer: *Kurt Owens*

Book Designer: *William Thomas, Rebecca Batchelor*

Indexer: *Heather McNeill*

Layout: *Ayanna Lacey*

Proofreader: *John Etchison*

Contents

Introduction

Imagine learning that there are over a billion people in the world, one sixth of humanity, who follow a religion that you never really studied in school. This little-known religion is called *Islam*. Perhaps you've heard the name before or developed some opinions about it based on what you've seen in the news. However, if you're like most people, you might not know a great deal about Islam. Well, you've taken the first step toward understanding more about this mysterious way of life, and you may come to find yourself pleasantly surprised to learn what it really teaches.

Islam shares many of the characteristics that are familiar to followers of Judaism and Christianity. In fact, Islam considers itself a related ideology that fits into a tight chronology with these two other religions. As the population of Muslims rises in many Western countries, and as the West continues its interaction with the traditional Muslim world, for good or ill, the challenges and need for tolerance and an accurate understanding of each other's faith and values has given rise to a curiously refreshing debate on both sides about the nature and place of the other in our increasingly interconnected world. In this spirit of dialogue and discovery (and even highly spirited debate), it is no wonder that some people have begun to speak of a Judeo-Christian-Islamic heritage for the West.

Islam is the fastest-growing religion in the West. If current trends continue, in a few years there will be more Muslims in America, for example, than Jews or Protestants! Mosques now dot the skyline views of many American cities, and the changing face of America's schools has its share of children wearing head scarves and round caps called Kufis. All of this serves to highlight the need for people to understand their Muslim neighbors and their religious and cultural traditions.

Islam is a way of life and a philosophy of living that millions of people consult in their daily affairs. It has its own answers to such questions as why are we here, who is God, what kind of life should a person lead, and what happens to us after we die? It also has its own program for improving one's heart, mind, and spiritual strength. Through a daily regimen of prayer, supplication, good works, and a strong commitment to faith, Muslims, or followers of Islam, try their best to live in harmony with their fellow men and women and even with their environment.

Napoleon Bonaparte once wrote that if people followed the way of Islam, there would be true harmony and brotherhood in the world at long last. Bernard Shaw also echoed the same sentiment in his writings, though he went a step further stating, *"One day the West will accept Islam."* On the flip side there are those who view Islam as a potential rival for Western dominance and present Muslims in a negative light. Samuel P. Huntington, Daniel Pipes, and Steven Emerson are three prominent writers who have published books or articles that paint a picture of Muslims that is highly critical and even dangerous. How should we here in the West view Muslims, then?

This book will help you understand who Muslims are, what they believe, what rituals they perform, what civilization they built, as well as what challenges they face. Although the history of interaction between the Muslim and Christian worlds has often been fraught with conflict, there have been many periods of peace and understanding that have enriched both societies. One of the greatest periods of peace and intellectual development for European Jewry was during the era of Muslim rule in Spain. This has often been called a golden age for the Jewish people. Indeed, Christian-Muslim-Jewish relations were not always as strained as they seem to be today, and through mutual respect and tolerance the followers of each of these three monotheistic religions can reacquaint themselves with that spirit of tolerance that reigned in so many places before.

The stamp of Islam and its civilization can be found in many aspects of our society today. Economic terms such as *bank* and *check*, as well as scientific words like *horizon* and *alcohol* come from the world of Islam. Did you ever study algebra or chemistry? Have you ever enjoyed lemonade or sugar? Do you dream of going on safari, or have you ever read an almanac? Do you enjoy the works of Plato (which Muslims transmitted to the West), or have you read the poems of Rumi? These and many other words, discoveries, and intellectual achievements are gifts from Muslim society to the West.

Islam has a very appealing belief system that has been embraced by converts for decades now, and its rituals give meaning to people from all walks of life. Many prison systems across the United States now actively encourage their inmates to learn about Islam, recognizing the discipline and civilizing effect it has on the prison population. In some urban areas, Muslims have been credited with ridding neighborhoods of drugs and prostitution and working with local officials to revitalize depressed areas. Islam can and will continue to make positive contributions in every society in which its followers settle.

I hope you will enjoy learning about Islam and discovering that Muslims are not as different as you thought. In the future you will be seeing a greater Muslim presence in the West. And as Muslims take their place in the melting pot, I hope we can all see that the flavors they will add will enrich our lives for the better.

Here's What You'll Find Inside

This book is divided into seven parts.

Part 1, Introducing Islam, opens for you the world of Islam from an insider's point of view. In this part, you will learn about some of the reasons for the unfortunate relations the Christian and Muslim worlds have had for centuries. You will also discover the reason why knowledge of Islam has often been lacking in modern school curriculums.

Part 2, The Spiritual World in Islam, introduces the Muslim concept of the four stages of life, the three levels of the soul's journey to truth, and the Day of Judgment. The Islamic view of Heaven and Hell and their purpose will also be reviewed. The story of creation all the way up to the Last Day will present a thrilling journey into an alternate conception of the universe and our place in it.

Part 3, The Five Pillars of Islam, explores the famous Five Pillars of Islam in great detail and shows how each pillar influences the life of a Muslim. This discussion includes a full account of the Islamic concept of social justice and action. *Jihad*, which is often mistakenly labeled as *holy war*, and the Islamic duty of activism will also be highlighted.

Part 4, Islam and Other Religions, gives a full account of the relations between Christians, Jews, and Muslims from the beginning of Muhammad's mission through the present. The Qur'an contains quite a lot of discussion on Muslim relations with the followers of other religions and goes into great detail about the merits and drawbacks of both Judaism and Christianity. In this part, I'll also touch upon the rise of interfaith dialogue.

Part 5, Regulating Life Within the Laws of Islam, introduces you to the sources for Islamic teachings, how they are interpreted, and how a code of life can be derived from them. You'll learn about issues related to Islamic Law, such as dietary restrictions, male/female relations, community life, ceremonies, and celebrations. You'll also explore the purpose of a mosque.

Part 6, The History of Islam, takes you on a panoramic overview of the breadth and depth of the world of Islam from the Prophet Muhammad to the present day. I also cover the influence of Islam on Europe, the Golden Age of Muslim Spain, the glorious Mughals and Ottomans, and the Christian/Muslim wars over Palestine and Eastern Europe. This will help you understand better how Islam and the Western world have interacted over the centuries.

Part 7, The Legacy of Islam, highlights the contributions of Muslims to the growth of civilization, globalization, and modern technology. Great Muslim thinkers and explorers will be introduced, and the era of Colonialism will be fully explored.

Extras

To make your learning experience even more enjoyable and insightful, you'll find sidebars sprinkled liberally throughout the text that include interesting tidbits of information.

DISPELLING THE MYTH

This sidebar confronts myths about Islam with authentic information. These can be quotes, points, or comparisons. This is one of the most important types of information you will find, given that stereotypes and misunderstandings about Islam are rampant today.

ASK THE IMAM

In this sidebar, you will find issues about religious application to daily life. Tough questions need equally strong answers, and Islam doesn't back down when solutions are needed. By the way, an Imam is the title for a religious leader in the Muslim community.

DEFINITION

This sidebar includes definitions of words common in Islam that you may have never heard before.

FROM THE SOURCE

This sidebar includes actual quotes from the Qur'an, the sayings of Muhammad, and the writings of prominent Islamic scholars and others through the centuries. What better way to learn than to let the sources speak for themselves!

Acknowledgments

I really want to thank the people who made this book possible. This is my first book in the *Complete Idiot's Guide* series, and the support I received has been overwhelming. To Jacky Sach, my literary agent, I extend my gratitude for encouragement and helpful feedback. A special thank you for Randy Ladenheim-Gil, my initial editor, for all the kind assistance she extended in the completion of this manuscript. The staff at Alpha Books has also been exceptional. Michael Koch deserves kudos for the hard task of making sense of my endless files in the first edition. Finally, and most importantly, I would like to thank my wife for shouldering more than her fair share of family responsibilities during my time working on this book.

Trademarks

All terms mentioned in this book that are known to be or are suspected of being trademarks or service marks have been appropriately capitalized. Alpha Books and Penguin Group (USA) Inc. cannot attest to the accuracy of this information. Use of a term in this book should not be regarded as affecting the validity of any trademark or service mark.

Introducing Islam

What is the religion of Islam really about? Although you might have already heard a lot about this religion, you might not feel like you've learned what its actual teachings are. Is Islam being given a fair hearing? Beyond all the hype and stereotypes, Islam is, in fact, a genuine spiritual tradition that more than a billion people worldwide are associated with. That's quite a lot of public support! Why, then, is Islam so often presented in such a disparaging manner? Have there been unfortunate circumstances in relations between the Muslim world and the West that would cause long-standing myths and prejudices to take root? Have essentially political events around the globe been used to unfairly taint an entire people and their beliefs?

In reality, Islam is a peaceful religion with teachings that cover every area of life. The philosophy of Islam begins with God and ends with the inevitable journey of all people back to their Creator. Concepts that are already familiar to people in the West, such as righteousness, Heaven, Hell, and angels, make Islam seem less mysterious and more comprehensible than most people would think. In this part, I explore the Islamic conception of God and why there is so much misunderstanding about this great faith in the world today.

Why Has Islam Become So Important?

In This Chapter

- Learn why understanding Islam is now more important than ever
- Consider how stereotypes have affected the Western view of Islam
- Take a brief look at where Muslims live and how they got there
- Understand how the Muslim world affects your life here in the West

It may be surprising to learn that Islam is the fastest-growing religion in the world today, outpacing Christianity, Buddhism, and all other belief systems through a mixture of conversion and natural increase. However, even more eye-opening is the fact that Islam is also the fastest-growing religion in North America. With over 2,000 mosques spread throughout the continent, and populations approaching 1 million in some urban areas, learning about this often misunderstood and mysterious faith has become more important than ever. In this chapter, I will be discussing the ways in which many Muslims have felt that their faith and way of life have been unfairly maligned by stereotypes, a lack of accurate knowledge about the religion of Islam, and the heinous actions of a select few who have offered their own twisted views as somehow representative of this ancient and otherwise noble religion.

The Muslims Are Coming!

Signs of the growth of *Islam* in the United States, Canada, and recently in Mexico are evident everywhere. Mosques are being built in neighborhoods where once only churches and synagogues stood. Women who wear scarves covering their hair are now a common sight in many towns and cities. Moreover, *Muslim* holidays are gaining official recognition in such places as Los Angeles, Toronto, and New York; and the U.S. Postal Service has even issued stamp designs commemorating Muslims and Islamic themes (Malcolm X and Ramadan stamps, for example). In addition, an increasing number of employers are accommodating the religious needs of their Muslim workers in the same way they responded to the needs of their Jewish workers in the past.

DEFINITION

Islam is the proper name to use when referring to the religion practiced by Muslims. It is an Arabic word that means two things: to surrender your will to God and to acquire peace in your soul. A **Muslim** is a follower of Islam.

On a personal level, many people are finding that some of their neighbors or fellow college students practice the Islamic way of life or that some of their children's classmates are Muslims. Others may be just curious about a religion they hear more and more about and never really learned much about. Clearly Islam is beginning to enter the mainstream of community experience, and the more you learn about your Muslim neighbors the better you will be able to understand each other and work together for the common good.

Why Didn't I Learn More About Islam in School?

So you made it through high school and maybe college and managed to learn a little bit of everything along the way. Then one night you sit down to watch the evening news and find yourself listening to a report about Islamic terrorists and their plots, followed by another one highlighting the holy month of *Ramadan* as it is celebrated in a major American city. The next morning you read an article in the newspaper about sectarian protesters demonstrating against their government in a Muslim country, and throughout the day or week you find more news about happenings concerning Muslims and things Islamic—some positive, but mostly negative.

For a moment, you may reflect on what a diverse world we live in; however, you also may become influenced by the slant of the reporting to view Islam as some monstrous religion with backward values incomprehensible to civilized people. If you are a thinking individual, however, who likes to form opinions for yourself after looking at all the evidence, perhaps, in times of quiet contemplation, the realization hits you: I really don't know much about Islam. What does it teach? Is it as bad and dangerous as it is often portrayed in the media? Why do so many people seem to be following it? What should I know about Islamic customs given that my new co-worker may be a Muslim and I saw a girl with a scarf on her head at my child's school? Heck, who is this *Allah* they always talk about? Is He the same God as ours?

Raising these questions enables you to confront the power of stereotypes and how they can damage relationships between people of diverse backgrounds. You also may realize, when you reconsider what you know about Islam, that your education has a gaping hole in it. It is no accident that in previous decades, the religion of Islam and Muslim culture were hardly given more than a cursory treatment in grade school history classes, even though the Muslim impact on world civilization was at least as great as that of European or Chinese culture. Until recently it was even difficult to find classes in colleges and universities that focused on Islam as a phenomenon, rather than just a footnote in Middle Eastern studies classes.

A combination of biased attitudes going back a thousand years coupled with a kind of cultural chauvinism has led generations of academics to dismiss the contributions of Islam and Muslims to world history. Although the situation is now improving dramatically, some of the old attitudes still remain, and the information about Islam that is being brought to the general public is often incomprehensible to Muslims, who see their faith being maligned or routinely misrepresented almost with impunity.

The Backlash Against Islam and Muslims

The outrageous events of September 11, 2001, in particular, have unleashed an equally outrageous Pandora's box of bigotry and prejudice against this world religion and its followers. The Council of American Islamic Relations (CAIR) released a report in May of 2004 outlining a 70 percent increase in anti-Muslim bias and violence in the United States, and that was just covering the prior year of hate-crime statistics. In addition, an attitude of blanket condemnation and guilt-by-association has made Muslims feel vulnerable, harassed, and humiliated, especially in places where they are more visible in the community. Consider some of what has been publicly said by leading politicians and opinion makers in the United States that has given fuel to this intolerable and un-American bigotry:

- "The nation has been invaded by a fanatical, murderous cult ... We should invade their countries, kill their leaders, and convert them to Christianity."
  —Syndicated columnist Ann Coulter, *National Review Online*, September 2001

- "We're not attacking Islam, but Islam has attacked us. The God of Islam is not the same God. He's not the son of God of the Christian or Judeo-Christian faith. It's a different God, and I believe it is a very evil and wicked religion."
  —Franklin Graham, *NBC Nightly News*, November 2001

- "Unfortunately, we have too many mosques in this country."
—Peter King, just before successfully forcing a hearing in Congress (in March of 2011) about the supposed "radicalization" of American Muslims.

- "I believe that Muslims in this country are a fifth column ... The vast majority of Muslims in this country are very obviously loyal, not to the United States, but to their religion ... the reason they are here is to take over our culture and eventually take over our country ... You think we should befriend them; I think we should kill them."
—Jay Severin, host of a popular Boston area morning talk show on WTKK-FM, April 2004

"[Muslims attacked us] because we're a Christian nation, because our foundation and roots are Judeo-Christian and the enemy is a guy named Satan ... We in the army of God, in the house of God, in the kingdom of God have been raised for such a time as this."
—Lt. General William G. Boykin, October 2003

These dramatic, prejudicial, and inflammatory statements are, unfortunately, all too common today, though for the most part it is Muslims who notice their frequency and their effect on our freedoms. This rhetoric of hate has now filtered down into the lives of ordinary Muslim Americans, who have become frequent victims of discrimination in public and private places as well as targets of harassment, verbal assault, and hate crimes.

The irrational fear of Islam (called Islamophobia) has even come to influence official United States government policy, with strong echoes of the unjust treatment of Japanese Americans in World War II. The infamous immigration registry program enacted just after September 11, 2001, in which tens of thousands of Muslim immigrants were forced to undergo a special re-registration (and the subsequent detention and expulsion of thousands of law-abiding Muslim immigrants) sent shock waves through Muslim America. The official congressional hearings into the supposed "radicalization" and disloyalty of American Muslims, sponsored by representative Peter King in March of 2011, certainly did little to bolster the sense of justice that Muslims have always expected from the government. The current climate of prejudice and bias has done much to damage many Muslims' faith in American freedom and fairness.

The unfortunate wars in Afghanistan and Iraq and the accompanying nationalist bravado have made Muslims, no matter where they came from or what they believe in, the new worldwide boogeyman that Red Communism used to be during the

Cold War. The situation has deteriorated so rapidly that Kofi Annan, the former Secretary-General of the United Nations, remarked in January of 2004, "One of the most disturbing manifestations of bigotry today is Islamophobia … Since the September 11 terrorist attacks on the United States, which were condemned throughout the Muslim world, many Muslims, particularly in the West, have found themselves the objects of suspicion, harassment, and discrimination." Clearly the time for a more thorough and accurate exploration of Islam and Muslims has come. Who better to ask what their religion is about than Muslims?

Muslims, Muslims Everywhere!

The Muslim world—where is the Muslim world? It can seem confusing at times: news about Muslims coming in from Africa, Europe, Asia, the Middle East, and even North America. Just where is the Muslim heartland, anyway? How can a religion we know so little about have followers almost everywhere on the globe from Suriname in South America to Bulgaria in Eastern Europe? The answer to this question lies not in geography but in history. Islam began in Arabia with the Prophet Muhammad in 610 C.E. and spread rapidly to the east, west, and north, mainly because of the zeal of Arab armies and the disloyalty of the peasantry who, under Persian and Byzantine rule, often looked upon the Muslims as liberators (even if only for their more lenient tax policies).

Within 100 years, converts from North Africa, Syria, Iraq, and Iran continued to expand the borders of the Islamic Empire until the classic heartland of Islam consisted of a broad swath of territory, encompassing all the land between Spain and western China. The Turkish Ottomans later spread their rule over much of southeastern Europe, resulting in the mass conversion of the Albanians and Bosnians, whose brand of Christianity had been under persecution from the Orthodox and Catholic churches. A further combination of immigration, trade, missionary activity, and displacement resulted in Muslims being in the far-flung places we find them today from South America to Indonesia.

DEFINITION

The **Qur'an,** which is often spelled *Koran* in English, is believed by Muslims to be the literal speech of God as revealed to the Prophet Muhammad. The word *Qur'an* means *The Reading.*

Muslim Missionary Efforts

The spread of Islam was accomplished not only through the conquest of land but also through the willing conversion of many of the inhabitants. Even as Christianity spread throughout Europe and the Americas by means of a mixture of missionary work and war, so, too, did Islam have its more prominent missionary side. A large tract of land stretching from central China down through Cambodia, Vietnam, Thailand, Malaysia, and the Philippines and into Indonesia saw the rapid conversion of huge populations, a result due almost exclusively to the efforts of individuals who were interested in teaching their beliefs to others. Most of these missionaries were either primarily businessmen or wandering mystics. No Muslim armies ever entered that part of the world. Ironically, Indonesia and the surrounding countries now boast the largest Muslim populations found on the globe.

FROM THE SOURCE

There is no forcing anyone into this way of life. The truth stands clear from falsehood. Anyone who rejects wrongdoing and believes in Allah, has grasped a firm handhold that never breaks, because Allah hears and knows everything. (Qur'an 2:254)

The Qur'an forbids forcing someone to convert to the faith. Despite popular stereotypes of fanatic Muslims with the Qur'an in one hand and a sword in the other, Islam does not teach this type of conversion method; modern Western writers who have taken a fresh look at history now almost unanimously declare that forced conversion was not a method used during the rapid Muslim expansion out of the Arabian Peninsula.

Today in America, Canada, Mexico, and Europe, the number of converts to Islam is rising each year. There are no organized soul-saving crusades, no TV shows in prime time, no magnetic personalities filling stadiums each month in a different city, and certainly no central planning unit to bring Islam to the Western public. Instead, religious and cultural trends among certain groups have continued to evolve. For example, the conversion rate of African Americans to Islam has remained steady since the days of Malcolm X and the old Nation of Islam. As the number of converts rises, so does the general acceptance of Islam as a viable life choice in the African-American community.

America now sports more than a million African American converts to Islam alone. Caucasian women who marry Muslim immigrants often convert to the faith, either before or after marriage, and it is estimated that there are more than 200,000 such converts in North America today. A surprising movement of Hispanic Americans, especially Puerto Ricans, into the Islamic religion has also continued to grow and expand in recent years. Thus, you can see how the conversion factor contributes to the growth of Islam in unexpected places.

How Did Muslims Get There? Thank the British!

In addition to land conquests and missionary efforts, another factor is responsible for the spread of Islam: the efforts of the British, who were looking for a cheap labor supply for their colonial plantations. In the eighteenth and early nineteenth centuries, the British imported tens of thousands of Muslims from India to South America, South Africa, the Caribbean, and elsewhere. Their descendants have continued to practice Islam. Suriname, for example, a small nation just north of Brazil, has a population that is over 30 percent Muslim, the rest being Hindu and Christian.

Recently, immigration from Lebanon has resulted in a sizable Muslim population in Argentina, and the Muslim immigrants of Britain and France are well known. In short, Muslims inhabit every corner of the globe, and their growth has been due to a wide variety of factors. The main Muslim heartland stretches from Morocco to Indonesia and from Bosnia down to Tanzania, with important fringe populations all over the world.

If it seems that news from the Muslim world is suddenly more prominent and noticeable these days, it's not because in the past Muslims were sleeping or because they previously didn't exist. It's because now each and every Muslim country has suddenly become more valuable to the West. Given the Western dependence on fossil fuels, especially oil and gas, and the need to ensure easy access to foreign markets for Western companies, the political events in every Muslim country are watched closely.

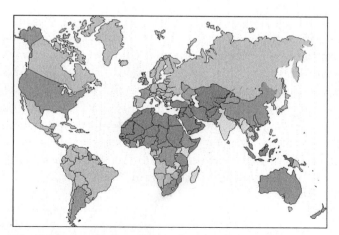

The Muslim world now stretches from South America to China.
The shaded areas have the heaviest concentrations of Muslims.

The Arab oil embargo and the rise of OPEC in the 1970s made people take notice that numerous people have a history and values that the West does not fully understand. Other events, such as the Arab/Israeli conflict, the Gulf Wars, and the shifting balance of power in the Middle East from dictators to "people power" activists, have confirmed the view that Americans need to know more about what forces drive people who live in those places. Stay tuned: as the years pass, the volume of news about or originating from the Muslim world will only increase.

Is There Really a Clash of Civilizations?

When Westerners think about Islam, well-worn stereotypes of veiled women, bearded men, exotic food, and an incomprehensible language tend to come to mind. Islam is considered by many to be an alien culture that can't possibly have any relationship or commonality with normal Western values. This belief has an unfortunately long history and dates back 1,400 years, to the era of the Byzantine Roman Empire when the Muslim world and Europe most often met on the field of battle. The Muslim world was still young then, and the vitality of youth caused it to expand its frontiers, much like the European nations did hundreds of years later, when they achieved near total world dominance.

From the year 622 C.E. when Muhammad, the Prophet of Islam, gained control of the Arabian city of Medina, until the close of the sixteenth century, the Muslim world was continually expanding in one direction or another. Although there were many setbacks, such as the loss of Spain in 1492 or the Mongol invasions in the thirteenth century, the Muslim world overcame most of these challenges and continued its outward march. During this time, the Christian world lost all of North Africa, the Middle East, and much of Eastern Europe to Islam.

As a counterstrike, the Crusades (the Christian invasion of Palestine in the eleventh and twelfth centuries) showed Europe that it could wrest land away from "the Saracens," as Muslims were called at the time. Vilification of Islam and Muslims reached a crescendo throughout Europe during this period, and European kings and Catholic priests portrayed Muslims as children of the Devil who must be forcibly converted or exterminated. Although the Crusades ultimately failed, the Europeans, who never shook off their image of Muslims as being nearly subhuman, came back with a vengeance in the eighteenth century and by the close of World War I came to dominate over 95 percent of the Muslim world.

DISPELLING THE MYTH

The growth of Islam during the early centuries of its existence was a difficult phenomenon for Western Christianity to comprehend, and misunderstanding, prejudice, fear, and, in some cases, hatred have characterized much of the history of encounters between the two faiths.

—Jane I. Smith, author of *Islam in America*

Sadly, in all of this fighting back and forth, little effort was made to understand the values of the other side, and the greatest legacy both Westerners and Muslims are struggling with today is the fear with which each civilization regards the other. These stereotypes have led many Americans and Europeans to conclude that Islam is incompatible with "modern" values centered on democracy, personal rights, equality before the law, and tolerance for the views of others. You may be surprised, however, to learn that the values of Judaism, Christianity, and Islam are not as different as you might think. It is imperative, then, that the truth be told and that the actual beliefs of Islam be examined closely. Western Christian civilization and Islamic civilization have looked each other in the eye for centuries and done nothing more than give each other bruises. The necessities of the modern world have made a re-examination of that mode of exchange a priority.

Bridging the Next Gap

Muslims are quite puzzled these days when it comes to sorting out their relationship with the rest of the world. On the one hand, many Muslim countries have allied themselves to Western interests, opened their markets to international trade, and have become valued trading partners. On the other hand, when someone like Saddam Hussein comes along, regular Muslims suddenly find themselves made out to be monsters and killers. Indeed, the number of anti-Muslim incidents during the first Gulf War in 1991 rose all across America as mosques were defaced and vandalized and ordinary Muslims were jeered at and taunted in the streets. These people, mind you, were American citizens who had nothing to do with the Iraqi regime and what it did during its invasion of Kuwait. Moreover, Muslims in America were almost completely unanimous in their condemnation of Iraq's unprovoked attack of Kuwait (as evidenced by the numerous press releases from organizations large and small denouncing the action). At the most, they wanted the war to end quickly because innocent civilians in Iraq were being harmed by the intense bombing raids that seemed to hit nonmilitary targets with ever greater frequency.

The coalition of nations that then-President George H. W. Bush assembled to oust the Iraqis included more than a dozen Muslim nations that contributed men and material to the war effort. Only one Muslim nation, Jordan, failed to express its disapproval, and it abstained out of fear of Iraqi retaliation. (Iraq is Jordan's neighbor.) Yet throughout this conflict, even though the Muslim world joined in to fight on the American side, the Western media failed to adequately identify Muslims as allies of the West. Instead, Muslims as a group were sometimes represented as *supporters* of Saddam Hussein simply on account of a few well-televised, anti-American protests in Palestine and Jordan, and the American public may have been given the wrong impression that the Gulf War was a war between the West and the Arabs (read: Islam). It only became worse in 2001 after the September 11 attacks, with Islam itself being blamed for anything and everything that a small cadre of zealots operating under the name of Al Qaeda carried out.

DEFINITION

The name Muslims use when referring to a mosque is **masjid.** This translates as *the place of bowing down.*

Indeed, even though the vast majority of Muslims had no allegiance to or sympathy for either Saddam Hussein or Osama bin Laden, a leader of a secretive group known as Al Qaeda, still Muslims have been made to feel like a suspected fifth column, ready to betray America in a second. This fear has been borne out at the local level through the vandalism of some religious centers and the daily harassment many Muslims face in the streets, in their schools, and in their places of work. Even the desire to construct a new mosque is now often met with protests in the community, innuendo, and outright bigotry of the worst kind. So now Muslims have been increasingly forced to ask themselves the question: What does it mean when Muslims, many of whom are American citizens, are made to look like the enemy on account of the actions of a few in far away places? This feeling is not unlike how Japanese Americans must have felt during World War II when they were rounded up and detained for "security" reasons. Hypocrisy and racism were obvious then, and Muslims feel as if they are the current "foreign" group suffering from misinformation, hysteria, stereotypes, and collective judgments.

Hollywood hasn't helped to dispel these erroneous ideas, either. Movies such as *Not Without My Daughter, True Lies, Black Hawk Down, Under Siege,* and *Delta Force* have served to paint Muslims as wife-beaters, bomb-throwers, and swarthy immigrants whose loyalty cannot be trusted. Caricatures of Islam and Muslims are staples of

American television, and the types of insults and barbs being slung against them would raise howls of protest and marches in the streets if they were directed toward African Americans, Jews, or Hispanics today, as they were in the past. But Muslims have not yet organized an effective, nationwide antidiscrimination movement to correct such stereotyping and maligning. Several organizations such as the Council on American-Islamic Relations (CAIR) and the Arab-American Anti-Defamation League have been established in recent years and have made some strides in influencing the way many news organizations report on Islam and the Muslim community in America. But there is a long way to go before Islam and Muslims achieve the same level of sensitivity from the popular media that other religious and racial groups have.

Grace Halsell, the former speechwriter for U.S. President Lyndon Baines Johnson wrote in 1994 that …

> Phrases such as *Muslim militant* and *Islamic terrorist* appear so often in the U.S. media it is as if word processors were programmed to produce only such pairs. Muslims, now numbering about one billion, are aware of the stereotype. Do these Muslims tend to see duplicity in U.S. Middle East policy? Do they perceive that the United States and Europe make the same stereotypical judgment for all Muslims, all over the world? If they are not seeing Muslims as authentic human beings, will they deem them expendable? Is this why, they ask, the Americans and the West can so easily turn a blind eye to a genocide of Muslims in Europe?

DISPELLING THE MYTH

I hope that in the next century we will come to terms with our abysmal ignorance of the Muslim world. Muslims aren't a bunch of wackos and nuts. They are decent, brilliant, talented people with a great civilization and traditions of their own, including legal traditions. Americans know nothing about them. There are people in that part of the world with whom we are simply out of touch. That's a great challenge for the next century.

—U.S. Supreme Court Justice Anthony Kennedy, December 1999

It would be nearly impossible for me to express in words, however, the frustration that Muslim Americans have felt in their efforts to undo the many forms of stereotypes directed against their religion and communities. But suffice it to say that many Muslims feel they have been treated unfairly by the media, entertainment industry, and political establishments. As Muslims gain a greater sense of participation in the modern melting pot of ideas and as more people become increasingly comfortable with their Muslim neighbors, realizing they are not as different as they thought, then real progress toward breaking down barriers can be made. Until then Muslims are watching anxiously as each wave of misinformation washes over the television screens and newspaper pages of this otherwise tolerant nation.

Muslims have been migrating to the West in great numbers over the last five decades for the same reasons that other people immigrate: a chance at a more prosperous economic life for themselves and their families. This movement of Muslims into the neighborhoods of North America has given Westerners the chance to come into contact with Muslims and learn directly from them about their values and beliefs. This opportunity is one of the many benefits of our current time. When your children meet Muslim children, they discover that Muslims are not very different from themselves. As mosques start to take their place alongside churches and synagogues in the landscape of the West, the opportunity to bridge one of the last great remaining cultural gaps becomes a possibility.

The Least You Need to Know

- The study of Islam in Europe and North America has been colored by false stereotypes that have hindered good relations and been the cause of much misunderstanding and hostility.
- Muslims are found in every corner of the world and have a history and culture that is as rich as any other.
- The population of Muslims is rising in North America and Europe due to immigration and also to conversion.
- Muslims in general feel they have been stereotyped and are being treated unfairly by the media and entertainment industries.
- Nearly all Muslim countries in the world are either allies of the West or are friendly to the West.
- It is unfair to point to a few villains in the Muslim world and then blame all Muslims for the actions of a very few.

Food for the Soul

Chapter

2

In This Chapter

- Understand how Muslims conceptualize their purpose in this life
- Discover the God of Islam
- Learn why Muslims say the physical universe is surrendered to God
- Discover the spirit world according to Islam
- Find out what Muslims believe about natural human morality

In Chapter 1, I discussed the reasons for the general lack of information about Islam among people in the West. I also explored some of the reasons for the cultural prejudice and bias that many Muslims feel as they attempt to make their homes and communities in lands that have been traditionally Judeo-Christian in their orientation. Now I will turn to the religion of Islam itself. What does this mysterious religion teach about God and our place in the universe? Does it have a well-defined cosmology as Judaism and Christianity do, with a definite purpose in the world? What are the codes of belief that Muslims live by? What happens to Muslims after they die? The answers to many of these questions may be surprising in that the ideas and concepts you are about to learn are not as alien or foreign as you might expect.

The Muslim lifestyle is based on having faith in God, leading a morally upright life, following a set of daily rituals to remind oneself of his or her allegiance to God, and doing good works to improve the lives of all living things. The reward for such a life-style is eternity in Heaven. The penalty for utter self-indulgence may be a stint in Hell.

The Core Beliefs of Islam

Islam has seven fundamental beliefs that every Muslim must accept as a part of his or her religion. Over the course of the next several chapters, I take a closer look at each of these teachings. In Arabic the title of this group of beliefs is the *Emanul Mufassil*, or *Faith Listed in Detail*. Every Muslim learns this formula as a part of his or her religious training. The seven core beliefs are ...

- Belief in God

- Belief in the angels

- Belief in the revealed Books of God

- Belief in God's many prophets

- Accepting that there will be a Last Day

- Belief in the divine measurement of human affairs

- Belief in a life after death

We All Have the Same God

The foundation of Islamic teachings begins with God, whom Muslims call *Allah*. The name Allah comes from the Arabic language and means literally *the one and only God*, as opposed to any old god with a small "g." The Qur'an itself declares that Allah is the same God that spoke to the Jews and Christians. Therefore, when Muslims speak about God, they have in mind that it is the God of Abraham, Moses, Jesus, *and* Muhammad. Even Arab Christians, who speak the Arabic language, say "Allah" when they talk about God.

The Qur'an states it this way:

> Tell [the Jews and Christians], "We believe in the Revelation which has come down to us [the Qur'an] and in that which came down to you [the Torah and Gospel]; Our God and your God is one; and it's to Him we surrender." (Qur'an 29:46)

Muslims prefer to use the name *Allah* no matter what language is being spoken. This is because this proper name for the supreme deity cannot be made plural or altered in any way grammatically in Arabic. I use the terms *Allah* and *God* interchangeably throughout this book.

One of the most memorized passages of the Qur'an, the famous *Ayatul Kursi*, or Verse of the Throne, gives a good introduction to the way in which Muslims view God. It goes like this:

Allah! There is no god but He, the Living, Who needs no other but Whom all others need. He is never drowsy nor does He rest. Space and the Earth belong to Him; who can intercede without His consent? He knows everything people have done and will do, and no one can grasp the least of His knowledge, without His review. His throne extends over the heavens and the Earth and He doesn't tire in their safekeeping. He alone is the Most High, the Lord Sovereign Supreme. (Qur'an 2:255)

The Islamic concept of our place in the universe hinges on the notion that Allah, or God, is the only true reality. There is nothing that is permanent other than God. Everything exists because of His will and everything depends on Him whether we recognize it or not. Allah is eternal and uncreated. Everything else in the universe is created. Created things will pass away and return to Allah for His review. Not even the stars will last forever.

According to the method of reasoning used in the Qur'an, the proof for God's existence is found in four areas:

1. The natural world with all its complexity and beauty. This is a sign of intelligence in the universe because only a designing mind could have constructed it.

2. Our human abilities and capacities for thought, belief, invention, creativity, and moral choices. No animal or plant can do what we do. We are like the other creatures of Earth but so very different and unique.

3. The revelation of God's guidance and the existence of religion. They show that there is a right way and a wrong way to live life. Prophets, holy books, flashes of insight—all these serve as proof that guidance is real and purposefully directed.

4. Finally, our inner feelings. These propel us to seek the meaning in things and show us that we have a soul or spirit that seeks harmony with nature, the universe, and a higher power. The human will is, by definition, inclined to seek the answer to questions that concern more than mere physical existence.

The Universe Is Muslim!

In the realm of creation, Islam makes a clear distinction: There is God *and everything besides Him*. With created things (the *everything besides Him*), there are two basic categories: whatever is *surrendered* to God's will and whatever is *resisting* His will. You are either following God's way or the wrong way. All inanimate matter, such as rocks, comets, water, and even atoms, follows well-defined natural laws regarding their motion, atomic structure, properties, and qualities. Islam holds that God established *all* natural laws, and thus every physical material in the universe is surrendered to His will—that is, everything does what it was created to do. In that vein of thought, then, the entire nonliving universe is considered to be *surrendered* to God. The whole universe follows Islam!

Thus, the Qur'an states that the entire physical universe is *Muslim*. How can this strange statement be explained? If the word *Islam* means to surrender to Allah and to acquire peace, then someone or something that does this is called a *Muslim*, or surrendered one. That is how the label *Muslim* can be applied to things other than people. Note the similarity between the words *Islam* and *Muslim*. Both have the letters *S*, *L*, and *M*. The way Arabic works is simple. You take a base of consonants that have a plain meaning (a root word) and then you add or subtract prefixes and suffixes and alter the vowel patterns to form new, related words. Think about the English word *cover*. You can have *covered, recover, unrecoverable, covering, uncovered, undercover,* and so on. Arabic works in a similar fashion. So the name of the religion is *Islam* and a person or thing that follows Islam is called a *Muslim*, or surrendered one, and because the term is generic it can be applied to nonliving things as well—whatever follows God's will (Islam) is a Muslim.

Animals and plants are also considered to be Muslim in that they follow their innate instincts, which are sort of like their programming. God states in the Qur'an that He taught animals how to do what they do, such as birds flying, bees making honey, plants growing in response to rain, and so on. He even goes so far as to declare that all living plants or animals praise Him in their own way, this praise being an expression of their submissiveness to their Creator. Have you ever wondered why birds sing, frogs croak, or cats meow all night? Not all of it is for mating and establishing territory! Some of it may be for the pure wonder of being alive. The great Sufi poet, Jalaluddin Rumi, said it best when he wrote the line: "I am joyful in the world because the world is joyful in Him."

Aladdin Rubbed the Wrong Lamp

Now let's move on and look at the other category of created things. These are the living creatures that are not *automatically* Muslim, or surrendered to God's will and laws. Primarily, I am talking about human beings and another type of creature called the *jinn*. *Jinns* are similar to the genies so often portrayed in Western literature as wild and crazy spirits. Despite popular folklore, however, Islam does not teach that there are *jinns*, or genies, in lamps or magic rings. Sorry, Aladdin. On the contrary, Islam proposes that these unique life-forms exist for their own sake and that we have no control over them in daily life.

Jinns are the real cause of supernatural phenomena and paranormal events, not ghosts. *Jinns* inhabit another dimension in which you cannot see them, and they have no substance you can detect. They can be good or evil in their disposition. The evil *jinns* prey upon human beings by goading us into doing wrong. Good *jinns* ignore us. They do not have as much free will as we humans do precisely because they already know without any doubt that Allah exists. The Qur'an declares that *jinns* are made out of the residue of scorched fire. Muslim scholars have long speculated that *jinns* may exist in the realm of thermal energy or in the x-ray or energy wave spectrums. They can contact us only through our thoughts, in which they can "whisper" suggestions and other types of information in our brains, possibly altering our brain waves. Islam rejects the idea that the spirits of the dead walk the earth as ghosts. Instead, Muslims believe that it is *jinns* who haunt houses, possess people, spook animals, give predictions to psychics, and cause many other inexplicable phenomena. While Christianity relies on the concept of fallen angels to explain the forces of evil, Islam teaches that all angels are good and cannot be corrupted. The angels are all Muslims and have no choice in the matter.

Touched by an Angel

Islam accepts the existence of angels, which are called *mala'ikah*. They are made of light energy and can materialize into any form they need to in the physical world. They have no inherent gender. They also have no free will and exist only to serve Allah. Although they're intelligent, they have no serious emotional shortcomings or foibles. Think of them as something like God's robots. They do as they are told, though God is not dependent on them. The following list presents the top four angels and their functions:

Jibra'il   (Gabriel) This angel brings revelations to the prophets.

Azra'il   This angel is the *Malikul Mawt*, or Angel of Death.

Mika'il   (Michael) This angel controls the weather.

Israfil   This angel will blow the horn signaling the end of the universe.

Islam assigns angels to many other types of tasks. One of these is to watch over people and note what they do. Another job of the angels is to look for people who are praising God and to join them. You will be learning more about the different types of angels and their functions as I cover other aspects of Islamic teachings in later chapters.

Accepting the Burden

The Qur'an says that long before God made people He offered the gift of self-awareness and responsibility for one's actions to every living and nonliving thing in the universe. The mountains, the animals, the angels, the planets, the stars, any of these could have accepted and become beings with a power unlike anything in the virtually programmed universe. Anyone or anything that accepted those gifts, called "the trust" in the Qur'an, would transcend nature and be able to conceive of itself and make decisions using an intellect and the power of reason.

Of course with such a gift would come a large measure of culpability for one's actions and spiritual orientation. There is no wrong if a squirrel steals a nut from another squirrel; it's just what squirrels do. Likewise, it is not sacrilege if a bird builds a nest on a place of worship. But when you can *choose* whether or not to do wrong, or to accept or deny God, then you ascend to a whole new level. Now you have *right and wrong, good and evil.* The Qur'an declares that every object in the universe declined this "gift" out of fear of the consequences of not being able to measure up to the task.

Soul Soup

At the time when all things and animals declined the offer of self-awareness, we find that God finally made the offer to us. Humans weren't around in physical bodies on Earth. Instead we existed only as a murky prototype and we were with Allah in a sort of primordial soup of spirit matter. Think of all our unformed soul material packed in one large ball, none being individual or unique. It is from this mass of spirit material that each individual human would later get its spirit or soul. (The word for spirit in Arabic is *ruh*.)

Allah offered the gift of self-awareness to that spirit-collective, and it accepted the challenge (though that was foolish, the Qur'an notes). Humans, when they appeared as physical creatures on Earth, would have the freedom to accept or deny God, self-awareness, intelligence, reason, and a moral compass called a *fitrah*, or natural inclination, to help guide them through life. Incidentally, this is how Islam explains our superiority over animal intelligence and abilities. Recent studies into the workings of the brain have even uncovered evidence that we are already "wired" for spirituality. That is, our brains respond to religious stimuli and cause us to feel euphoric.

DEFINITION

Fitrah means your inner nature or moral compass. It steers you to seek out religious experiences and ultimately directs you to accept the existence of God.

Our Compass Points Inward

Why were we implanted with a moral compass? Isn't rational intelligence enough to guide our free choices? That is the claim that humanists and some scientists have put forward in recent years. This theory, however, has failed in many respects. The mere application of reason alone as a means of solving the world's problems may appear a valid procedure on paper, but as Islam points out, all of us have an inherent weakness. We all desire personal pleasure and the fulfillment of our animal urges. These are the instinctual motivations that cause us to hoard food, gather wealth, and procreate. A secular rationalist, thinking himself or herself free of religious obligations, could still act from selfishness, desire, emotion, or anger. As an example, global warming could be solved tomorrow; all the science is there. But people, many scientists and humanists included, want their stereos, their big cars, their air-conditioned homes, and their lighted walkways. Reason would dictate we all need to sacrifice for the common good, but the desire for self-fulfillment and comfort overrides what would otherwise be good common sense.

Reason alone cannot guide us to right actions given that our animal urges plague us. We need a nudge from inside to counterbalance the animal in all of us. That nudge is our *fitrah*, or inner nature and inclination to seek God. Think of the *fitrah* as that little voice in your head that takes you to task when you do something wrong or that makes you look longingly upon someone performing a selfless act of religious devotion or sacrificing for the greater good. The Prophet Muhammad once said that every child is born with the natural inclination to surrender to Allah, that is, to be a Muslim, but parents make the child a Jew, a Christian, or a Zoroastrian. This is a way of saying that our environment can shape and mold us into life patterns that are far from our real nature.

When a child is born, the child enters a world in which the signs of God's creative power found in nature and the child's own *fitrah* seek to influence him or her to believe in God. Other forces, as we shall see, attempt to take the child's focus away from God. At birth we are also equipped with a kind of free will. What does that mean in practical terms? It means that we humans have the choice of surrendering ourselves to Allah or of rejecting Him, preferring to focus only on creature comforts and temporary worldly interests. Thus we are given the power to choose whether to become Muslim; that is, whether to surrender to God's universal way.

ASK THE IMAM

A person who decides to convert to Islam will find an easy entry into the faith. All the person has to do is recite a two-line statement, called the *Testimony of Faith,* in the presence of two witnesses and, *voilà,* the person is in! All past sins are erased and the person starts out as fresh as if just born. This is "born-again" religion Islamic style.

Can You Stand on One Leg?

Interestingly enough, Islam teaches that our physical bodies are already *Muslim* in that our blood flows, our organs work, and our cells reproduce, just as they were made to do. It is within the heart and mind where we have control over our choices and beliefs. It's as if we're half Muslim and half not. The very purpose of our existence, then, is to use our eyes, ears, brains, emotions, and *fitrah* to come to the realization that God is real and that we must surrender our will to His will. By doing so we can join the rest of the universe and exist in harmony with the only true reality that is. There is a faint echo here of the Buddhist and Taoist ideal of being at one with the universe.

By deciding not to fight against Allah's good way, we live a stress-free life in harmony with all things around us. When we say, "I will not fight against you anymore, God," we float peacefully in the great river that is life until we ultimately reach our final destination and return to God as sincere as we can make ourselves.

The Least You Need to Know

- The word *Islam* means peace and surrender to God.
- Humans have a kind of free will that God is testing.
- Islam believes in a spirit world populated by angels and by creatures called *jinns.*
- People have a moral compass called a *fitrah,* which directs them to look for God.

Looking at Life the Islamic Way

In This Chapter

- Find out about the three stages of the soul according to Islam
- Be aware of the major sins and how to obtain forgiveness from God
- Understand the meaning of accountability
- Learn about the Islamic concept of reward and punishment from God

Philosophers throughout the ages have attempted to tackle the issue of good and evil. What makes a good person go bad, and how can a bad person reform himself or herself? Every religion has its own answer to these questions, and Islam is no different. But whereas other spiritual traditions may emphasize external forces as the primary cause for our sinful behavior, Islam first looks inward. It does so, not with a broad brush by claiming we are born with original sin, such as the Christian New Testament asserts in Romans 5:12, but by delving into the soul and its secrets.

Islam holds that we are all born basically good but have a natural weakness attributable to our physical nature. Social scientists call this our desire for pleasure and aversion to pain. Through these creature instincts we have the capacity to fall into sin. Islam also has the concept of an evil enemy, a Devil that preys upon our hearts and minds. However, this being has only limited power over us and God has given us the tools to combat him. The result is that we can elevate ourselves to a higher level of spirituality or descend to a deplorable moral state. God will judge our faith (*Iman*) and conduct (*'Amal*) in this great struggle after our physical death and resurrection on the Day of Judgment, and we will be punished or rewarded as a consequence.

The Three-Fold Journey

All human beings have three levels of self-development through which they must pass during their lives:

- **The Animal Self**   Acting on basic instincts and desires
- **The Accusing Self**   Higher-order questioning of our purpose
- **The Restful Self**   Transcending worldliness as a focus

These are the stages we pass through as we struggle to come to the final realization that God is, in fact, real and that we ought to move closer to Him. Islam teaches that we are all born sinless and free of sin. This is the condition of our soul upon birth. But being creatures of the flesh, we can be drawn into the pleasures of the flesh as embodied in the world around us. This is best demonstrated in the spoiled child syndrome. No child is born evil, but if a child's every urging and craving is fulfilled, if the child never learns any self-control, then the child becomes unruly and impatient. The soul's journey, Islam would say, got off to a bad start.

The aim of our *fitrah*, or inner nature, is to countermand this trend and elevate our minds to seek God. The journey out of the first stage, our binding tie to seek ever greater resources unto ourselves, is perhaps the hardest of all. The reward for reaching the end of this struggle, however, is an eternal reward, though not everyone will reach his or her full potential. As the Qur'an says, "By the soul and the proportion and order given to it; And its innate knowledge of wrong and right; Whoever purifies it will succeed. And whoever corrupts it will fail!" (Qur'an 91:7–10)

The Animal in All of Us

The first stage of our soul is activated from birth and is called the *Animal Self*. During this stage our basic desires for food, sex, creature comforts, and wealth guide our life choices. People who remain stuck in this stage as they grow older wind up living only for themselves and their own pleasure. Think of all those people in the world who do nothing but indulge their whims. No matter how rich or poor, educated or ignorant, famous or unknown, all of us are susceptible to the temptations of our earthly desire for self-satisfaction. Christians call such people hedonists. The Qur'an often refers contemptuously to "the life of this world," describing it as nothing more than "play and amusement, mutual rivalry, hoarding wealth, and boasting." "How can you turn down God?" the Qur'an asks, "when He gave you life when you had none. Then He will take back your life and you will return back to Him."

The struggle out of our Animal Self stage is made even harder by the efforts of an evil *jinn* named *Shaytan*. *Shaytan* and all those *jinns* who follow him seek to corrupt and ruin us so that we will eventually forget our Creator. They do this by playing upon our fears, desires, and emotions, ultimately causing us to make bad choices if we succumb to their intimations. As you might have noticed, the spelling of the name *Shaytan* is close to that of *Satan*. But although some of the concepts are similar, there are some important differences between the Islamic view of the Devil and what is believed in the Christian and Jewish religions. You find out more about *Shaytan* and where he came from in Chapter 6.

DEFINITION

The name **Shaytan,** which is the Islamic term for Satan, means to pull away from. Thus, *Shaytan* seeks to pull us away from God. He does this by goading us into seeking ever greater physical pleasure and ignoring our *fitrah,* or inner inclination to seek our Creator.

Stepping Up to the Plate

When we discard the life-is-a-big-party attitude and begin to pay attention to our *fitrah*, we receive a flash of insight, a deep thought. Here is the chance to enter into the second level of our soul's development, the *Accusing Self.* Now the big questions come flooding in: Why am I here? What's it all for? Is what I'm doing right? What happens to me when I die? Is there a next life?

A person may reflect on the meaning of life for weeks, months, or years until finally becoming motivated to seek spiritual guidance. The person has become ready to look for God. Generally, a person will move toward what is familiar, and thus you can see people becoming fervent practitioners of Christianity, Judaism, Buddhism, and so on. This is all very natural and from the Islamic perspective the practice of any noble spiritual path is better than none at all. Some people fail to have their hunger satisfied by their traditional religion, however, and may begin to explore or experiment with other religions. The Qur'an expects this and postulates that with enough study and research a spiritual wanderer will eventually move beyond those previously revealed (and compromised) religions and into the Islamic way of life that God revealed as His last religious "installment" to the world. (I discuss this topic in further detail in Chapter 9.)

Regardless of the initial path to *enlightenment*, after this second stage has been entered and we realize through our heart and mind that we need God and wholesome values, we can now try to mold our life according to His universal way. We become less attached to the life of this world, more introspective and less irritable and stressed. If we were lucky enough to find the Islamic path, then even greater progress can be made. Through a daily regimen of prayer, reflection, fasting, and study, and a consciousness of morality, our heart becomes more and more at ease.

The Supreme Achievement

One day, through devoted effort, we may achieve complete peace and tranquility in our heart. Now we have entered the third and final stage of our soul's development. Nothing in the world has a hold on us any longer. We lead lives of quiet contemplation and are not overly discomfited by any tragedy or bounty that may come our way. We realize we will die and return to God and that this whole life is a test for us. It's not that we become unfeeling, but that we put things in *perspective*, the ultimate perspective.

ASK THE IMAM

Islam teaches that God sent prophets to every nation and that every racial and ethnic group received some form of divine guidance. Most of the major Jewish prophets and, of course, Jesus, are accepted by the Qur'an as true guides from God. The original Torah, Psalms, and Gospel are considered revelations from God that came before the Qur'an.

This third stage occurs when a soul becomes a *Restful Self*, awaiting the meeting with the Creator. The individual still has a job, family, and vacations: Islam has no place for monasteries or asceticism. While still maintaining a normal life, the person is no longer living only to satisfy himself or herself, but realizes the higher purpose of life. Thoughts of charity, self-sacrifice, truth, and the simple beauty of life blend together to create a noticeable aura of peace and wisdom around people whose souls are truly *at rest*.

Sin and Redemption

I've talked a lot about following God's way in your life, so what does it mean to *surrender* to God? For a Muslim, surrendering to God means to believe in Him, to follow a lifestyle that promotes harmony on Earth and among people, and to follow a personal code of morality that can lead to an ever higher understanding of God's nature. God's revelations have guided people throughout history in how to do this. The original Torah, Gospel, scrolls of Abraham, Psalms of David, and countless other religiously inspired texts detail how to achieve such a goal. Islam accepts the validity of them all, though the Qur'an points out that no previous revelation from God has survived without alteration or editing by human hands. The Qur'an, which is considered the last installment of divine guidance to the world, declares itself the culmination of all of God's previous revelations to us and thus is the source for how to live a Godly lifestyle. The Qur'an, incidentally, says it is the one book that God won't allow people to change.

Islam makes a clear distinction between good and evil. Islamic Law, which is derived from the rules contained in the Qur'an and the oral traditions of the Prophet Muhammad, is a detailed code concerned with do's and don'ts, good and evil, and relations among people. A Jewish or Christian person might be very surprised to learn that nearly every virtue one can think of in the Western religious tradition has its counterpart in Islam. Charity, honesty, thrift, compassion, self-control, and integrity are the goals of a Muslim, while dishonesty, violent behavior, greed, jealousy, gossip, and sexual promiscuity are considered sins that deserve to be condemned. Although Islam has no definitive listing of a "Ten Commandments" or a "Seven Deadly Sins," there are ample Qur'anic verses and prophetic teachings to put together a list of over 100 virtues and vices for a Muslim to be aware of. Some of these are listed next.

The major sins in Islam are ...

- Committing idolatry.
- Stealing from an orphan.
- Committing adultery or fornication.
- Disobeying parents.
- Collecting interest on investments.
- Accusing a chaste woman falsely.

- Giving false testimony.

- Committing murder or suicide.

- Committing infanticide.

- Enslaving a free person.

- Engaging in slander and gossip.

The virtuous deeds in Islam are …

- Speaking the truth.

- Being kind to family.

- Honoring parents.

- Giving in charity.

- Feeding the poor.

- Fighting against injustice.

- Freeing slaves.

- Returning borrowed property.

- Studying and learning.

- Being kind to animals.

How Does God Forgive?

Islam teaches that when you commit a bad deed, or a sin, it will be held against you on Judgment Day. The only way to remove the stain of that sin is to follow a four-step process of repentance called making *tawba*. To receive God's forgiveness, you must …

- Feel remorseful about the sin.

- Repent of your action to God by saying, "My Lord forgive me."

- Make restitution for the sin if possible.

- Resolve sincerely never to do the sin again.

God has promised to forgive our sins if we seek His forgiveness sincerely. If we, despite our best efforts, repeat the same sin later, we can repeat this process again.

ASK THE IMAM

There is no concept of confession to a priest in Islam or of burnt offerings to atone for sins. Likewise there is no virtue in airing a person's own bad deeds in public. Sin is a private matter between the sinner and God. Only when a person breaks civil laws should the public know about it.

Law and Order

In addition, for some sins in which other people's rights or safety were harmed, there are prescribed penalties that must be paid in this life. These are a kind of deterrent to show people that theft, murder, arson, and other social crimes have consequences. Unfortunately, the way the Western media presents it, you would think that in Islam chopping off a hand or a nose or a toe was the norm for punishing people. In fact, there are only a few crimes that incur physical punishment and even then Islamic Law allows the judge to forgo those if mitigating circumstances allow. (The only physical punishments are cutting off the hand for repeated theft, flogging for certain crimes like fornication, and capital punishment for murder or treason.) Personal moral sins require only the four-step process of repentance previously outlined, which is done by an individual in private. As you may have noticed, Islamic Law mixes personal morality and civil and criminal law into one overall code in keeping with the religious view that there is no difference between the secular and spiritual realms, though only criminal activity is prosecuted in front of a judge.

FROM THE SOURCE

Muhammad said, "Allah has recorded both good and bad deeds. Whoever intended to do a good deed and did not do it, Allah writes it down with Himself as a full good deed. But if he intended to do it and did it, Allah writes it down with Himself as worth from ten to seven hundred good deeds, or many times over. But if he intended to do a bad deed and did not do it, Allah writes it down with Himself as a full good deed, but if he intended it and did it, Allah writes it down as one bad deed."

Everything Counts When It Counts

Islam does not accept the idea that you need to ask a priest to forgive you or pray to the Son of God for deliverance. Even more incomprehensible to Muslims is the common Protestant Christian belief of being "saved by grace" in which a person who asks Jesus into his or her heart automatically goes to heaven no matter what the person does later in life, good or bad. Islam teaches that you can save or damn yourself every day through your belief, or lack of it; your actions, good or bad; and your overall record. God's mercy will play a major part on Judgment Day because no human can ever hope to be perfect enough to earn heaven. God, in His mercy, will forgive much and overlook much, but this doesn't absolve us of our responsibility to try to be as virtuous as possible. The Muslim is taught that there is an open line from each of us to God, and when we pray for forgiveness we must each ask God ourselves, every day, until the day we leave this earth.

Our sins, if we don't repent of them, will be held against us. Likewise, good deeds are considered the hallmark of our true faith. Every time we do a good or bad deed it is recorded with God and will be a part of our record come Judgment Day. Islam, however, does not teach that you *earn* your way to heaven, as some Christian theologians have charged. Salvation in Islam is founded on believing in and surrendering your will to God and nothing more. Avoiding sin and leading a righteous life are merely proofs of your faith. A Muslim would respond to the false accusation that Muslims get to heaven by deeds by quoting the Apostle Paul who said, *"Faith without works is dead."* So the emphasis on good deeds in Islam is for another, more noble purpose: to give us a way to measure the strength and veracity of our convictions.

FROM THE SOURCE

Once a man came to the Prophet Muhammad and asked, "What is faith?" He replied, "When doing good makes you feel good and when doing bad makes you feel bad, then you are a believer." The man asked again, "What is a sin?" The Prophet answered, "When something bothers your conscience, give it up."

The Last Payday

God will reward good even as He will punish evil. This being the case, the more good you do, the more rewards you will get from God. A Muslim, then, is basically given more incentive to do good in the world than to do evil. Think of why Communism failed all over the world. Weren't its precepts noble? No one owns anything; everyone is paid the same, regardless. In practice, however, what happened was that few people worked hard because so many took the attitude that diligent work didn't matter. A hard worker would get no special recognition. Capitalism, on the other hand, succeeds on a certain level because the promise of greater returns for greater effort propels people onward and forward in a mad rush. The Qur'an says, "Every soul has a goal to work towards. Make your goal doing good and race with others for this purpose." (Qur'an 2:148)

Allah rewards us according to the amount of our good deeds. It's a kind of religious capitalism with results that can only make life better for everyone. If more people were eager to help the poor, visit the sick, adopt orphans, and assist the elderly, there would be no need for government welfare, nursing homes, and the like. In addition, the Prophet Muhammad emphasized the inherent value of doing good for others by saying it would make our own faith stronger and increase our satisfaction in life.

Our Report Card

All of our good and bad deeds are recorded in our own individual record. On the Day of Judgment, which will occur sometime in the future, we will be confronted with our book of deeds. Using the yardstick of our faith, deeds, and motivations, we will then be sent to either Heaven or Hell, barring Allah's extra mercy upon souls who would otherwise deserve punishment. Quite simply, the Day of Judgment is when we get our grade for our test in life. Were we greedy and immoral or kind and hopeful in God? An interesting caveat is that on Judgment Day, when our record is read, anyone we ever wronged will be brought in front of us and they will be told to help themselves to our stash of good deeds in order to compensate them for what we did to them in our earthly life. This gives new meaning to the phrase, "Get your affairs in order before you come to regret it!"

FROM THE SOURCE

The Prophet Muhammad once said, "When a believer sins, there is a dark spot put on his heart, and if he repents and asks for pardon, his heart is polished. But if he keeps on sinning, the dark spots increase until darkness gains ascendancy over his heart."

Christianity teaches that people are already doomed to Hell unless they believe that God's son died for their sins going back to the sin of Adam and Eve. Islam, however, does not teach that people are born sinful. Rather, Islam teaches that we are all born spotless and that throughout our lives we can do either good or bad based on the interplay of our *fitrah*, intelligence, and God's revealed guidance versus *Shaytan* and our lowly animal desires. Salvation in Islam comes from making the choice while alive to accept God and mold your life according to the way of life He has established. That life is based on morality, daily and annual rituals, and repentance for your weakness or misdeeds.

There'll Be Hell to Pay

Why is there the punishment of Hell if we fail God's test? The consequence of rejecting God and staying in the Animal Self stage is that our soul becomes corrupted, or warped. We took our gifts of free will and intelligence and wasted them, burying our *fitrah* in a life filled with meaningless pleasure. In that case, our soul must be repaired before it can enter again into God's presence in the *akhirah*, or next life. Thus, we may find ourselves in Hell where our soul is cleansed by fire of all the dirt we heaped upon it through our immorality and misdeeds in the world. The Qur'an explains the two fates this way:

> Shaytan makes them promises and creates in them false desires, but Shaytan's promises are nothing but deception. [His followers] will have their dwelling in Hell, and they won't find any way to escape it. But those who believe and do what is right will soon be admitted by Us into gardens beneath which rivers flow to live there forever. Allah's promise is the truth and whose word can be truer than Allah's? Anyone who does what is right, whether they are male or female, and has faith, they will enter Paradise and not the least bit of injustice will be done to them. (Qur'an 2:120–123)

When the deserved punishment is finished, the newly cleansed soul may again rejoin God's presence and receive its reward in Heaven for any true belief he or she had and any good done. Some souls, however, are so warped by their owners that they will never get out of Hell and will remain there forever. Think of Hitler or Charles Manson—can anyone ever imagine their redemption? Although, as we are taught to say in Islam, God knows best. In other words, He knows the secrets of our hearts better than we know them ourselves. You will find more about Heaven and Hell in Chapter 6.

The Least You Need to Know

- Muslims believe that people are in this life to be tested on whether or not they will surrender to God's will and lead a moral lifestyle.

- There are three levels of personal spiritual development: the Animal Self, the Accusing Self, and the Restful Self.

- Islam does not teach that humans are inherently sinful. In Islam, sin is not a consequence of birth but rather the result of a choice that the individual has made to commit a bad deed.

- God can forgive any person who asks for forgiveness and is sincere. God is more likely to forgive than to punish.

- Muslims believe people will be held accountable on a Day of Judgment and will be rewarded by God with eternity in Heaven or punishment in Hell.

All About Allah

In This Chapter

- Learn in detail about the Muslim concept of God
- Revisit the main religious beliefs prevalent in Arabia during Muhammad's time
- Discover the Ninety-Nine Names of Allah
- Learn what God means to the ordinary Muslim

Islam has a very well-defined concept of what God is and what He is not. Perhaps no other religion has spent as much time defining God and trying to understand how much we *cannot* understand about Him. Given that Islam categorically forbids making any representations of God, Muslim ideas of God are not affected by changes in social values or mores. For example, until recently in the Western world, God has traditionally been referred to in the masculine gender, and representations show God as a man. Now, as a result of the women's rights movement, some people are using the feminine gender when making references to God. Muslims take a different approach and are content with a concept of God that has far-reaching implications in our modern world.

For the Muslim, God is not personified into forms or shapes created by the imagination of men and women. (How can you paint or carve what you never saw?) The corpus of literature and the arts produced in Islamic civilization are also strangely absent of divine imagery. Although many other religions have prohibitions against making pictures and statues depicting God, only Islam has succeeded so well that the concept is unknown. As you will see, what Muslims lack in artwork about God they make up for in a compelling intellectual and spiritual ideology. In this chapter, I will clarify just who and what God is to Muslims.

God and Hollywood

The Islamic concept of God has often been called the most uncompromising *monotheism*, next to Judaism, in the world. Islam has a very definite concept of God and how to understand Him, and it has no time for concepts that bring God down to the level of human imagination. With the establishment of Islam as a third major influence in the religious life of North America, Muslims must face a new set of challenges and opportunities. Chief among these is battling the distortions about God and His nature that appear in the mind of the general public and in popular culture.

In addition to promoting disbelief in God, a trend that Islam abhors, today's movies have transformed God into a fun-loving old man, such as in the *Oh, God* movies (starring George Burns) or have typecast Him as a stern, yet fickle being as portrayed by Dustin Hoffman in *Joan of Arc*, or even as a kind of glutton for punishment as in Mel Gibson's *The Passion of the Christ*. In Hollywood, God seems to be whatever the director wants Him to be. Hey, and you don't even have to pay Him!

During the Christian-organized protests of the movie *The Last Temptation of Christ*, Muslim organizations asked their followers not to attend the movie theaters that were showing this controversial film. But whereas Christians were defending the honor of their God, Muslims were more interested in upholding the honor of a man who is considered to be one of the greatest prophets. The same holds true with *The Passion of the Christ*, a movie in which Jesus is beaten up for over an hour. Even though many Christians embraced this movie, Muslims still counseled each other not to view it. By the way, Muslims shun all movies and cartoons about prophets. Disney's kid-oriented portrayals of such figures as Moses and Joseph and the never-ending stream of made-for-TV movies about David and Jesus are considered in poor taste by Muslims, who see any attempt to represent the physical features of a prophet as wrong.

 ASK THE IMAM

Islam forbids all realistic representations of people or animals. Muhammad said that on the Day of Judgment God will command people to put life in what they fashioned. Exceptions are made for children's toys and art for kids.

By showing the face of a prophet, these movies and cartoons give people a false idea about what the prophet looked like, and thus they begin to judge that prophet by the actor's looks and performance. People become less interested in the prophet's *teachings* and more so in his *charisma*. When was the last time you saw an unattractive man playing the part of a prophet? How many such movies made you desire to transform your life? These kinds of cinematic portrayals offer a good story, not a God-inspired way of living, which is, incidentally, what the prophets really stood for.

There Is Only One God

Muslims look aghast these days at the efforts of popular culture to promote the idea that we are all gods inside our hearts or that God "lives within us," and we can "tap into" His power like some sort of personal energy reservoir. It seems people are creating God in their own image and justifying any action they engage in by claiming that "God is Love" and so will condone all types of behavior.

It seems sometimes that authentic knowledge of God and a seriousness about what He represents have descended to the level of a personal opinion. Muslims stand, along with sincere people of every monotheistic religion, like lighthouses in the storm, calling people to resist the false suggestions of *Shaytan*, or Satan. Muslims have been among the staunchest defenders in the world of their ideology about God. The Qur'an warned us long ago that the desire of *Shaytan* is to separate us from God, and what better way for him to succeed than to get all of us to call ourselves gods and goddesses or to make up gods of our own!

Does God Show Himself to Us?

Has anyone ever seen God? If you were to believe the claims of some televangelists, God comes and visits people in their living rooms all the time. Islam records only one incident in which a person came close to seeing God. The Qur'an records that the Prophet Moses, who is considered to be one of the greatest prophets in Islam, asked Allah if he could see Him. Moses was all alone on Mount Sinai and thought now would be his chance to look upon the Being he loved more than any other. Allah asked him, "Don't you believe in Me?" Moses affirmed that he did but that he wanted to see Allah to satisfy his own longing. Allah said that if Moses could keep his eye on the next mountain then he would see Him. Allah began to materialize His power on the mountain, which shook and rumbled in a great cataclysm. Moses couldn't withstand the sight, however, and passed out without seeing what he wanted to see. His faith was given quite a boost, though! So no one has ever seen God in this life.

Islam on God

As explained in Chapter 2, Islam teaches that its God is the same God as the God of the Jews and Christians. So how does Islam see God in its own terms? How is its view alike yet different from the Judeo-Christian tradition? The first cardinal belief in Islam about God, or Allah, is that He is only one being, without division, children, or partners. This doctrine is called *tauhid*, or oneness. God is strong enough and capable enough not to need anyone's help or to divide Himself into parts to do different jobs. The Islamic phrase that is most often repeated by Muslims on a daily basis (during prayer) and that reflects these teachings is *La ilaha ill Allah*, which translates as "There is no god other than God." In addition, Muslims are taught that He is not the God of a chosen people nor can any racial or ethnic community lay claim to His exclusive attention. Even Muslims cannot claim exclusive rights to Him as He is, as the Qur'an explains, the *Lord of All Creation*.

Understandably, the Qur'an completely rejects the Christian Trinity theory. It answers the idea of a three-in-one God with these words: "They are blasphemers, those who say that God is the third of three in a Trinity. There is no god except the One God." (Qur'an 5:73) In the same spirit, Islam would also respectfully disagree with the Jewish belief that God has an all-time covenant with them and a special relationship that divides the entire world by race into Jews and Gentiles. The idea that God makes any kind of racial preferences is reprehensible in Islam. The Qur'an says in this regard, "The Jews and the Christians declare, 'We are the sons of God and He loves us.' Ask them, 'So why does He punish you for your sins (like everyone else)? But no, you are only some people from among the (many) nations He has created.'" (Qur'an 5:17)

Needless to say, the practice of idolatry in which there are many gods, each with its own sphere of influence, is considered ludicrous by the Qur'an, which says, "God has birthed no son nor is there any god along with Him. If there were many gods, behold each god would have taken away what it had created and some would have lorded it over others!" (Qur'an 23:91)

Pagan Arab Beliefs Before the Coming of Islam

The Prophet Muhammad was born in Arabia in 570 c.e. He grew up in the southwestern city of Mecca, which at that time was a major trading town. Although a handful of Christians lived in or around the city, the vast majority of people were Arabs who worshipped idols. Prior to Muhammad's birth the Meccan leaders even banned Christianity outright in the city limits, seeing that it would threaten their age-old way of life. (Little did they realize what new message was about to come!) The Meccans, to be fair, did believe in the concept of an overall Creator (in a fuzzy sort of way), but they felt that the main deity was too remote to be concerned with human affairs. Thus, they venerated idols, thinking they were "convenient gods" who would bring luck, safety, good business deals, and other bounties on a daily basis.

DISPELLING THE MYTH

The pagan Arabs accepted a supreme God over all the demigods they worshipped, but they considered Allah to be too powerful and remote to make any difference in their lives.

It is in this context that Muhammad grew up. Interestingly enough, from his earliest age he disliked idol worship, equating it with superstition, and he never engaged in its practice. This is partly why Muslims believe God chose him to be His last prophet to the world. In this he was not entirely alone. An informal tradition of quasi-agnosticism was practiced by a few in the peninsula. These people, who were nicknamed *hanifs*, believed in God but shunned all idolatry and even well-developed religions like Christianity.

Beginning with Muhammad's first exhortations in 610 c.e., we find the earliest revelations of the Qur'an concerned mainly with the evils of worshipping anything else besides the unseen God (a sin called *shirk*) and of the dangers of living an immoral or unjust lifestyle. The Qur'an declared that God is not remote and is not contained in a wood or stone carving. He hears our prayers. He knows our thoughts and actions, and He needs no partners or lesser gods to do His will in the universe.

The Middle East

Mecca is located in southwestern Arabia at the junction of several ancient trading routes.

The Qur'an Speaks

One of the most memorized portions of the Qur'an is the short chapter titled "Sincerity," which states:

> Tell people that He is One God; Allah, the Eternal Absolute. He neither gives birth nor was He ever begotten, and there is nothing equal to Him. (Qur'an 112:1–4)

For the pagan Arab this message was completely new. In their world, magic, spirits, shamans, luck, totems, and idols were the defining characteristics of religion. Islam challenged the very core of their belief system. Thus it was inevitable that they would oppose Islam when it was first offered to them by the Prophet Muhammad as an alternative belief system.

FROM THE SOURCE

Every soul draws the results of its actions on none but itself: no bearer of burdens can bear the burden of another. (Qur'an 6:164)

Man and God

Contrary to the beliefs that the pre-Islamic Arabs held, Islam teaches that every person has to face God alone. No one can look to another god or person to save himself or herself in this life or in the next. The Qur'an goes so far as to declare that on the Day of Judgment the false idols in which people placed their hope will be brought forward and made to speak. The idols will reject the people who used to worship them and will taunt them, saying that they were fools for believing in gods of their own making. In desperation the idol-worshippers will even start to blame *Shaytan*, but he will shrug off the blame, saying he only suggested it. He didn't make them call on false gods. The Qur'an is very clear about blame being laid squarely upon our own shoulders. Listen to how cold *Shaytan's* response will be when we try to blame him for our misdeeds.

> And Shaytan will say [on Judgment Day], "It was Allah Who gave you a true promise. I made a promise to you also but I failed in my promise. I had no authority over you except to suggest things to you, but you listened to me. So don't blame me, only blame your own souls. I can't listen to your cries nor can you listen to mine. I reject your former act in associating me with Allah. For wrongdoers (like you) there must be a terrible Penalty." (Qur'an 14:22)

Do Muslims Believe in Original Sin?

If Islam teaches that we all have to bear our own burdens on Judgment Day, how does this idea stack up to Christianity's view that Jesus takes on all our sins? Is there a doctrine of original sin and atonement in Islam? To answer this question, we need to realize that the entire edifice of Christianity hangs on the assumption that because Adam and Eve sinned all human beings have the taint of that original sin on their hearts. According to this theory, everyone is automatically doomed to Hell because of it. God had to send His own begotten child to earth to be killed by people to atone for the sins of man going back to the Original Sin. Believing in Jesus' death and rebirth, Christians say, is what saves us from a curse that can't be lifted otherwise.

Before going further, we need to mention that the Christian concept of God having a son is directly addressed in the Qur'an. Islam considers Jesus to be a prophet of God, born of the Virgin Mary as a special miracle from God. Muslims accept the Virgin birth but consider the lack of a father in Jesus' creation as being on the same level as the lack of parents in Adam's creation. Muslims do not take Jesus' birth as a sign of godhood or as a sign that Jesus was the son of a god. The Qur'an states, "The likeness of Jesus in the sight of God is that of Adam. He created him from dust and said, 'Be' and he was."

ASK THE IMAM

Sometimes God refers to Himself as "We" or "Us" in the Qur'an. A few Christian scholars have suggested that this shows that there is room for the Trinity theory in Islam, but this plural usage of pronouns is merely a common technique called the "Royal We," which is used in many languages. In other words, a powerful king might say, "We decree that ..." even though he is one man. What he is emphasizing by saying *We* is "I *and* My power are decreeing that ...."

The Qur'an even denies that Jesus was killed on a cross. It says that he was neither killed nor crucified but that it was "made to appear so." What happened to Jesus, then? Did he run off to India and study Buddhism like some New Age proponents argue? The Qur'an states only that God saved Jesus and "took him to Himself." Muslims interpret this to mean that God took Jesus to paradise and is keeping him there until he must return to Earth to defeat the anti-Christ. For more details, see Chapter 9.

Islam flatly rejects any notion of original sin and says we are all born pure. Yes, Adam and Eve sinned, the Qur'an says, but God forgave them when they asked for His mercy. No sin was passed on to their descendants. Thus, it is our cumulative faith and actions that determine our salvation. The Qur'an declares that Allah can forgive any sin He wants to, whenever He wants to, and that He has no children nor any need for them to act as sacrifices. Certainly God would never allow Himself to be tortured and killed by His creatures before He would forgive them! The Qur'an explains that it is beneath the majesty of God to do such things. It is no sign of love for a Muslim that God would die for him or her. So the doctrines of original sin and the Trinity have no room in the Islamic concept of God because Islam asserts that God's power is great enough for Him to forgive anything without requiring His death first.

How Close Is Close?

But does God's absolute power make Him remote and unconcerned? Islam says no. We can build a personal relationship with Allah because He can hear all our thoughts and because He knows our feelings. He is not far away and cold. "He's as close as our jugular vein" says the popular Qur'anic verse. In the Qur'an Allah says, "Call upon Me. I listen to the call of every person when they invoke Me." Although we don't phrase our creed in quite the same way as Christians might—"Accept Allah into your hearts and be saved"—we do have a similar phrase: *Ataqullah*, which means, "Be aware of God in your heart." The word *taqwa* means consciousness or awareness of God in your life. It also implies self-control, knowing that God is watching you. The more *taqwa* you have in your heart, the closer you are to God. Islam teaches that prayer, fasting, reflection on life and its brevity, and selfless action can cause your *taqwa* to grow.

Allah Has Many Names

The Qur'an provides a very clear picture of God, but not in the style of the Bible. The Bible begins by saying that God made man in *His image*, that is, God looks like a human; whereas the Qur'an declares emphatically that God has no form we can comprehend and that He resembles nothing at all in creation. Like Judaism, Islam completely forbids making representations of God, such as paintings or statues. The Qur'an says, "He is not like anything you can imagine." God is not a human, an animal, or a fuzzy spirit. The rule in Islam is that if you make a mental picture of what God looks like, then God does not look like that at all!

So if God has no form, how can we understand Him? Are we doomed to endless reprimands of "It's a mystery"? In Hinduism or Christianity, there are statues and paintings of God, but Islam says these are all false imagery. How does a Muslim imagine God, then? Islam has a unique answer to this human need to rely on appearances. Instead of focusing on God's physical form, we look to His *qualities*. What does God *do?* What is His *nature?* What is He *like?* These are called Allah's Names and Attributes. Muslims use adjectives to describe the nature of God, and through studying them and emulating them come to a closer understanding of who God really is. The Muslim approach is not to passively look at pictures but to actively participate in knowing the Divine.

FROM THE SOURCE

Tell them, "Call on 'God' or call on 'the Compassionate' by whatever name you call upon Him (it is well), for to Him belongs the Most Beautiful Names. (Qur'an 17:109)

There is a famous listing called the Ninety-Nine Names of Allah. The list includes such descriptions as the Merciful, the Strong, the Mighty, the Loving, the Everlasting, the Beginning, the Last, the Acceptor of Repentance, the Caring, the Bringer of Peace, the Avenger of Evil, the Living, the Faithful, and so on. Through these Names of Allah we get a feel for the essence of Allah, and thus we no longer have to worry about what He physically looks like. We can know Him by His qualities and actions. The Prophet Muhammad once said that whoever knows and lives by the Ninety-Nine Names of Allah will go to Heaven. This is a way of saying that God's qualities are the best ones to inculcate in yourself, for by doing so, you bring your life closer to His way.

Islam also teaches that God is neither male nor female. After all, if He has no form that we can understand, how can He have a gender? So why, you may ask, do we use the pronoun "He" when referring to God? In Arabic, as in Spanish or French, all nouns are either male or female in gender. A house is considered feminine but a chair is masculine. It's just the way these languages work.

In Arabic there is no word for "it," so the pronoun "He" is used to refer to God, with the full understanding that Allah is not a male. Interestingly enough, the base word *Elah*, which means *a god*, is a feminine word (the *ah* ending signifies femininity in Arabic); yet when you take the proper name *Allah* (*the* God) and use the masculine pronoun *Hoowa* (He is), you are canceling out both male and female genders. The phrase *Hoowa Allah* combines both genders and thus each negates the other. This is the closest thing to "it" that you can get in Arabic and applies to no other words in that language.

To summarize, Islam teaches that God is a single entity with no divisions, partners, wives, or children. He has no beginning or end. He does not reveal Himself to people, and no human eye is strong enough to behold His power. He can do all that He wishes with no need of a helper. He is not male or female. He has no form we can comprehend. We can know what He is like only through the names He used to describe Himself in the Qur'an. He did not burden us with original sin nor does He ever need to die for any purpose. Idolatry is false. Allah is not a remote God; rather He is active in human affairs and is testing us in this life and giving us the chance to choose to surrender to Him.

The Least You Need to Know

- Islam is a monotheistic religion with no concept of the Trinity.
- Muslims believe that God is all-powerful and that He knows all, sees all, and can do whatever He wishes.
- Original sin has no place in Islamic teachings. Every person has the potential to be good or bad, and there is no need for any atonement or redemption.
- Muslims have no physical description or representation of God. They have an abstract concept that consists of God's qualities, which are embodied in the Ninety-Nine Names of God.
- In Islam, God is not male or female, nor was He ever born on Earth. He never begets any children and He does not show Himself to people.

The Spiritual World in Islam

What is the meaning of our lives here on Earth? What is the soul, where did it come from, and what happens to it after we die? Islam provides its followers with answers to these and many other questions related to both this earthly sojourn and the life to come. Muslims believe that we all have four stages to go through on our great journey called life and that each station has its own unique challenges and rewards.

Islam also has an explanation for the creation of the earth and the appearance of living beings upon it. The Muslim Holy Book, the Qur'an, tells us that life arose for a purpose. All lifeforms on this planet, and beyond, have a special duty to live in quiet praise and obedience to the Lord of the Universe.

Although Islam says all nonhuman creatures accomplish this automatically, our kind is the one exception. We have the free choice to accept God or not. The path of Islam gives us a way to surrender ourselves to God if we so choose. Free will is our great burden, and there will be rewards and consequences on account of it. In these chapters, I explain the four stages of Islamic life as well as our earthly purpose as detailed in the Qur'an.

The Four Stages of Life in Islam

In This Chapter

- Learn what Islam says about the significance of conception, life, death, and beyond
- Discover the main duty of the angels who watch over us
- Find out what happens to a person's soul after death

There has been a lot of controversy in recent times about the meaning of life and death. When does life begin? When does it end? Does our quality of life determine how long we should live? Islam would say that all of these issues are wrapped up in a larger one—our purpose for being alive. Given that the Qur'an teaches that people exist solely for the sake of learning to surrender to God, it stands to reason that Islam's answers on many of these tough issues would be framed in that context. So in this chapter we will be exploring the journey of life as envisioned by Islam.

So let's begin, then. To put it plainly, Islam puts forward the proposition that human life begins at conception, that the unborn attain personhood at a definite time, and that life after birth is no less than a crucial testing ground where either contentment or frustration will be our lot. However, Islam goes even further by asserting that there exists an undying soul within each one of us that will live on after our physical body has ceased to function. We will still be around after death while we're waiting for Judgment Day, but unlike the fun-loving ghosts in such movies as *Casper* and *Beetlejuice* or the vengeful spirits of *Poltergeist*, Islam tells us that our souls will be put into a kind of storage bin, so to speak, and will get a foretaste of our eventual fate. This is called the Life of the Grave. As you'll see, Islam has quite a lot to say about what will happen there.

Four Lives for Each Life

According to Islam, we all have four well-defined segments of life that we will pass through from our conception in the womb until our death and beyond. These are the stages from the time a soul is joined with the flesh in the womb until we are ultimately in either Heaven or Hell. Each of our four life stages has its own unique challenges and features, and each is considered separate from the others, like a series of doors we must pass through on our journey back to our Creator.

Indeed, the whole concept of life in Islam is that our soul is on loan to us from God. Remember that primordial spirit lump from which all of our souls came and that accepted free will eons ago? Well, that's Allah's property, and when we die He takes back our souls. Of course, now that we have become fully realized individuals we won't be stripped of our uniqueness. He has a different purpose for us then.

The four stages of life are …

- Life in the womb

- Life in the world

- Life in the grave

- The next life (Heaven or Hell)

I will be discussing the first three stages in this chapter, and the expansive topic of the next life in Chapter 6. As you learn about each stage, notice how the Islamic emphasis on our utter dependability on God is interwoven with the events and features therein.

Life in the Womb

Physical life begins at conception, according to Islam. This is the beginning of the first stage of life for us. In the womb we are in our most vulnerable state. Our bodies are growing and developing, and our soul becomes one with our physical self. It is understandable, then, that Islam has teachings concerning the welfare of the fetus.

Islamic Law recognizes the right of the mother to have a protected pregnancy and the right of the fetus to be brought to term. If anyone assaults a pregnant woman and the fetus dies, the perpetrator must pay penalties and compensation, though the act is not classified as full murder in the same sense of killing an already born person. But the very fact that there are penalties for harming a person in the womb shows that Islam considers this stage of life important and worth protecting.

Life in the World

In the teachings of Islam, the moment we are born we enter the proverbial life of the world. This is the second stage of life. In this new reality we will need to learn how to lead a moral and upright lifestyle that is pleasing to God. If we are denied the opportunity to learn a godly lifestyle and orientation as children, either because of neglect or abandonment by our parents, then our *fitrah* will help to guide us in seeking such knowledge. When we enter puberty, the standard for adulthood in Islam, God will hold us accountable for our beliefs and actions.

Shaytan and his minions will continually attempt to corrupt us by whispering evil suggestions into our minds. All the pleasures of the world will present themselves on a platter, tempting our lower animal desires. Our primal motivations will rule over us until such time as we begin to use our reason and inner spiritual motivations to train our hearts and minds to seek God. The Qur'an describes this world as an illusory place of deception and play, rivalry and amusement, boasting and hoarding. If we enter adulthood and aren't careful, we just might fall into the trap of becoming an unabashed hedonist.

FROM THE SOURCE

The Prophet Muhammad said, "A Muslim, male or female, remains subject to trials [in this world] in respect of self, children and property till he or she faces God, the Exalted, [on the Day of Judgment] in a state in which all his or her sins have been forgiven [on account of their struggles]."

The span of our life, which was recorded in our book of deeds, will not last a minute longer than it is supposed to. While we are alive, however, we will be confronted with a series of challenges and tests in life: the car breaks down; whom I should marry; I got a big raise; someone stole my credit card; my mother passed away; and so on. All of these daily life circumstances happen in order to give us the opportunity to improve ourselves and to draw closer to God. According to Islam, these tests and challenges in life serve a purpose. They can bring out the best in us and cause us to dig deep within ourselves where bravery, courage, perseverance, and fortitude reside. Without being tested, how would we know that we have the guts to carry through in times of crisis? The Qur'an asks, "Do people think they can just say, 'We believe' and they won't be tested in what they claim? You can be sure We tested those before them and Allah will make clear those who are true and those who are false." (Qur'an 29:2–3)

Many people take the opposite approach, though, and choose not to rise to the occasion. They fail their tests and forget about God. They resort to lying, cheating, backbiting, corruption, violence, or worse when faced with life's difficult choices. The Qur'an describes them as people who are sitting on the edge of a fence: when times are good, they are satisfied; but when the going gets tough, they engage in evil deeds with no regard for the rights of anyone else.

Careful! You're Being Watched

The Qur'an says that we all have two angels who follow us around throughout our lives. They are called the *Kiraman Katibeen*, or the Noble Writers. One figuratively sits on our right shoulder while the other sits on our left shoulder. Their only job is to write in our book of deeds every action, thought, or feeling we have each day. The right-side angel records our good deeds and the left-side angel notes our bad deeds. (Imagine if someone followed you around all day with a video camera!) Muslim parents often joke with their children that one of their two angels is very busy writing: which one is getting a tired hand?

This metaphorical book in which the angels are writing is our cumulative record, which we will be confronted with on the Day of Judgment after our death. There is a widely circulated story in the Muslim world to bring home the point of God's omnipotence. A religious scholar, or *Shaykh*, wanted to test his young students. He gave each one a piece of candy and told them to go and eat it where no one could see them. All of the students went away and came back some time later. The teacher asked if everyone had eaten their sweets, and they all raised their hands except one boy. When the *Shaykh* questioned the boy about eating the candy, he answered, "I couldn't find a place where Allah couldn't see me."

The Qur'an calls this life a time of trial and testing to show who among us has the most consciousness of God and behaves the best. "O People!" the Qur'an announces, "We created you from a single pair of a male and a female and made you into nations and groups so you can come to know each other. Certainly the noblest among you in the sight of Allah is the one with the most *taqwa* [awareness of Allah]." (Qur'an 49:13)

The preferred lifestyle Islam envisions is one based on prayer, repentance, contemplation, responsibility, and morality. Islam doesn't demand that we become perfect. It merely states that we have to use this life to be the best we can be in all spheres of life. The Prophet Muhammad said, "Allah loves a person who, when they do something, they try their best." In the end, though, Allah makes allowances for those who were sincere, regardless of their success.

A Muslim who lives a normal life span is expected to work, marry, have a family, participate in social activities, and do his or her part to advance the cause of Godliness. Waste and extravagance are to be avoided, and thrift and conservation are praiseworthy values to acquire. In every sphere of life, religious guidance must be consulted and followed. You often see the bumper sticker that reads, "God is my co-pilot." Islam says that if you really believe this, then you must act like it and not merely feel smug and do whatever you want. Follow the straight path of surrender to God in your life and you will please the One whom you will have to face regardless of your personal opinions about His existence on a day that you cannot avoid.

FROM THE SOURCE

According to the Prophet Muhammad, Allah said, "O son of Adam, so long as you call upon Me and ask of Me, I shall forgive you for what you have done, and I shall not mind. O son of Adam, were your sins to reach the clouds of the sky and were you then to ask forgiveness of Me, I would forgive you. O son of Adam, were you to come to Me with sins nearly as great as the earth and were you then to face Me, ascribing no partner to Me, I would bring you forgiveness nearly as great as that."

A person may live for 20, 50, or even 100 years, and every day will still be a continuous challenge to remain on the path of surrender to God. There are no easy tickets to Heaven. There is no salvation moment whereby we are guaranteed admittance to Heaven regardless of what we do for the rest of our lives. If we believe in God one day but reject Him a day later and then die, our whole life will be judged by the condition of our belief when we left the physical world. I'm reminded of a tombstone inscription from a graveyard in New York that begs the reader to consider every moment of life and its implications: "Behold and see as you pass by, as you are now so once was I. As I am now so you must be. Prepare for death and follow me."

Life in the Grave

One of the more graphic and compelling teachings of Islam begins with the moment of our death. Islam teaches that when we are dying, our soul rises in our body and collects in our throat. An angel called *Malikul Mawt*, or the Angel of Death, arrives and is given the task of removing the soul. This angel isn't the handsome young Mr. Death like Brad Pitt in *Meet Joe Black*. He's stern and unflinching in his duty and has no crisis of identity.

So how does the angel remove our soul from our body? Our soul, or *ruh*, is an other-worldly substance. The angel merely takes hold of it as it separates from our physical body and *pulls*. If the person believed in God and led a virtuous life, then the Angel of Death and his assistants gently draw out the soul from the body. But if the soul was that of a person who denied God or a person who led an evil life, then the angels will tear out the soul violently, like yanking cotton through a metal grate.

The exact moment when death is inevitable is described in the Qur'an as a moment of complete realization: "When a dying person breathes his last, when, 'Can any doc-tor save him?' the people ask, then, in the pangs of death he'll know his time is due. His knees will shake as death approaches and then he will return to his Lord." (Qur'an 75:27–30)

When you take your last breath, you finally know your time is up and you may panic or be filled with regret. But repentance is too late then. God accepts no repentance from a person who is that close to death. When the process is moments away from completion, the cutoff point has arrived. The Qur'an records the final minutes of the pharaoh's life, just before he was drowned in the Red Sea while chasing the fleeing Israelites. The pharaoh said, "Now I believe." But God answered by saying he was too late.

ASK THE IMAM

Muslims don't view death as final. It is merely passing on to another stage of life. Pain is naturally felt at the removal of a loved one from this world. However, no believing Muslim feels that the person is gone forever. Appropriate words of sympathy to tell a grieving person who has lost a loved one are: "To Allah we belong and to Him we return." One may add the line, "May Allah forgive them and grant them a high place in Paradise."

Spirit on a Wing

What happens to the soul now? Islam teaches that there is another world, or paral-lel reality, if you will, in which only spirit material and energy beings like *jinns* and angels can exist. When we die, our soul is released from every cell of our body and is now in that other realm. The angels who took us out will now hold our soul fixed over our corpse. We can see all of the people gathered around our body, but they cannot see us. We try to speak to them, but they can't hear us. We see everything that happens to our body. When it is finally time to take the corpse to the graveyard, our soul floats along with it. A person who has been good will say, "Take me forward," but a person who has been immoral or faithless will say, "Curses, where are you taking me?"

A good soul will be carried gently by the angels and clothed with shrouds from Paradise. The angels will ascend upward into Heaven and will pass through its gates announcing who the soul is. When they reach the highest place in Heaven, Allah gives the command, "Write My servant's name in *Illiyun*." (*Illiyun* is the record of who will get into Heaven after Judgment Day.) Then the angels are told, "Take him back to Earth because I promised them that 'from it I created them, into it I will return them and from it I will resurrect them once again.'"

The soul of an evil person is also carried to the gates of Heaven, but when the angels bring the soul there, the gates will not open for the soul to pass through. It is written in the Qur'an that the doors of Paradise will not be opened for someone who rejected Allah. Allah will then command that the person's name should be written in *Sijjin*, which is the register of Hell. Next He will order the angels to return the soul to Earth for the same reason He also returns good souls.

Soul Storage

Even as a person's body is being lowered into the grave and buried, his or her soul is brought down with it by the angels. We will hear the dirt being shoveled in and also the footsteps of the people as they walk away. Then we are alone, but not for long. By the way, it doesn't matter whether our body is destroyed or remains intact. Our soul will stay near the place where our body was last placed. So a person who dies in a fire and whose body is destroyed will find his or her soul sinking into the ground there. Even if the body is cremated and the ashes put in an urn and displayed on a shelf, the soul will sink into the earth somewhere along the way.

Now the life in the grave begins. The term for this life stage is *Barzakh*, or the Partition. It is sometimes referred to as "soul storage." Our soul will wait in this timeless existence until the Day of Judgment. No contact with the living or the souls of the other dead is possible, and we will be aware of nothing except our own selves. Islam does not believe that the spirits of the dead can be contacted by clairvoyants or that departed souls can inhabit the bodies of the living. Muslims believe that evil *jinns* work with psychics and spirit mediums and fool people into believing that they really did talk to their long-dead aunt or grandmother. Islam says death is final and there is no coming back.

So what happens to us in the grave? According to the Prophet Muhammad, two angels with black faces and blue eyes are sent to us shortly after burial with an interesting mission. Their names are *Munkar* and *Nakir.* When they arrive, they force our soul to snap to attention. These angels are the Questioners of the Grave, and they ask us three questions: "Who is your Lord?" "What was your way of life?" And finally, "Who was your prophet?"

Islam accepts that there were other prophets sent by God to the world before the Prophet Muhammad. In fact, as mentioned earlier, Islam teaches that all people in the past received some type of divine guidance through an authentic prophet. Muhammad is merely the last of the prophets in a long chain. So the correct answers to those three questions are: "God," "Surrender (or obedience) to God's will," and then the name of the prophet we followed, whether Muhammad, Jesus, Moses, or whoever.

If we answer all three questions correctly, then something amazing happens. Our good deeds become personified into a being resembling a person who says to us, "I'm here to give you good news. Allah has accepted what you did, and you will receive eternal gardens of delight. This is the day you were promised. I am your good deeds. By Allah I only knew you to be quick in obeying Allah and slow in disobeying Him. May God reward you with good." Then a window is opened to Heaven and another to Hell. We are shown where we would have gone in Hell if we were bad and then we're told to look at the place we will go to in Paradise instead. Then the angels expand the size of our soul storage bin to the size of a large room. A soft warm light fills the space, and we will be told to go to sleep and to dream peacefully until the Day of Judgment. Every day an angel will come and nudge us in our dreams and open a window through which we will see our place in Heaven again.

If we don't answer the questions correctly, and only a true rebel against God will fail the test, then something horrible happens. The angels appear terrifying to us. They strike our spirit body with a heavy mace, and they command our soul storage bin to squeeze in upon us until we feel suffocated. Our bad deeds become personified into a being resembling a grotesque ghoul who says, "I'm here to give you some bad news. I am your evil deeds. By God I only knew you to be slow in obeying God and quick in disobeying Him. May God repay you with evil." Then the angels come to us daily to strike us and force us to look through an open window through which we see our future spot in Hellfire. We stay tormented and screaming until the Day of Judgment.

Islam teaches that animals can hear the screams of those being tormented in the grave. The Prophet Muhammad said that if we could hear their cries, we would faint in terror. He often encouraged us to pray for protection against the Punishment of the Grave, as it is called. Time has no meaning there in the real sense, but this experience can be either a pleasant or a terrifying one, and, as Islam says, we will all have to undergo it, whether Muslim or not. Chapter 6 will explore what happens after the life in the grave is over.

The Least You Need to Know

- Islam counts our time in the womb and our lying in the grave after death as distinct stages of life.
- Islam says faith can render any situation, good or bad, into a way to please God.
- When we die, our soul lives in the grave until Resurrection Day.
- Faith and at least an attempt to lead a virtuous life are essential prerequisites for a contented earthly life and a successful afterlife.

Islam on Heaven and Hell

In This Chapter

- Understand what Islam teaches about the coming Judgment Day and why it is necessary
- Understand the process of our soul's final judgment from the Islamic perspective
- Learn about the terrifying bridge that spans Hellfire and leads to Heaven
- Discover the delights of Heaven
- Know what fate awaits those who wind up in Hell

Nearly every religion in the world teaches that there will be some sort of reward or punishment for our actions in this life. Whether it is belief in Heaven, Valhalla, union with the light, or Paradise, a realm of eternal delight for the deserving motivates the followers of any given religion to invest in their ultimate future by straight-jacketing their lives here in order to reap rewards later. In the same way, whether you're talking about Hell, Hades, or the Fire, visions of never-ending suffering are powerful incentives for avoiding immorality and wickedness in this world.

Islam offers a very clear picture of each of these possibilities to its followers, which I outline in this chapter. For the Muslim, there is no vague union of our souls in a great nothingness nor a bland pearly gate leading to a street paved with gold. No, for the devoted follower of the Prophet Muhammad, Paradise is presented with such clarity and detail that we can almost taste it. Likewise, Hell is given such a vivid treatment that it can give us nightmares if we're not careful. All of this serves to accentuate the very reason that religion teaches us about an afterlife in the first place: so that we can feel the immediacy of the importance of our beliefs and actions in everything we do and know what is to become of us after death.

Judgment Day, Then What?

Over one quarter of the Qur'an's verses deal with issues related to the next life or the spiritual world. For the Muslim, this is a naturally appropriate ratio given that Islam teaches that the *real* life is yet to come. This life, the Prophet noted, is like a dream. When we die, we will truly awaken to reality. In Chapter 5, you learned about some of the things that every person will experience after death: the angels drawing out the soul, being placed in the grave, and being visited by angels in *Barzakh*. Now I will turn to what happens afterward. I mean, you can't stay in soul storage forever! Because Islam teaches that the earth will cease to exist one day, all of those stored souls have to go somewhere!

Life in the grave will last, then, until the Day of Judgment (known as *Youmul Qiyamah*), when God will gather together every human being and *jinn* who ever lived. No dead soul can rise from its grave and walk the earth in the meantime like a ghost or an apparition. To reiterate, the only time the soul gets out of the grave is after God has caused the world to end in a cataclysmic Last Day. Only then is it time to bring all departed souls together for their final reckoning. The fourth and final stage of our life now begins.

To understand the reasoning behind a Judgment Day, we have to remember what the purpose of life is for each one of us. We are here to be tested by God in our ability to master our very selves, thereby making us worthy of entering His paradise. The two main proofs of this worthiness lie in our faith and in our actions. Throughout this test, we try to raise our souls to the highest of three levels of development, passing from our animal self, to an accusing or self-reflective self, and hopefully becoming a restful soul at peace. We accomplish this ascension in status through a combination of belief in God, seeking His guidance through His revealed Books and emulating the example of His prophets; and then of a life devoted to good deeds, asking repentance when we stumble. From this philosophy of our purpose, then, the logical conclusion is that there must be an end to this test and that each of us will receive our grade eventually. This is what Judgment Day is for.

The Long Arm of the Law

According to Islam, the idea that criminals and evil people in this world can escape punishment simply by dying is unimaginable. Can Adolph Hitler, with the blood of millions on his hands, escape a more severe retribution than merely expiring in a bunker? Think of all the children who have been abused, animals who have been mistreated, thefts and rapes that have occurred—what kind of universe would say that miscreants can get away with such deeds? The modern mechanistic view of life, which says we are all just intelligent animals who live only once, is the greatest danger to human safety ever conceived. To tell someone that because you live only once go ahead and have fun while you can is a license for any deranged person to harm others with abandon. If it feels good, do it, is not an acceptable mantra for a Muslim.

We must police our own behavior if we are to have safe societies, says the Qur'an. If there is no punishment for crimes, there is no peace. If man-made laws are not enough of a deterrent, then an appeal to higher laws that transcend humans' existence will help for many people. Those who flout both levels of law will get more than a slap on the wrist from God! The Qur'an is very clear about the need for just retribution for those who did wrong and redress for those who were wronged, and it is on Judgment Day that injustice will be paid back. "That will be the Day of ultimate recompense," the Qur'an declares, and Islam is very firm in promoting the full justice that is everyone's right. Even plants and animals that we have wronged for unjust or cruel reasons will be able to make their claim.

When Will It Come?

So when does Judgment Day begin? Is a date given in Islamic sources? Unfortunately, no. The Qur'an records that a group of idolaters went to the Prophet Muhammad and taunted him about this whole concept of a final judgment. They dared him to make it happen right there or to at least tell them when it was supposed to be. A revelation came to him and he recited this argument in rebuttal, "They ask you about the hour, tell them only God knows when it will occur. When it does happen, they will be taken completely by surprise and will wish it never came."

We do know how it will commence and proceed. According to the chronology given in Islamic sources, one day God will initiate a process that will bring about the end of the world. Even as He began it, He will shepherd it to a close. An angel named *Israfil* will sound a note on a massive horn, and the shock wave will permeate the whole of space. In the beginning, Allah had created the universe in a huge explosion (the Big Bang) and was expanding it. Now He will roll it up like a scroll and shut it down. People will still be living on Earth at that time, and they will run in terror as the globe begins to shake and break apart violently. "What is happening with the world?" they'll cry. The Qur'an has many vivid passages describing what will be going on when the earth is covered in darkness, and following is one of the more famous ones.

Without a doubt, I call your attention to the Day of Resurrection. And further still, I call your attention to the accusing voice of every person's own conscience. Do people think that we can't resurrect them or knit their bones together again? Without a doubt we can recreate them down to their very fingertips! Even so, people choose to deny what lies ahead of them, asking, "When will this resurrection day be?" But on that day when fear overshadows their sight and the moon is darkened and joined together with the sun, on that very day people will cry out, "Where can we escape to!" But no, there will be no escape. The journey will lead back to your Lord, alone. People will be informed, on that day, of all that they did and left undone. Without a doubt, every person will be their own accusing witness, even though they may try to hide themselves in excuses. (Qur'an 75:1–15)

All living beings will die, including the angels and the *jinns*, and all matter in the universe will be destroyed. This is called the Last Day, and it signals that the show is over. Next stop: Judgment. The angels will then be brought back to life, and *Israfil* will sound another note on his horn. All human beings and *jinns* will suddenly appear standing on a huge level plain. The souls of all the dead will be instantly brought out from Barzakh and given new bodies that will look like their physical bodies from Earth in every respect, though without the flaws. We will be stunned by what we see and will feel we had lived on Earth for less than a day. Everyone will be naked and without any symbol of status or power. This is called the Resurrection.

Next, all people will be sorted according to what they used to believe in or follow in the physical world. A Muslim, Christian, or Jew will be standing behind Muhammad, Jesus, or Moses. A Hindu follower of Ganesh will be standing behind a representation of the elephant god. Those who followed Communism will probably be standing behind Karl Marx and so on. This sorting will be absolute, and we can't cut lines or hide in other groups. The angels will be moving us into place, and we have no choice but to cooperate.

The Prophet Muhammad said that the Day of Judgment will last 50,000 years because of the large number of people present. Think of it: Every human being who ever lived will be there. But no one will be concerned with anyone but himself or herself because of the gravity of the situation. The Qur'an says a person will ignore his or her own parents and children because of the worry and suspense on that day. Think back to grade school and how you felt on report card day; then imagine getting a report for your whole life!

People who denied God outright (called *kafirs*) will be agitated and filled with stress on that day. All the more so because the pit of Hell will be visible in the distance, and all the terrifying moans and booming sounds of massive explosions within it will be heard. The sinners will approach the people who were faithful and virtuous in their lives because these good persons will be bathed in a sheen of light. The sinful will beg for some of that light but will be cordoned off from the righteous.

> **DEFINITION**
>
> *Kafir* is the term used in the Qur'an to describe someone who does not believe in God. Although the word is often translated as unbeliever, that is not what it means. In fact, there is no equivalent word for *unbeliever* in Arabic. *Kafir* comes from the word *kaffara,* which means to cover up, conceal, or hide. Thus a person who is a *kafir* hides God's truth and covers his or her heart and mind, refusing to accept the existence of God.

Allah will be hidden behind a huge veil and will not show Himself, though He will be conducting the judgment proceedings. (He will reveal His true self in Heaven only to those who desired to seek Him alone.) He will run a tight courtroom, and no excuses will be accepted. People will try to bribe the angels or offer to pay a ransom to God for their salvation, but what can they pay with when everything belongs to God? This gives new relevance to the saying, "You can't take it with you."

The Judgment Cometh

How will the judgment proceed? The Qur'an and the hadiths (see Chapter 2) give a very detailed picture of the whole affair. There will be no breaks from the assembly. We won't need to eat or drink or sleep. We just wait. When it is our turn to be judged, two angels, one walking in front and the other in back, will escort us before the Judge, Almighty God. The angel in front will announce, "I have his record here with me." Our record will be given to us in our right hand if we were a good person. Those of us who must receive it in our left hand or from behind our back are in big trouble.

Next our whole record will be read in our presence. Every thought or deed we ever did will be there, so much so that we will exclaim, "What kind of book is this? It leaves nothing out, great or small!" Our faith in God will be examined in detail and our sincerity measured. We will then be questioned about what we did and why. If we try to lie or be evasive, our body parts will be made to speak and bear witness against us. For example, if we stole something and denied stealing it, we may be surprised to hear our hand talking, saying, "He did it! He did it!"

Other witnesses will be brought forward. Anyone we ever harmed in our earthly life will come and state their claim against us. Our good deeds and evil deeds will be gathered near us in a pile, and people we wronged will be told to help themselves to some of our good deeds. We will be powerless to stop them. We will try to blame *Shaytan*, but he will disown us. People may call to their idols for help, but they will say, "You're on your own!" Then we truly will realize that we are held completely accountable for what we did, and no one can save us.

After the review of our record, our good and bad deeds will be placed on a scale and weighed. We had better hope our good-deed side is heavier! However, our record of prayer will be examined first; if it is found to have shortcomings, then all our good deeds will be thrown out. What good are our deeds if we were deficient in calling on our Lord and praying to Him? Why, you might be wondering, are our deeds weighed if Islam teaches that faith is what brings us salvation? Good deeds are the proof of our faith, as even the Apostle Paul in the Christian Bible noted. So if we did little that was good or right in the world, then what was the value of all our declarations and assertions?

After the review, our victims' payback time, and the weighing of our deeds, we kneel humbly before Allah's presence. He will explain to us the meaning of the evidence, and no injustice will be done or favoritism shown. If we are guilty or innocent, we are made to understand completely and beyond the shadow of a doubt what we deserve. But Allah is a merciful and a loving God. He loves to forgive those who asked for His forgiveness in their worldly life, and thus He will display that great magnanimity that is only His on Judgment Day as well. He may forgive extra sins of ours for no other reason than that He wants to. People who hoped for Allah's forgiveness may find themselves with a spotless record, and the worst criminal may find that due to some small but poignant act of kindness done to a person, plant, or animal, his record may be wiped clean. Other factors that could cause God to forgive unconditionally include taking orphans under our care lovingly, raising and educating three daughters in the best way, being martyred in battle or oppressed by a tyrant, and being dutiful and faithful to our aged parents.

The Bridge over Hell

Finally our verdict is given: guilty or innocent. We either rejoice or hang our heads in shame as we return to our places in line. Then, when all of the judgments are finished, we must travel on to the next segment of this process. From the Plain of Judgment everyone will move forward to the brink of the pit of Hell. It will be a monstrously huge, gaping hole that you can't even see across. The flames will leap up for miles, and sparks the size of logs will shoot out. The intense heat will be felt by all, and people will be terrified of it. The angels will throw the worst sinners, who were found guilty of the worst crimes, into the flames headfirst without any fanfare or ceremony. The rest of us, whether guilty or innocent, will have to take a harrowing journey over a bridge called the *Sirat*, which spans the chasm of Hell and leads to Paradise on the other side.

The Sirat is as thin as a razor and is studded with jagged edges and spikes. The righteous people and the prophets will zoom right over it and make it to the other side. Good people who had a few sins that were not forgiven will be cut and bruised as they journey over the bridge to remind them that there are consequences for all bad deeds, but they will make it over as well. Some people will be in tatters when they step off! (We all are healed on the other side.) Sinful people will be able to make it only so far because they will suddenly become snagged by the thorny bridge and will tumble headlong into the pit. Their screams will echo and terrify everyone else. Incidentally, more people will fall in than will make it over.

What if we were not too bad but also not good enough for Heaven and our good deeds weighed exactly the same as our bad? We might find ourselves in an elevated spot between Heaven and Hell called the Heights. It is not exactly the same as the Christian conception of purgatory or Abraham's Bosom, but the idea is similar. We will stay there, seeing Hell and fearing it and seeing Heaven and longing for it, until such time as we fully realize that we almost slipped up and went to Hell. Then we will eventually go to Paradise.

The topics of Heaven and Hell are covered quite extensively in the Qur'an and in the hadiths, or the sayings of Muhammad. The details are unerringly stunning. Wherever we end up will be the culmination of our fourth and final stage of life. Our soul, on loan from God, has now been returned to the other realm and is receiving its rewards or torment based on what we did with it in the world. Now I'll explain what Islam says about Heaven and Hell.

Use Your Time Wisely

Islam presents a very vivid picture of the afterlife. According to a saying of the Prophet Muhammad, we should live in this world as if we were merely strangers or drifters. The idea is that we only have a few years to live here on Earth and then we die, so shouldn't we look to the realm of the soul? Isn't the afterlife the most important thing to know about? Shouldn't we spend our life investing in the kind of capital (faith and good deeds) that would make our permanent life worthwhile? But all too often we spend our time running after what is only temporary. Regardless of our awareness of what is to come, however, Heaven or Hell is our final destination.

The Gardens of Paradise

Jannah, or Paradise, is the place where our soul is rewarded for listening to its *fitrah*, or inner nature. Because we had lived a life of faith and good deeds while avoiding bad deeds—which wasn't always easy in a world where *Shaytan* and animal desires compelled people to commit evil actions—we demonstrated that we are the best type of creature God created. Our souls have been purified and are ready for the good life after so much struggle and hardship. The Qur'an tells us: "History is a witness! Indeed, humanity is truly lost. Except for those who have faith, do what is right, and who teach each other about truth and perseverance." (Qur'an 103:1–3)

DEFINITION

Jannah is the word for Heaven in Arabic. It literally means a garden, and thus the English equivalent, *Paradise,* is more often used by Muslims to describe the "good place."

When we step off the *Sirat* (assuming we passed our judgment successfully) and make it to Paradise, we will find a huge wall in front of us with eight gates. Each gate is named after one of the main religious rituals that God established on Earth for us (which are enumerated in Chapter 10). For example, there will be gates named after Prayer, Charity, Fasting, Struggling Against Evil, and so on. We will enter through the gate that corresponds with the activity we were best at. Some very holy people will be called by the wardens of all the gates simultaneously to enter. In that case they can go through whichever gate they wish! Angels, who will be standing guard in front of each, will greet us as we enter and say, "Peace be upon you! You have done well! Enter here and dwell within."

The Muslim greeting that is equivalent to "Hello" is *Assalamu alaykum*. This means "Peace be upon you." The reply is the reverse, *Wa alaykum assalam*, which translates as "And upon you be peace."

The total wonderment of Paradise cannot adequately be described in human language, and God says as much: "I have prepared for My servants what no eye has ever seen, nor ear heard, nor any human being ever conceived of" (hadith Qudsi). The Qur'an can merely give us mental images drawn from our own life experiences in this world, and thus Heaven is described in very earthly terms, though Muslims understand that many of these descriptions are metaphors to appeal to what we know now. It will seem to us as a land of lively cities, exquisite gardens, rolling meadows, primeval forests, and river valleys. Soulless servants who will resemble us, and who only aim to please, will pamper us at all times. The colors and scents that will greet us at every moment will be so vibrant that we will never grow tired of looking at them.

Whoever was handicapped, lame, infirm, or blind will find that they, along with everyone else, will have perfect bodies. Once an old woman asked the Prophet Muhammad if she were going to go to Heaven. He told her that there will be no old women in Paradise. She bowed her head sadly, but then the Prophet smiled and lifted her head up and said, "There will be no old women in Paradise because you will all be made young again." The woman was overjoyed. We will all be about 30 years of age and in the prime of our physical shape, and we will never feel sick or hurt again. Babies who died will remain as infants, but they will have the run of the place, scurrying around "like pretty green birds all aflutter."

Heaven has seven layers, each more fascinating than the next, and each of us will be taken to our home, which will be located on one of those levels. The level is determined both by the extent of our goodness and by the amount of our prophet's scriptures that we learned by heart while we were alive in the world. Each level is so fantastic, however, that we will not feel any slight or jealousy because of our assigned level. In fact, such sentiments will be unknown in Paradise; no ill talk, gossip, or lying will ever be heard.

We will be able to visit people who live in different levels. Friends and family will meet and lounge in leisure. Husbands and wives will be reunited, if they choose, and socializing will be a major activity. There will be special servants and pleasure mates (called *houris*) in Paradise. They are intelligent yet soulless creatures made only to serve and please us in a world that knows no more vice. Islam is very matter-of-fact about sex and says straightforwardly that guiltless sex is one of the benefits of Heaven.

Wine, another vice that was forbidden in the world, will be allowed there also, and the best food will always be brought to us. We don't need to eat to survive any longer; there we will eat for the joy of it. Paradise contains markets to shop in, fountains to relax near, roads to travel, and endless delights. Boredom will never occur. We will be given silk clothes with jewelry and brocade of the finest quality. The people of Paradise will be quite a sight indeed!

Paradise is forever. No one has to leave and we will be at peace with everything in all of creation. Every question we ever had will be answered. Every delight we ever imagined will be ours for the asking and more besides. Even greater than these, however, is the ability to see God, Himself. He can be seen beyond the seventh layer in a fantastic spectacle of indescribable light and sound.

Such is Heaven according to Islam. There are so many vivid descriptions in the Qur'an and the hadiths that the immediacy of the next life is brought to the forefront of the Muslims' mind. People of other faiths may have pearly gates and gilded hymnals in mind, but Muslims have a closer look at what's there and can envision it that much more!

No Dancing with the Devil Here!

Hell. The word conjures up images of fire and suffering. Nearly every society has some conception of an ultimate place of punishment for those who committed great evil or seemed to get away with their crimes here on Earth. But the purpose of Hell in Islam is not only to punish, but also to purify. Christianity teaches that Hell is forever for anyone who goes there. Islam, while teaching that some will never get out, also says that some souls will get out after their fixed term of punishment is reached. Then they, too, will go to Heaven. So in Islam, Hell isn't forever for everybody.

Even as the Qur'an describes Heaven in stunning detail, so, too, does it give a very immediate depiction of Hellfire. To begin with, Hell is not the headquarters of *Shaytan* and his devils, as is the popular idea in Western culture. *Shaytan* has no throne in Hell from which he directs his plans against true believers in God. Hell is a place that God created only for punishing. *Shaytan* does not want to go there, and neither does anyone else. Hell is so tremendous that it will never be completely filled. The Qur'an has a verse in which God says that He will ask Hell one day if it is full yet. Hell will respond, "Are there any more to come?"

Hell has seven layers, just as Heaven does. The lower the level, the worse it gets. Nineteen angels patrol the rim of the chasm and push back anyone who tries to escape. The Prophet Muhammad once remarked that the fire of Hell is 70 times hotter than fire here on Earth. That's worse than an incinerator! Our level in Hell will be determined by how bad we were and how little we believed in God and the afterlife. The inmates of Hell will frequently hear the phrase: "Didn't any Warners come to you? Didn't you listen to what your religious guides were saying?" Angels will administer the many varieties of punishments and will not flinch in executing their duties.

Among the more terrifying punishments of Hell are these:

- Endless columns of fire will enclose the inmates of Hell, and flaming chains will fall upon them. Snakes and scorpions will continuously harass them.

- The inmates of Hell will wear clothing made of burning pitch, drink from fountains of burning oil, eat barbed fruits that look like devil heads, and never have a moment's rest from it. Every time a person's body will be burnt up or destroyed, a fresh body or layer of skin will materialize so that the punishment can be felt anew.

- There will be no communicating with anyone else. Isolation will be complete, and nothing but screams and moaning will be heard. No pleas for mercy or cries for a relief will be entertained. Instead, every time the inmates of Hell cry for relief, their punishment will be doubled.

- People will be punished according to their crimes: faultfinders will scratch their faces with iron nails, liars will rip out their cheeks with iron bars, gossipers will cut off their lips with razors, the greedy will be bitten by snakes, and those who dressed to incite lust in others will be disfigured and made grotesque.

Fountains of pus and blood and boiling muck will be the only refreshment, and utter hopelessness will be everyone's lot.

DEFINITION

Jahannum is the name for Hell in Arabic. It is related to the Hebrew word, *Gehenna*.

Western writers have tried to envision the afterlife for centuries. Dante Aliguieri's *Inferno* is probably the most detailed European concept about the subject. The more dramatic movie starring Robin Williams, *What Dreams May Come*, also attempts to paint a picture of the next life but ultimately falls short of a full representation of how wonderful it will be. Whereas traditional Christianity gives the one-size-fits-all Lake of Fire, Islam provides a closer look at what awaits those who denied God and spent their life hurting other people and harming the world in general. The Qur'an quotes God as saying, "You forgot this possibility so this day I will forget you."

Why Does God Punish?

Hell is not the province of a cruel God. It serves a purpose: to purify warped souls. Once a woman and her son were sitting in a gathering listening to the Prophet Muhammad as he gave a sermon. The child wandered away from his mother and tried to put his hand in the fireplace; the mother instinctively snatched her child away to safety. She thought for a moment about what she had done and asked the Prophet how Allah could punish those He loved in Hell when she as a mother wanted only to protect her little one. The Prophet bowed his head and cried softly and then answered her by saying that Allah does not like to punish. He punishes only those who have rejected Him and committed evil actions. Wouldn't the mother also correct her son when he did wrong? Thus, we find the purpose of Hell justified.

If we have been cast into Hell temporarily but have finished our sentence, the angels will locate and remove us, though we will be mere charred skeletons by then. A substance called the Water of Life will be poured over us, and our bodies will regenerate and be restored to us as good as new. Finally, we will be escorted to Paradise and given our full rewards for any good we might have done. Who will stay in Hell forever? Only God knows, and He is never unjust. The lowest level of Hell is for the worst inmates who will have no way out of it ever.

The Least You Need to Know

- Muslims believe in a Day of Judgment where all injustice will be paid back and no one will be treated unfairly.
- Islam teaches that Heaven is eternal, whereas a person's sentence in Hell can range from temporary to forever, depending on his or her misdeeds.
- Heaven is presented as an ideal adult playground with the best delights in food, comfort, friendship, activities, environment, and physical pleasures of all kinds.
- Hell is described in great detail in Islam. Punishments there often mimic crimes done in this life. Anyone who has any small amount of faith in God will eventually be released and admitted to Heaven.

In the Beginning ...
An Islamic Perspective

In This Chapter

- Learn about the Qur'anic account of the creation of the world
- Find out where Islam stands on the evolution and creationism debates
- Learn about the role of science in the Qur'an
- Compare the Islamic version of the story of Adam and Eve to the biblical account
- Discover how Satan became the enemy of humankind

The Qur'an has its own explanation for how the world began and also for how it will end. The Qur'an, however, is not structured in chronological order as the Bible is. Rather, it consists mostly of essays on spiritual topics and then uses scattered references to history and science to prove the validity of the religious points as they are presented. Most chapters of the Qur'an employ this kind of technique. The history of ancient prophets and nations, the formation of space, the natural world, and the miracle of life are the most common proofs given. When you gather together all of the statements in the Qur'an related to natural phenomenon, for example, and examine them, you'll find an amazingly detailed description of how everything came to be.

In addition to a well-structured explanation of the elements of creation, Islam also has its own account of how people were made and what human activity means throughout history. Such familiar Judeo-Christian concepts as Adam and Eve, the prophets, God's hand in history, and the coming of an anti-Christ have their counterparts in Islam. But as you have already seen with the subjects covered in earlier chapters, Islam has its own version of what each means. Throughout this chapter you will find that the Islamic explanation for how we came here and what it all means is wide in its scope and complexity as well as independent in its own right.

The Creation of the Universe

"Let there be light" is a familiar phrase for Jews and Christians. It signifies the beginning of the universe according to the Bible. In fact, if one were to read the book of Genesis, a very clear and ordered picture of creation would be presented. Does Islam have its own version of creation? You bet. Is it similar to the biblical account in any way? The answer is both yes and no. As you'll see, the Qur'anic presentation of the creation of the universe is both unique and startlingly accurate.

To begin the Islamic narrative of creation, I must go way back to the time when there was *nothing but God.* Muslims believe that God has no beginning and no end and that He exists independently of time or place. His omnipotence is complete, and He is present everywhere, though He is not a part of anything. In a way, you can *almost* compare Him to the concept of the Force in the *Star Wars* movies, except that God is very much alive and cannot be used by people for their purposes like some sort of tool. Given that Muslims do not personify God as other religions do, the mental energy involved in understanding His place in the universe has to come from a higher conceptual level. Trying to explain the origin of God is not something Muslims even try to do.

DISPELLING THE MYTH

Muslims are supposed to look into the natural world for proofs of God's existence. Evidence of His creative genius, says the Qur'an, is found in every aspect of our environment. Science strengthens a Muslim's faith and there has been no conflict between science and religion in Muslim history.

Allah's Notebook

Before God even started the ball rolling, though, He made some rules for Himself to follow. One of these was that He would be kinder and more generous with His soon-to-be-made creatures than He would be stern. He also made laws for the governing of the natural universe that would not change. (God invented physics!) Where did He record all of these rules and laws? Muslims believe that God has a ledger of some sort in which He records whatever He wishes. He does not need this ledger, however, just as He doesn't need the angels to help Him. He just willed it.

In this ledger He also wrote down how long the universe would last and how it would end. Everything in creation, as you learned in Chapter 2, would be *Muslim*, or surrendered to God's will. The only exception to that rule would be those creatures in whom He endowed free will. The Qur'an says, "We did not create space and the Earth and everything in between them except for just ends and for a fixed term." (Qur'an 46:2–3)

Creation in the Qur'an

How did God proceed to make the universe? Did He announce, "Let there be light"? Actually, no. There is no such verse in the Qur'an. What He *did* do will sound very familiar from a scientific point of view. He said the word "Be," and an object like a ball (or something equivalent to it) appeared, and then He split it into pieces. The materials from this initial explosion were the building blocks for all things in the universe. The force of that blast continues to expand and spread this matter in all directions even to this day. The Qur'an is very clear when it says, "Don't the people who hide the truth see that space and the earth were all joined together in one unit of creation and then We split them apart?" (Qur'an 21:30) Does this statement ring a bell? Scientists would call this description amazingly close to the modern concept of the Big Bang.

After this great explosion of matter, the Qur'an mentions that the heavens were filled with a kind of smoke. (For Arabs in the seventh century, this is how interstellar gases would have looked.) The formation of planets and stars soon followed, and the fact that they have regular orbits is stated in the Qur'an, as well: "By the rotation of the stars and the orbit and setting of the planets, by the night as it falls and the morning as it passes, certainly, this is the speech of an honored Messenger." (Qur'an 81:25)

Interestingly enough, the Qur'an also describes the movement of bodies in space by using the Arabic word for *swim*. Planets and stars are *swimming* in their courses. As we know today, space is not empty and the objects within it move at a measurable pace not unlike a person gliding underwater. The Qur'an even correctly identifies the sun as a giver of light (*siraj*) and the moon as a reflector of light (*munir*).

Six Days and Still No Rest

God finished the creation of the universe in six segments, ostensibly called days, and then mounted the throne of power to govern the universe on the seventh. He did not rest, for as the Qur'an says, He never tires. With that said, Muslims do not believe that the universe is only a few thousand years old, as some religious groups assert. Islam can accept the proposition that the universe is *billions* of years old. How can this be when the Qur'an declares that it took God six *days* to create everything? The answer lies in the meaning of the Arabic word for day, *youm*. The term *youm* can mean a day as we know it or a segment of time independent of a 24-hour Earth day. The Qur'an further points out that a day to God is not like one of ours. In one verse it says a day to God could be like a thousand years. In another it says that the time it will take the angels to ascend to God for Judgment Day will be a day that is equivalent to 50,000 years of our own time. We simply can't conceive of time in the same way God does. After all, He *made* time. So the length of time in years that it took for creation is negotiable for us.

Adam and Eve: A New Perspective

The Qur'an teaches that human beings were created by God to dwell upon the earth. People who are familiar with the biblical account of Adam and Eve will find some similarities with the Qur'anic version. The Qur'an begins their story with an announcement. God told an assembly of angels that He was going to create a *khalifa*, or caretaker, for the earth. When the angels realized that this new creature, the human being, would have free will, they objected, saying, "Will you create beings there that will cause trouble and shed blood, while we praise Your Holy Name?" From the angels' point of view, to make someone who could choose to be bad was unwise, especially because God already had perfectly obedient creatures like them. Allah told them frankly that He knew what He was doing (and He would later prove it to them). In other words, He had something in mind, and they could never really know the reasons behind His plan.

DEFINITION

Khalifa means a steward or caretaker. Humans are the stewards of the earth. This is also the title given to the worldwide head of the Muslim political entity. The English spelling is *caliph*.

Then God created the first man and woman from dust and placed them in a tropical garden paradise. Their names were Adam and *Hawwa*, or Eve. Where was this garden located? Many Muslims believe that it was in Heaven and that later on the pair were sent down to Earth after having been expelled from it. Others believe the garden was on Earth in a highland area in East Africa, and when Adam and Eve were ejected they settled down in lower country not far from there. There is a friendly debate over this, as the Qur'an and sayings of the Prophet Muhammad are vague about its exact location. This issue, however, is not essential to Islamic teachings and is peripheral to our story.

The Education of Adam

The Qur'an tells us that God taught Adam all the names of everything in his environment. An examination of the root meaning of the Arabic word for name, *ism*, shows that Adam was made to understand the meaning of nature around him and how to use it. He could understand his world and could grasp what each plant and animal was useful for. When the education of Adam was complete, God called the angels to participate in a demonstration of sorts. God wanted to show the angels what He had meant earlier when He said that He knew what they didn't know about humans and their value.

God commanded the angels, "Tell Me about all of this (natural phenomena on Earth)." The angels, who were light-based creatures, had no real understanding of how the physical world worked, so they expressed their ignorance about such matters. Then God commanded Adam to tell the angels what he knew about the world. When he finished fully explaining about the plants and animals and how to understand their uses, the angels realized that humans were creatures of great worth and had greater insight than they did. Allah declared, "Didn't I tell you before that I know what you don't?"

The First Racist

To signify that they were wrong and deserved to pay their respects to Adam, God commanded the angels to bow to the human beings, much in the same way a defeated opponent in a chess game or martial arts school might bow to the victor. They all bowed together. But that was not the end of this episode. Do you remember the *jinns*, those fire or energy-based creatures that God had also created? They have a habit of following angels around, and some were in the garden, watching the proceedings.

When the angels lost their contest and were commanded to bow, the *jinns* began to bow, too, because when the Creator of the universe says to bow, even if you are not mentioned by name, you bow! But one *jinn* remained stiff and refused to bow. He must have stood out like a sore thumb! His name was *Iblis*. God asked him why he didn't bow along with the angels, and *Iblis* gave a reply that echoes to this day in the prejudices people hold against each other: He said, "I am better than him."

 DEFINITION

Iblis is the original name of *Shaytan*, or Satan, and literally means frustrated.

God had just proven that humans were better than angels, and angels were certainly better than *jinns*, so for *Iblis* to make such an arrogant statement was foolish and uncouth. God ordered him to get out of the garden, saying that he, and his jealousy, were to be rejected. But *Iblis* didn't want to go quietly. He laid down the gauntlet and dared God to another contest of sorts: "If you give me time," he shouted, "I can corrupt [your precious humans] and in the end you will find most of them ungrateful to You."

Now God isn't one to back down from a challenge. Of course, He doesn't need to participate in them, either, because He is God, after all. But the way that the Qur'an tells it, God accepts all of our challenges against Him so that in the end when we lose, we finally understand how wrong we were. God punishes only after someone fully realizes the folly of their ways. For that reason, He lets us stray as far as we want into sin and evil so that when He seizes us, we can't protest the receipt of our just desserts.

So God accepted the challenge and granted *Iblis* time until the Day of Judgment to do his worst to us. *Iblis* boasted, "I will attack them from their front and back and their right and left, and I will create in them false desires and superstitions." (He does this by "whispering" thoughts into our minds.) But in return for allowing *Iblis* virtual eternal life until Judgment Day, God laid down one ground rule of His own that *Iblis* had to obey. He said that *Iblis* could have no power over those who seek protection with Him.

Iblis's name was then changed to *Shaytan*. The word *Shaytan* means to separate, which is an apt description of his goal: to separate us from our Creator. A segment of the *jinn* population decided to follow *Shaytan*, and they are called the *Shayateen*, or Separators. *Shaytan* is evil and frightening and wants to have us sent to Hell, but we have our *fitrah* and God's revealed religious teachings to help us combat him and our animal desires. Note that Islamic thought does not portray him as a red devil with a pitchfork, nor is he a fallen angel as some religions present him. He is a being with the free choice to do good or evil and he chose the latter and will go to Hell one day himself because of it.

The Great Test

God warned Adam and Eve about *Shaytan* in a revelation. He told them that *Shaytan* was their declared enemy and was out to corrupt them. These first two people were so innocent that they had no need of clothes, for they felt no shame, nor did they engage in lying or theft because everything was free. Food was within easy reach, and they never experienced hardship of any kind. Sounds like an idyllic life, doesn't it? What could possibly go wrong? How could *Shaytan* hope to corrupt these two virtuous people?

Although Adam and Eve had complete freedom to do as they pleased in the garden, they had to follow one rule: Do not go near or eat the fruit of one particular tree. That was it—one off-limits tree. Was this the *Tree of Knowledge of Good and Evil* spoken about in the Bible? Well, not exactly. You see, in the Bible we read that the forbidden tree had the power to let everyone know about good and evil deeds. Yet in the Qur'anic telling of this story, God is never quoted as saying that this tree was anything special. In addition, the Bible also mentions a *second* tree, called the Tree of Life, which could give anyone enough power to rival God. The Bible says in Genesis 3:22 that God was apprehensive lest Adam and Eve eat from that one as well.

The Islamic version of the story just has the one tree, and nobody tells Adam and Eve it is special—no one except *Shaytan* that is. According to the Qur'an, *Shaytan* came into the garden and tempted both of them to eat from the tree. He told them it would give them eternal life and that their power would never end. This was *Shaytan's* first big lie to humanity. Well, they went ahead and did it. They ate from the tree (and gained no special power). Why, you may ask, would they do what God Himself told them not to? Here we see the strategy of *Shaytan's* sly appeals to our animal self, our desire for more and more. Adam and Eve slipped up because they gave in to their greed for what they weren't supposed to have.

After they ate from the tree, *Shaytan* left them, probably laughing at the fact that it was so easy to corrupt God's "best creation." The Qur'an does not blame Eve for goading her husband into taking a bite, nor does it let Adam off the hook, as the Bible seems to do in I Timothy 2:14. In fact, Islam does not specify who ate first at all! The Qur'an lays the blame on them both equally. "They both did wrong," the verse says. Even though other religions assert that women brought sin into the world, Islam makes no such claim and places no stigma on being female. So what happened next? Adam and Eve realized they did wrong and felt ashamed because of it. As their sense of shame grew they wanted to hide and this caused them to question even their nakedness, they began to sew leaves to wear as clothes. The tree they ate from didn't give them any insight into good or evil; rather they felt the shame from within their own conscience. Their innate *fitrah* (orientation) made them feel inadequate and disgraceful.

As a consequence of their disobedience, God ordered Adam and Eve to be expelled from the garden. They were forced out into the wild world to fend for themselves with nowhere to go and nothing to shelter them. God declared that humans would have discord and hatred for each other from now on because of the inherent struggle to survive in the world. Imagine the world hundreds of thousands of years ago: no other people, dangers everywhere, and no safe place to hide. Life was harsh for the first two humans for a while. Even worse was their feeling of separation from God. Their *accusing self* was soon activated, and they sought to find the reasons for their disobedience.

Now whereas Christianity would say that Adam and Eve's failure in the garden put the taint of sin on us all, resulting in an unforgivable *original sin*, Islam states that after a while God had mercy on the repentant and humbled pair and taught them how to ask for His forgiveness. Then, when they implored God for His grace, guess what? He forgave them. End of story. Although they could not return to the garden, the sin was erased and redemption was complete. *Shaytan*, not realizing that people had a way to remove the stain of corruption from their hearts, was furious! Perhaps he realized that his self-imposed mission was going to be harder than he thought.

Pass It On

God gave Adam and Eve some important instructions that they were to pass on to their descendants:

> If, and it will happen, there comes to you guidance from Me, whoever follows My guidance will not lose his way, nor fall into despair. But whoever turns away from My message, certainly he will have a life narrowed down and We will raise him up blind on the Day of Judgment. (Qur'an 20:123–124)

Thus God promised to send prophets and guides throughout human history to help combat the ignorance of following our animal desires (and *Shaytan's* prompting). The entire history of the world, from the perspective of the Qur'an, is nothing more than an expression of this eternal battle.

Do Muslims view Adam in any other way than being the first man? Yes, Islam teaches that he was the first prophet of God on Earth, because he taught his children how to serve God, though in a far simpler way than our modern organized religions.

And so it all begins. By now you might be asking what the future holds for God's people. Do we have a hand in our fate, or is it sealed? In Chapter 8, I will explore what Islam teaches regarding destiny and fatalism.

The Least You Need to Know

- The Qur'an has a complete chronology and explanation for how life and the universe began.
- Islam accepts elements of creationism and evolution in explaining the origin of life.
- The Qur'an contains its own version of the story of Adam and Eve. The woman is not blamed for the pair eating from the tree, and there is no original sin.
- God sends prophets to guide people. The messages of the prophets were sometimes lost by later generations.
- The structure of the Qur'an is completely different from the Bible, as is the style and theme.

The Measurement of Life

In This Chapter

- Gain an Islamic perspective on the concept of destiny
- Discover how Islam looks at time and its role in our lives
- Understand the difference between the principle of Divine Measurement and fate or fatalism
- Learn what Islam says about God's knowledge of the future and what we can do about it

Destiny. This word evokes a wide range of responses in people, probably because many of them don't have a clear idea of its meaning, so they unwittingly use the word incorrectly. For example, in popular culture, destiny is often portrayed romantically as a vision of what a person is *supposed* to do. "I go to my *destiny*," intones the motion picture hero as he leaps into the fray, not knowing if he will live or die but trusting to some ultimate purpose in the universe to decide his fate. In real life, too, people call upon destiny, but their use of the word is more therapeutic than romantic. Usually they are trying to justify whatever circumstance befell them that was beyond their power to stop. In such cases, destiny transforms into an undesirable *fait accompli*, of having no say in a matter. The synonymous, yet less desirable term known as *fatalism* then is bandied about. Yet most people would strongly disagree with the idea of an inescapable fatalistic end that must happen despite all our best actions to stop it. So why is destiny often considered benign but fatalism, which is basically similar, considered outrageously negative and self-defeating? Aren't both terms two sides of the same coin?

Muslims have a unique concept about their lives both in the present and the future, but it does not involve either fatalism or destiny in the usual sense. Islam has been accused of teaching fatalism and of promoting an attitude of acceptance that results in inaction and hopelessness. This false notion, which grew out of eighteenth-century European criticism of Islam, is actually a highly inaccurate misinterpretation of Islamic teachings on the subject. Islam has a unique concept called *Divine Measurement*, which gives Muslims hope that they can affect the future with personal effort and which provides a clear explanation for the reasons why things happen the way they do.

Destiny, Fate, or Free Will—Which Is It?

Islam asserts that God is omnipotent. He had no beginning and He will have no end. Because He is outside the realm of time and space, He knows everything that has happened and will happen. He knew that human beings would be valuable creatures when He made them, even though the angels didn't think much of us. He also knew that the first pair of people would sin, and He made a plan for the salvation of their descendants—if any would choose to take it. This would be the test we are all taking in this life.

When Adam and Eve were expelled from the garden, they were sent into a world full of choices. All of us today have just as many challenges to face as they did. We can do right or wrong. We can lead a successful life, or we can blow our chances and miss golden opportunities. But if God is all-powerful and knows the past, present, and future, and has already written for us the span of our life, our economic condition, and so many other things, are we, in fact, locked into an inescapable destiny? Does Islam teach that each of us has an inevitable fate? Are we destined for Heaven or Hell?

This is an important issue. Christianity, especially, has had to wrestle with this topic for centuries, and it took great thinkers such as St. Augustine and Meister Eckhart to provide some answers. Even then, appeals to *Divine Mystery*—or things that only God can know—permeate Christian literature on this and many other subjects. After all, asking why God made the universe when He already knows the future is a pretty powerful question. What does Islam say about this? Free will and the ability to shape our own future must mean something if our test is to be fair.

It's Not Written in the Stars

You might be pleasantly surprised to know that Islam does not teach *fatalism*, or hopeless reliance on what is destined for a person. At the same time, Islam also does not promote the idea of destiny as it is usually understood in the West. *Destiny* implies that there is a future plan designed for each individual that will unfold no matter what happens. On the flip side, Islam rejects the notion that the universe and everything in it is an unplanned exercise in random events. There is order in life, and people can sense it. Some put their faith in a Higher Power and work as they can in life while others seek to discover the ultimate meaning of things and what is to come through their own devices. Many people, in fact, become apprehensive when they think about tomorrow, and they begin to believe that their destiny or future part in the great plan of life can be learned if the right way to discover it can be found. Some claim that destiny is "written in the stars." Such people have devoted followers who throw thousands of dollars their way for a glimpse into tomorrow. Psychics and astrologers are an integral part of Western culture, and their influence is everywhere in newspapers, in society, and even in politics. (Former President Ronald Reagan's own wife is reputed to have contacted psychics while she lived in the White House!)

DISPELLING THE MYTH

Orientalists have charged that Islam teaches abject fatalism, or the belief that personal actions do not matter because we cannot escape what will happen to us. Islam is actually against this kind of a concept. Muhammad said, "Work as you are able because if you don't help yourself, God won't help you either."

Islam, however, says that the position of the stars and planets has no bearing on what will happen to us. For this reason, Muslims are forbidden to engage in astrology. The Arabs had strong superstitions in Muhammad's time, and he worked very hard to dispel them. When his infant son died, an eclipse of the sun happened to occur a few hours later. People started to say that it happened on account of the baby's passing. When Muhammad heard people were saying this, he came before them and said, "The sun and the moon are two signs of God; they are not eclipsed on account of anyone's death or on account of anyone's birth. So when you see an eclipse, glorify and supplicate to God."

On another occasion, Muhammad said that God Himself commented on astrology by saying:

> This morning one of My servants became a believer in Me and one a disbeliever. As for him who said, "We have been given rain by virtue of God and His mercy," that one is a believer in Me, and a disbeliever in the stars. And as for him who said, "We have been given rain by such-and-such a star," that one is a disbeliever in Me, and a believer in the stars. (hadith)

Watching Time Go By

So if astrology is out, how can people know what will happen to them in the future? Islam says that we don't *need* to know what will happen tomorrow at all! The reason is that *God* knows; and if we truly trust Him and believe in Him, then we have nothing to worry about. How does this differ from fatalism or destiny? Islam teaches that even though God knows the future, we can still act and make a difference in our ultimate fate. How does Islam balance God's knowledge of the future with our ability to act? The synthesis comes in a grand concept that can almost be described as *managed time.* What do we mean by this?

The Islamic answer begins with God's foreknowledge. God knows the past, present, and future all at the same time. He can do this for one simple reason: He created time and so is not bound by it. Picture a timeline that begins with your birth. As you move to the right you pass through your teen years, college, marriage and family, and ultimately your death. Look at what you just did! You saw it all at once as if you were outside of your own timeline. Islam teaches that God is in this position. Muhammad said that God declared: "People struggle against the passing of time, but I am Time. In My hand is the night and the day."

So God sees us in any life stage at any time He wants. He won't end our share of time until we reach the amount allotted for us. In the Qur'an, God has laid out the principle that all of us must live, be tested, and then wait for His Judgment. So for Muslims, knowing that God is outside the timeline means that God's foreknowledge is not a worrisome issue for us. That's just the way it is. God's *seeing* what we will do is not Him *making* us do it. Yes, there are times when God is active in the timeline by sending prophets, allowing catastrophes to befall evil rulers or nations, or answering someone's prayer, but this is balanced by a passiveness in which God allows things to take their own course. "Not a leaf falls but that God knows of it," says the Qur'an in many passages of this type. The only caveat is that God's ultimate objective is that truth and justice prevail in the end. That is why He doesn't plan to have the universe just go on forever, left to its own devices. He will nudge the timeline here and there to keep things more or less on track to a just end (at a time of His choosing) but most of what happens he lets happen because it is what naturally must come in the great interplay of events.

By the way, Islam does not teach that every time there is a disaster that it is God's punishment to man. If an earthquake strikes in a remote, uninhabited region, we may scarcely take note. But if, over many years, people began to settle in the area and another earthquake strikes, then people speak of Divine retribution. But the earthquake would have happened, based on built-up pressures in the earth, no matter whether people lived in the area or not. It was just a case of being in the wrong time and place.

What about evil rulers, such as Hitler or Stalin? People have asked how God could allow such abominations to occur under their rule when He is supposed to be a merciful God in charge of everything. The perspective in Islam is that people are given the freedom to act, whether for good or ill, evil or good, and even if it will harm others. The perpetrators of crimes will be punished by God, either by his nudging another people to have the courage to fight back and vanquish them, or by taking them to task on Judgment Day and then sending them to Hell. Their victims, if they don't get justice in this world from the society of men, will get justice on Judgment Day. The chance to reward people for their courage, especially martyrs who fight to uphold the revealed truths of God's revelations in the face of tyrants, also comes into play. God is only as passive as necessary to let people have a level and fair test of their free will.

Thus, no matter how many times the question pops up: Are we *destined* to do what we do? Does God *force* the criminal to be bad by *decreeing* his future? Islam says no, we are not forced to do anything. To reiterate, God's foreknowledge is not *making* us do what we do. He is merely outside the timeline, looking at us in every stage of our lives. He knows where we will end up tomorrow; however, He is letting time flow, so we can live out our natural lives and experience life for ourselves. Should we still worry then? Is our fate sealed in a way because God knows what will happen? Not at all.

All Things Great and Small

Islam provides a unique mechanism to free ourselves from this kind of worrying about the future. This doctrine is called *Qada* and *Qadr*, loosely translated as Determination and Measurement. *Qada*, which means to determine or to set parameters, covers the span of life for the universe and how it will operate. Gravity causes apples to fall; fire burns combustibles; illnesses can be treated with the right medications; our genes contain a blueprint for how our body will operate, and so on. Using this principle we can live life confidently, knowing that we can make sense of our world and the rules with which it operates.

The second principle to make our lives a little easier is *Qadr*, which means to measure. All things, including people, are dependent on God, and He has measured our life circumstances to provide a varied and challenging test for us to pass. What does this mean in practical terms? Beyond measuring the length of our lives, the interplay of all the different trends around us throws a specific set of challenges our way, so we can make choices and learn to live by faith and virtue—or descend into a life of nihilism and immorality. All along our timelines are stumbling blocks and situations that we must react to. When we consider that God can make sense of everyone's intertwined timelines and how they create a never-ending web of actions and reactions, we can become dizzy trying to conceive of His power of computation!

DEFINITION

Qadr, or Divine Measurement, is the term Muslims use instead of destiny. It is sometimes translated as *power* in the sense that the ultimate control over the future is with God.

How does this concept of measurement help us to live free from anxiety? Basically, if we say that God has measured the overall circumstances in our life, we can free ourselves from being overly stressed about what happens to us every day. When we are stricken with calamities, our anxiety is reduced and our despair is mitigated because we trust in God's measurement or foreknowledge of our tests. Life, therefore, can really be looked at as a test and not as a series of punishments, and thus a Muslim's belief in the goodness of God and the essential rightness of His overall plan remains intact.

The question remains: Can we change what will happen to us? Does prayer or our active participation in a situation have any effect on the outcome of events? Islam says yes. Muhammad said, "Nothing changes the Divine Measurement except fervent supplications (to God)." As God looks at our timeline, there may be a place where we decide to call on Him for His help. In that case, God may change the course of our future. In so doing, His foreknowledge is not affected because He knows what alterations will occur and when. In His mercy, He may decide at any moment to revise our timeline and respond to our prayers, so Muslims are asked to make supplications to God often.

As you can see, then, Muslims put their trust in God's foreknowledge and accept that what happens to them will be a test. But because we have the power to act and react and even to ask God to change things, Muslims always hold out hope that their active participation can influence the course of their lives. In the end, they trust in God and in His knowledge of their ultimate fate: "Whatever good happens to you is from Allah; but whatever evil happens to you is from your [own] self." (Qur'an 4:79)

What You Can and Can't Do

To gain a greater perspective on how the teaching of Divine Measurement affects the Muslim outlook on life, we can look at what our reactions mean. Islam divides daily life into two spheres: what we have control over and what we do not. We have no control over the circumstances developing around us. The car breaks down; we get laid off at our job; an earthquake topples the city; we bump into a long-lost friend; we find a bag of money; the dog runs away; and so on. These things just happen. We couldn't prevent them because we didn't know they were coming. Islam says all of these things are a test for us. They were predetermined challenges or merely things that, because of a complex confluence of events, just happened. They were a part of our Divine Measurement.

Now we come to the essence of the Islamic worldview. Even though we often have no control over what happens to us, we do have control over *how we feel and respond*. When a tragedy strikes, do we blame God? When we see a diamond, does covetousness well up within us? When someone does evil to us, do we reciprocate or forgive? When we are alone, do we feel lonely or jubilant? Islam says we have control over our feelings, emotions, and personal actions. *Our test lies in how we respond to what happens around us.* Do we exercise patience (*sabr*) with life's challenges or do we panic and create disorder in our lives and in others? Now if we really think of the complex web of actions and reactions that go on every day in all of our lives, we can begin to appreciate how little our capacity is compared to God's. The Hindu concept of karma might help here, but Muslims believe in God's *Qadr*, or measurement, not in a passive, impersonal web of actions coming back to us.

Living Free of All Worry

God sees the timeline and knows what we will do. He sees what everyone else is doing as well. He knows what challenges will erupt as lives cross, and He knows how natural processes such as tornadoes, rainfall, or sunny days will affect the mix. At the end of each person's timeline, his or her soul is stored in *Barzakh* to await the end of all time when Judgment Day will occur. By then, the universe, which began with the Big Bang, will be "rolled up" (scientists call this the *Big Crunch*) and time will no longer have any meaning.

FROM THE SOURCE

When We give people a taste of Mercy they celebrate and when some hardship afflicts them because of their own failures, behold they're in despair! Don't they see that Allah enlarges provision and restricts it to whoever He pleases? Indeed in this are Signs for those who believe. (Qur'an 30:35–38)

Muslims live their lives, then, trusting in God and His knowledge of the future. The future is not a threat, nor do we fear what is to come. Whatever challenges meet us in our lives we have to try our best to face them. When we have done our best, we leave it in God's hands. If we are rich or poor, fortunate or sorry, we don't get too worked up about it. Life's tests come from God. We try our best and accept what happens and then try some more. The Qur'an says:

> "No disaster can come on the Earth, or on yourselves, that isn't already recorded by Us in a book, and that is indeed easy for Allah. [Remember that] so you don't despair over what you have lost or brag about what you have gained, because Allah doesn't love the arrogant and boastful who are greedy and who urge others to be greedy also." (Qur'an 57:22–23)

Peace from the Pulpit

This next story is a practical example of the peacefulness that belief in *Qadr* can bring. A story is told about a famous Muslim scholar of the past named Abu Hanifa (703–767). He was giving a sermon in a mosque when a man rushed in through a side door, ran up to him, and whispered something in his ear. Abu Hanifa merely answered, "Praise God." The throngs of people gathered there were puzzled as the man ran back out, but they said nothing and the scholar continued his speech. A little while later, just as Abu Hanifa was concluding his talk, the same man came running back in and whispered again into his ear. Abu Hanifa replied once more, "Praise God." When the sermon was finished and the scholar was leaving, a crowd gathered around him and asked him what happened and why he said, "Praise God" twice. Abu Hanifa explained:

> The first time the man came to me, he told me all my merchandise was lost at sea in a shipwreck. When I realized that this loss had no effect on my faith in God, I said, "Praise God." The second time he came to me, he told me it was a mistake and that the ship with all my goods on it was now coming into port. When I realized that this also did not cause my heart to become altered I again said, "Praise God."

Islam never teaches that we should sit around and wait for whatever is supposed to happen to us. We must participate, take action, and, when results come in, accept what happened and not be filled with endless "what if's." The Prophet Muhammad advised us to say, "God has planned; He has carried out His plan, and I will be patient." Just because we don't like the results of our life's challenges doesn't mean they weren't good for us. At the same time we have to ask ourselves if we lived up to the challenges and tried our best.

In another famous story about Abu Hanifa, he was leaving a mosque one day when he was accosted by a beggar. The man was not disabled or old so Abu Hanifa asked him why he didn't get a job. The man replied that he was following the teachings of the Prophet Muhammad, who said, "If you would put your trust completely in God, He will provide for you in the same way He provides for the birds: They go out in the morning with their stomachs empty and return in the evening with their stomachs full." Abu Hanifa shook his head and told the man that he had misinterpreted the saying of the Prophet. The man failed to take note of the fact that the birds had to *go out* in the morning and work for their food. The man dropped his bowl and went looking for employment.

Trusting in God and His plan while taking action and then accepting the outcome reflectively is the Muslim way. "Tie your camel and then put your trust in God," the Prophet once told a man who asked which he should do first. On another occasion the Prophet said, "Whoever says our actions don't matter and we must rely on destiny has failed to understand the teachings of Muhammad." God knows the future, and we can rest assured He is the best Planner.

The Least You Need to Know

- Islam does not believe in fatalism or in an ultimate destiny that is inescapable.
- God is the creator of time and is outside of the flow of time, seeing the past, present, and future happening all at once.
- Muslims are taught to have perseverance no matter what happens to them, good or bad. This stoic attitude is the hallmark of an individual's level of faith.
- Muslims believe that God does not test people with more than they can bear. It's up to us to rise to the challenge.

From Adam to Armageddon

In This Chapter

- Learn how Islam explains the diversity of religions and cultures in the world
- Know the function of prophets and Divine Revelation according to Islam
- Discover the meaning of history in the Qur'an
- Discover what Islam has to say about Armageddon and the anti-Christ
- Learn about the role Jesus will play in the end-of-time scenario

The history of the world is filled with a dizzying array of cultures, customs, religions, and beliefs. Islam has its own explanation for the origin of this incredible diversity in our species' spiritual and religious mosaic. All true religion, Muslims believe, began with God. It is merely the fault of people through the centuries that beliefs mutated over time or were lost. Along the way, new values and customs would sometimes emerge, resulting in the great variety of unique local expressions of faith and culture we see today. With regard to our racial and ethnic differences, Islam says that humans are descended from one male and one female and that it is the environment that shaped how we look. So what is the meaning of history for a follower of Islam?

According to the nineteenth-century German philosopher Georg Wilhelm Friedrich Hegel, there are patterns to history, and those who do not know the past are doomed to repeat it. These two maxims describe the entire saga of the human story and, quite lucidly, mirror the message of the Qur'an. The rise and fall of civilizations is a manifestation of our collective desire to establish a permanent presence in this world. We can gain lessons, the Qur'an suggests, into the purpose of our lives by seeing how previous nations either exalted or ignored God and their ultimate fate. In fact, history for a Muslim can be considered no less than the playing out of episodes in a cosmic script culminating with the inevitable journey of all people back to their Lord.

From the first human couple, Adam and Eve, through the innumerable generations of humanity, the struggle between order and chaos and good and evil in our world has ebbed and flowed. But this process of history will not go on forever. Even as humanity had a beginning, so, too, will it have an end, and Islam provides us with prophecies about how the conclusion to our story will proceed. The prophets that God sent to the various races and nations of the earth all warned of a coming Last Day. Some gave more-detailed narratives than others, but the basic theme remains the same—at the moment when human civilization is at its height, it will come crashing down, and God's promised Day of Judgment will be upon us all. In this chapter, I will be discussing what Islam says about the End Times and the various players who will help to bring it about.

No Tower of Babel Here

How does Islam explain the variety of human cultures, languages, religions, and historical experiences we have in our world today? The Bible certainly offers a creative explanation. It says that all people in the ancient days were one nation, and in their arrogance they tried to build a high tower to the sky. This was called the Tower of Babel. Then God decided that it would be a good idea to break people up into different groups lest they become too powerful, so He magically made them all speak different languages. People scattered in a hurry and became the various nations of the earth. Is this how the Qur'an explains the linguistic and cultural diversity in our world? No, in fact, there is no Tower of Babel mentioned in the Qur'an.

FROM THE SOURCE

According to Muhammad, "There is no superiority of a white over a black or of a black over a white. All of you are the children of Adam, and Adam was made from dust." (Hadith from the Abu Dawud collection)

Islam gives a very reasonable and balanced explanation for the spread of people over the earth and their unique experiences. To begin our narrative, the Qur'an states that the earliest human beings did live together in one community or tribe. Then we learn that the group became too large to sustain a cohesive social life. The Qur'an says that "they fell into disputes with one another and scattered" over the earth. Another interesting verse even gives us a beneficial side effect for this dispersal around the world. It states, "O People! We created you from a single pair of a male and a female and made you into nations and tribes so you can come to know each other. The noblest among you in the sight of Allah is the one with the most spiritual awareness." (Qur'an 49:13)

So Islam views the diversity of languages and cultures in our world as a natural process caused by the movement of people here and there. It is a source of richness, wonder, and discovery. Multiculturalism has a treasured place in Islamic ideology; and according to the Qur'an, the only criterion for differentiating among people lies in the strength of their religious sentiment. Muslims are thus taught that race is not a legitimate standard of measurement. Islam has often been praised for its emphasis on the equality of all people regardless of race, creed, or color. Malcolm X, who had been reared in a racist hybrid of Islam, Christianity, and Black Nationalism, otherwise known as the Nation of Islam, came to discover this when he broke with the movement and undertook a Hajj to Mecca. There he found himself living and praying alongside whites, blacks, browns, and all the other races of the earth.

Given this understanding of natural human movement throughout the world, Muslims thus can agree with anthropologists who have proven that all people can be traced back to a single region in east Africa. What about the diversity of our colors and physical features? Islam makes an allowance for that as well. The Prophet Muhammad once commented on the differences of appearance among people in the Arabian peninsula by pointing out that people in the south of Arabia were darker skinned because the sun was harsher and the climate more extreme. People in central and northern Arabia, he explained, were lighter skinned because the climate was fairer. Thus, environmental factors account for how people look from region to region.

The Rise of the Prophets

The descendants of Adam and Eve spread throughout Africa, the Middle East, Europe, Asia, and finally the Americas. This process took countless generations, and different groups of people developed a variety of cultural expressions. The Qur'an says that God sent prophets to all those nations during this process of dispersal. Prophets were always chosen from among local people because those born into a community know best how to reach it. Islam makes allowances for the varied rituals and customs that each nation followed by saying that every community received religious features tailored to its specific needs: "To every civilization We have appointed rites and ceremonies which they had to follow, so don't let them dispute with you on this matter, but invite [them] to your Lord, for you are assuredly on the Right Way." (Qur'an 22:67)

If you think about the many peoples and communities that have existed for the last 500,000 years, the sheer number of prophets must be staggering. There is an unconfirmed saying of the Prophet Muhammad in which he said that God sent 124,000 *nabi*, or prophets, to the world and 313 *rasul*, or messengers, who also received an organized body of laws to pass on. Do we know the names of all these prophets? No, the Qur'an's unique style doesn't include countless names and genealogies. Where stories are pertinent to illustrate a spiritual precept or lesson, there you will find mention of ancient prophets.

The Qur'an clearly states:

> We have already told you the story of some Messengers, but of others We haven't. And Allah spoke directly to Moses. The Messengers gave good news as well as warnings so that people after [the life time] of the Messengers would have no plea [of ignorance] against Allah, because Allah is Powerful and Wise. (Qur'an 4:165)

Only 25 prophets and messengers are mentioned by name in the Qur'an; and their stories, following the Qur'anic method of teaching, are given mainly in the context of providing an example for the religious idea being taught.

How Religion Becomes Lost

What happened to those prophets and their teachings? Does Islam teach that a prophet must always be successful, as some Western scholars have asserted? In general, the Qur'an does not require that a prophet complete his mission successfully. The prophet of the day is only required to try his best. In fact, the Qur'an is very critical of the responses that most people have given to religious guidance. Under the pretense of protecting their cultures, most communities and tribes fought against their prophets. In some cases they even killed or tortured the prophets and their followers, who were mostly drawn from the ranks of the poor and downtrodden in society.

Even though God did His part—sending prophets who spoke with inescapable logic, providing signs in nature of His creative energy, possibly bringing about natural disasters to wake up the people, and sometimes performing miracles to aid the prophet's mission—*Shaytan* was able to convince many civilizations to cling to their old ways:

> Before you We sent [Messengers] to many nations and We afflicted them with suffering and adversity that they might learn humility. When the suffering sent by Us reached them, why didn't they learn humility? On the contrary their hearts became hardened and Shaytan made their [sinful] acts seem alluring to them. (Qur'an 6:42–43)

In a few instances, the people accepted the message of their prophet and became faithful believers. Other peoples might have adopted their prophets' teaching after the prophets had long since been dead. In any case, with the passage of time any given community was likely to alter, forget, or add to the precepts that had been passed down from generation to generation. If there were written revelations, they were probably edited, added to, or lost during wars or natural disasters. After many centuries there often was nothing left of a true prophet's doctrines but a name and a few snippets of advice. The rest of the religion might now consist of legends, idolatry, myths, superstition, and elaborate rituals.

When a prophet's message had been almost completely obliterated, God would send a new prophet who would again likely meet with opposition. Thus, the Islamic explanation for the existence of so many religions in the world is to say that all religions began with a true prophet but mutated over the centuries until they had little in common with their roots. The core message every prophet taught was *surrender to God and do what is right*—in other words, the tenets of Islam—but this message was lost successively until the last revelation given to the Prophet Muhammad.

Because Muslims believe that every nation received guidance from God and also that this guidance did not survive the passage of time unaltered, we automatically must respect the beliefs of other people. This is because a true prophet probably founded that person's religion many thousands of years before. The goal of Muslims, then, is to figure out what remains of authentic guidance from God, as determined by the yardstick of the Qur'an, and then to call upon that person, using any beliefs held in common, to take a look at Islam, the last installment of Divine Guidance.

The End Is Near!

Islam asserts that one day the world will end. The march of history from our hunter-gatherer days to our modern space age will not travel onward forever. The earth will be destroyed, and humanity will have to stand for judgment. Before this occurs, however, fantastic events pitting the forces of good against evil will take place. Christians have their Book of Revelation; Jews have their Messianic Prophecies; and Hindus have world-ending scenarios of their own. What does Islam say? Will the end come with no warning, or are there signs to watch for? The Qur'an and the words of the Prophet provide a definite scenario for the end of the world and its portents. They also give us a reason why it has to end.

As I've mentioned before, all Islamic teachings are derived from only two sources: the Qur'an and the Hadith, the sayings of the Prophet Muhammad. Muslims consider the Qur'an to be the literal Word of God while the prophetic sayings are Muhammad's explanations of how Islam should be lived, comments about the Qur'an's teachings, and also reveals prophecies of the future. Islam, unlike all other religions, did not develop its doctrines over many centuries through the efforts of many men. Every important aspect of Islamic beliefs and practices came within a span of 23 years, from 610 to 632 C.E. Islam combines both of these sources in its narrative of how the end-of-time scenario will play out.

To begin with, Islam teaches that the life span of the universe is fixed. God began it and will end it one day. The Day of Judgment will follow afterward so that evil can be punished and good rewarded. In Islam, God is considered a righteous Being who will right wrongs and show appreciation for those who listened to His guidance. The Last Day is necessary, for the ultimate *payback* time will come. Leading up to the Last Day, God will give many signs so that those who are disheartened may gain spiritual strength and those who are rebels against God's teachings may have one last chance to repent and reform. The twin sources of Islam give a complete picture of what these signs will be.

There are two major areas of focus when we look at the end-of-time scenarios. The first concerns human society and the final battle between the forces of *Shaytan* and the forces guided by God. The second concerns physical disasters that will overcome the earth causing its destruction. With regard to the human component, there will basically be tremendous conflicts and battles between nations. Unlike the Book of Revelation in the Bible, however, there is no mention of a climactic melee between angels and demons up in the clouds. All of the battles on Earth will be between people who are either for or against God. The actual destruction of Earth will follow after that. I will begin with the first topic, that of war between nations and people.

Prophecies About the Muslim World

Are Muslims expecting the end of the world soon? Modern conditions, as foretold by the Prophet Muhammad, lead many to believe that the end is indeed near. The greatest of these signs lies in the worldwide condition of the Muslim community. There is no unified Islamic nation encompassing the whole Muslim world, as is called for in the Qur'an. Muslims are not victorious against their foes anywhere in the world, and only recently did the armies of Europe end their military occupation of over 90 percent of the Muslim world. (From the 1800s until the 1960s, most of the Muslim world was ruled by France, the Netherlands, Russia, or Great Britain.)

ASK THE IMAM

The Jewish Old Testament of the Bible warns Jews of God's wrath and the destruction of Zion and its later rebirth by the Messiah. The Christian New Testament warns of a great disaster to befall true believers who will be saved later by a triumphant Jesus. Islam also has a prophetic tradition of predicting the downfall of Muslims until a hero, called the *Mahdi, or Guided One,* comes along who will revive the community.

To make matters worse, in most Muslim countries the free practice of Islam is suppressed. It was so bad for so long that in Turkey, the former seat of the last Islamic Empire, it was until recently illegal for females to wear head scarves in school or for children to be sent to academies to learn about the Qur'an. It would be akin to outlawing yarmulkes in Israel or Bible study groups in America! In Syria, if you speak publicly about corruption in the political system, you may wind up in jail. In Uzbekistan, the prisons are full of people whose only crime was that they wanted to promote basic Islamic moral teachings in their communities. In Algeria, the military canceled democratic elections in 1992 simply because a Muslim political party won the popular vote. From country to country in the so-called Muslim world, similar restrictions on the free exercise of Islam exist. How is it possible that the traditional religion of so many countries is suppressed? Many governments in the Muslim world happen to be ultra-secularist dictatorships or corrupt monarchies that consider organized religion a threat to their power. That's one of the grievances commonly heard in street protests that pop up from time-to-time throughout the Muslim world. Bet you didn't know that!

Turmoil exists on the economic front as well. Although it may seem that some Muslim nations are generally prosperous, especially when you think of the big oil countries, in fact, the rulers of those nations do not look after the welfare of their people. They spend the nation's resources on building palaces and enriching their relatives in typical despotic fashion. Because of the petty wars being fought in the Muslim world today between tin-pot dictators, Muslims now make up the majority of the world's refugees. The resources of the Muslim world do not benefit their countries of origin, because the oil, timber, gas, diamonds, and other treasures are largely exported to other countries, with the resultant cash being skimmed off by the ruling elite. The Prophet Muhammad warned that a day would come when the nations of the earth would feed upon the resources of the Muslim world like people eating at a banquet. A man asked the Prophet, "Will we be so few then?" The Prophet answered, "No, you will be numerous."

The Signs of the Hour

Muhammad gave many prophecies about these dire times, and he said that when the signs are evident, we should look for the coming of the anti-Christ, or *Dajjal* as he is known in Arabic. Given these conditions, many Muslims feel that we have entered the beginning of the end-of-time process. In this there is commonality with fundamentalist Christians, who also feel the end of the world is near. Though to be fair, the Muslim world had it far worse during the Mongol invasions, and writers back then thought the end of the world was coming soon as well.

DEFINITION

The starting point of the Islamic calendar is the migration of the Prophet Muhammad from the hostile city of Mecca to the friendly city of Yathrib in the year 622 C.E. This event is called the *Hijrah,* or migration. Muslims use the initials *BH* (Before *Hijrah*) and *AH* (After *Hijrah*) in the same way Christians use B.C. (before Christ) and A.D. (Anno Domini, or the year of our Lord—in other words, after Christ was born).

What are these signs of the end-of-time? Islam teaches that after the Muslim world is vanquished and broken up into many competing nations, the practice of Islam will be increasingly difficult for true believers. Muhammad once described this period by saying that holding on to Islam will be like holding on to a hot coal. He also said that Islam came into the world as a stranger and will end up as a stranger again one day. Other signs of the end-of-time include the following:

1. Abundant riches (oil?) will be discovered under the Euphrates River in Iraq, and people will fight over them, causing much death and destruction.

2. Children will no longer obey or respect their parents.

3. Poor nations will compete with each other to build tall buildings in their cities even as the populace starves.

4. It will be hard to tell men and women apart physically.

5. Women will outnumber men by a huge margin (50:1).

6. Religious knowledge will decrease dramatically and authentic pious scholars will be rare.

7. Wealth will be widespread, and corruption will be rampant.

8. Music, female singers, and alcohol will be prevalent.

9. The worst people will be chosen as leaders.

10. There will be family turmoil in every household.

Looking at this list, you might think that the Day of Judgment is coming tomorrow! But things would have to become a whole lot worse, and other similar signs have still to be met. Muslims in the Prophet's own time were often under the impression that the Last Day would soon come upon them. However, the Qur'an (and the Bible!) teaches that only God knows when it will occur. It could still be a long way away by our timetable. Perhaps it won't come for thousands of years or more. It is this realization that has prevented the formation of doomsday cults or movements in the world of Islam.

The False Prophets

When all the signs do start to fall into place, a series of false prophets will arise in the world. There will be nearly 30 of them, with the last one being the anti-Christ, or *Dajjal*. Before the *Dajjal* appears, though, a great Muslim leader will arise who will unify all faithful Muslims under his banner and will wage many successful campaigns against the enemies of Islam. This leader's title is the *Mahdi*. Muslims look forward to his appearance and expect that many victories from Palestine to India will be achieved. Invading armies from Europe will be vanquished as well. After unifying the Middle East, peace and prosperity will fill the earth, and the economic benefits for all, Muslim and non-Muslim, will be overwhelming. The main base of Muslim authority will then be centered in Palestine when, after an indeterminate amount of time, rumors about the appearance of the *Dajjal* will begin to circulate among the region.

ASK THE IMAM

The *Mahdi* will be a descendant of the Prophet Muhammad and will have the same name. He will be a man whom God will inspire with the mission of uniting the Muslim world.

The Prophet Muhammad described the *Dajjal* in great detail. However, whereas the Bible envisions him to be a handsome man who will woo people with his magic and charm, Muhammad said that he will be blind in one eye and will have a mark on his forehead that looks so prominent that you can sense the disbelief in his face. He will have brown, curly hair and will travel throughout the world spreading mischief and trouble wherever he goes with chicanery and deceptive activities. Not surprisingly, the name *Dajjal* translates as liar, or man of deception.

The *Dajjal* will claim that he is a new prophet of God. He will be wealthy and have amazing powers to cure people of their illnesses. *Shaytan* will send some of his evil *jinns* to impersonate the dead so that the *Dajjal* can claim to bring people back to life. Later he will make the claim that he is a god on Earth. The majority of the people in the world, including a few misguided Muslims, will follow him and believe in him. He will therefore amass a lot of military might, which he will use to harass and destroy all vestiges of true religious expression.

The *fitnah*, or turmoil of the *Dajjal*, will last for 40 days. During that time, he will gather an army and begin to conquer the Middle East, which had been unified under the *Mahdi*. He will even try to invade the city of Medina in Arabia but will be prevented from entering it by angels who will deter his attacks. The remnants of the Muslim army will gather in Syria and will very quickly find themselves under siege by the *Dajjal's* army. Battles will rage for several days, with the Muslims taking heavy casualties. When all appears lost, the *Mahdi* will call his soldiers together in the evening and receive their pledge to fight to the last man and woman on the following day.

While the darkness of night is still upon the Muslim camps in and around central Syria, a rumor of deliverance will spread like wildfire and a voice will be heard saying, "The one who listens to your pleas has come." When the time for the pre-dawn prayer arrives, the Prophet Jesus, whom Muslims believe had been saved from dying on the cross thousands of years before and had been kept in Paradise by God, will descend in the midst of Damascus. After joining the Muslims in prayer, he will lead the *Mahdi's* forces against the *Dajjal's* army. The *Dajjal's* soldiers will number 70,000.

On the battlefield, Jesus will command his troops to move aside so that there will be a clear view between him and the *Dajjal*. Upon seeing Jesus, the *Dajjal's* powers will fade and he will make a panicky retreat into Palestine. The Muslims will come down from the mountains and crush the remnants of the enemy army. Jesus will pursue the *Dajjal* to a place named Lydda, which is near an airport south of the present-day city of Tel Aviv in Israel. There Jesus will strike down the *Dajjal* with a lance, and his reign of tyranny will be over.

The Rule of Jesus

What will happen next? Is the game finally over? Is it time for Judgment Day? Not yet. According to the sayings of the Prophet Muhammad, Jesus will speak to the Christians and Jews of the world and convert them to Islam. He will succeed in breaking the worship of the cross and will stop the eating of pork. The army he led will disband and disperse back to their home countries, and only a small contingent will remain with him to serve him. Jesus will be the spiritual head of a transnational government of peace. Everyone in the Middle East will convert willingly to Islam, and there will be no more war for a long time. He will visit Mecca and Medina while on pilgrimage. He won't reign for a thousand years, as Christianity teaches, but will live only 40 more years—the rest of his natural life span. Along the way he will marry and have children. While he is in the world, peace and prosperity will bring countless benefits for all people.

Gog and Magog

The next great challenge for humanity will occur when the nations of the East, the *Yajuj* and *Majuj*, known as Gog and Magog in the Bible, will begin an invasion with forces such as the world has never before seen. They will invade the Middle East and destroy every city and resource in their path. They will completely drain Lake Tiberias in Palestine because of their armies' large requirement for water. Jesus will command the faithful to retreat to Mount Sinai in Egypt because no one will be able to withstand the massive onslaught of the invaders.

When the carnage wrought by the *Yajuj* and *Majuj* becomes so great that all looks lost, Jesus will pray to God for deliverance. His plea will be answered because God will unleash a pathogen or some type of disease upon the enemy that will infect their soldiers and cause their army to crumble from within. The power of the invaders will be broken, and Jesus and his followers will leave the mountain redoubt and return to their homes. Now, many more people around the world will start to convert to Islam, but before this can be fully accomplished Jesus will pass away. He will be buried in Medina next to the grave of the Prophet Muhammad.

The Last Day

We enter the final phase: the end of the world. Three massive sinkholes will open up in the earth. One will be in the east, one in the west, and one in Arabia. A mysterious cloudy haze will envelop the world, making people feel hot with fever, and the sun will rise in the West. Many of the remaining people in the world who do not believe in God will want to convert now, but no conversion will be accepted then. A strange and fantastic beastlike creature will rise from the earth and warn people about the end of the world. A ground fire will ignite in the land of Yemen, driving the people in Arabia to flee to Syria.

A new wave of hypocrisy and heresy will sweep over the world. Vice, crime, and state-sponsored oppression will become rampant. All the remaining faithful Muslims will gather in Syria once more. But by this time, even the few remaining Muslims in the world will have forgotten the Qur'an, and copies of it will not be found anywhere. The earth will start to quake, and the mountains will begin to crumble. As the Qur'an says, "Everything will be in a commotion."

FROM THE SOURCE

The Trumpet will [just] be sounded when all beings in the heavens and on earth will pass out except such as it will please Allah [to exempt]. Then will a second one be sounded when behold they will be standing [on the Plain of Judgment] and looking on! (Qur'an 39:68)

The stars will begin to fade; the skies will start to "roll up." The seas will rise, animals will gather in the few remaining patches of land, and terror and fear will grip the people who remain. God will order that all the souls of the dead be raised from their graves and reunited with new bodies on the Plain of Judgment. A breeze will pass over the world, taking the souls of any living believers, and they will feel no pain. The earth will be crushed, and the souls of the remaining living people (the sinners) will also be taken. God will then create a new universe with a new Earth, but for humanity the game is over. Everyone will stand before God on a level plain and await his or her judgment.

This is the Islamic view of the end of the world and the establishment of the Day of Judgment. As you can see, there are some similarities with the Christian concept of Armageddon, but the Islamic view has many twists and turns to the story that make it unique in its own right. Again, when will this process start? Only God knows the hour. Muslims today are expecting it to happen sooner rather than later, but thus far people have not been convinced enough to quit their jobs or sell their homes. Undue panic over this issue has no tradition in the Muslim community.

The Least You Need to Know

- The diversity in world religions is caused by the alteration of each prophet's message over many generations.
- Islam does not believe in the superiority of any race over another. The only valid criterion for establishing the value of people is their religiousness and level of faith.
- Islam has its own view of Armageddon in which Jesus plays a part, though he will be on the side of Muslims when he returns to Earth.
- Muslims believe in an end-of-time scenario that includes the destruction of Earth and the beginning of Judgment Day.

The Five Pillars of Islam

How do we live a godly life? Countless sages and seers for millennia have posed this question. Every religion and spiritual tradition seeks to answer this dilemma with its own program of faith, personal improvement, and social activism. Islam also has its own unique system designed to bring about a heightened awareness of God in our lives. Through a constant reaffirmation of faith and the practice of the Five Pillars of Islam, a Muslim orders his or her life according to the dictates of the Prophet Muhammad.

These religious practices encompass a variety of activities, from fasting and pilgrimage to prayer and active struggle against wrong. It is in this last one, otherwise known as *jihad*, where a large amount of misunderstanding among both Muslims and non-Muslims occurs. In this part, I take a look at the pillars and practices of Islam and the unique reason behind each one. I also discuss the role of *jihad* in Islam and why it has become such a misused term.

Declaring Faith in Islam

In This Chapter

- Learn about the Five Pillars of Islam and their significance
- Understand how the rituals and practices of Islam affect Muslims' daily lives at home and in the community
- Read up on the Muslim confession of faith
- Discover how belief in one God helps Muslims to transcend the material world
- Know how Muslims view the place of Muhammad in their religion

Islam has a very detailed philosophy for looking at life and provides a definite statement about our purpose in this world. Beliefs and philosophy, however, must be backed up with a program of life-changing action: daily rituals, meaningful practices, and annual reaffirmations of what it means to be a follower of God. Only when faith is reinforced by action can religious concepts be truly realized. From the perspective of the Qur'an, Muslims can't simply say they believe and then get away with leading any kind of lifestyle they want. What good is faith if it doesn't improve the way you live?

Although every religion asks its followers to engage in rituals to reinforce the precepts of the faith, only Islam requires its followers to keep a daily and yearly regimen of testimony, prayer, fasting, pilgrimage, and charity, commonly known as the *Five Pillars of Islam*. When a person commits to following the Islamic way of living, the commitment is no joke. However, it's not so hard that only a select few can do it. People from every walk of life live Islam every day. The idea is that we gain discipline through the application of Islamic rituals in our lives. The rituals teach us to master ourselves and our motivations so that we can gain control over our physical urges and elevate our minds for a higher purpose. In this chapter, I will be exploring in depth the first of the Five Pillars of Islam as well and the importance of monotheism and the role of the Prophet Muhammad in the Islamic faith.

Introducing the Five Pillars of Islam

Islam has a system of rituals designed to translate our religious beliefs into concrete reality. This serves to keep us constantly aware of our duty to God and helps us avoid the dangers of temptation and complacency. This system is called the *Arkan al Islami,* or Pillars of Islam. In order, they are …

1. **Shahadah**   Testifying our allegiance to God.
2. **Salat**   Daily prayer.
3. **Zakat**   Annual charity.
4. **Saum**   Month-long fasting.
5. **Hajj**   The pilgrimage to Mecca.

ASK THE IMAM

There are four categories of religious action with regard to daily duties in Islamic Law. They range from what you *must* do as a Muslim to what you can choose to do for extra credit on your record or leave off entirely. The categories are as follows:

Fard   Required duties for all Muslims, such as the five canonical prayers, fasting, etc.

Wajib   An action that should be done every time the opportunity comes up, such as certain extra prayers or lifestyle practices.

Sunnah   The Prophet's personal example or things he asked people to do without making them a religious duty, such as brushing your teeth after every meal or shaking hands with the right hand.

Nafl   Extra or optional actions that the Prophet did sometimes but not on a consistent basis, such as fasting on certain days, keeping night vigils, etc.

These practices are integrated into the daily routine of every Muslim's life, and they help keep us on the straight path. The Five Pillars remind us of who we are and what we have pledged ourselves to follow. These rituals are so important that they have the legal status of a *fard*, or required duty on the part of a believer. To neglect a required duty is a sin, and the angels will record it as such in our book of deeds. On the Day of Judgment everyone will have to answer for his or her lack of compliance in God's multi-step program for life change and personal transformation. As you learn about each of the pillars, try to put yourself into the Muslim frame of mind and think about how these types of activities could influence your own faith on a daily basis.

The Five Pillars are crucial from the standpoint of Islam, because through their practice we remind ourselves of our real purpose in this world. By praying, fasting, giving in charity, and such, we train ourselves to become God-oriented people. Islam has often been praised for its disciplining effect, and the five pillars are the core of that program. Prison wardens throughout the United States, for example, are giving greater freedom to the propagation of Islam among their inmate populations precisely because it makes the prisoners calmer, easier to manage, and more mature.

The Shahadah

Did you know that there is one phrase said at least 17 billion times a day? It is called the *Shahadah*, or *Declaration of Faith*. It is said a minimum of 17 times each day within the daily prayers of each of the 1 billion Muslims on Earth. Anyone who says that people don't praise God enough obviously hasn't met a Muslim!

In Arabic, the most basic *Shahadah* formula is said this way: *Ashahadu an la ilaha ill Allah, wa ashahadu anna Muhammadar Rasulullah.* The English translation is: "I declare that there is no god except God, and I declare that Muhammad is the Messenger of God." This phrase includes the two founding principles of Islam and is sometimes called the Muslim Creed. It is a very strong ideological statement in that it lays out the Muslim frontline position: There is only one God, and Muhammad is His last Prophet.

What are the benefits of reciting the *Shahadah* so many times each day? Think about it: All Muslims have the chance to remind themselves about the reality of God in their lives. Whereas the hustle and bustle of the daily grind may cause us to forget that we are living through a big test and will have to face God one day, the *Shahadah* and its recitation focuses our hearts and minds on our ultimate purpose. We are here to surrender our wills to God and lead virtuous lives. The Qur'an asks, "Who will take a reminder?" The *Shahadah* is one way to remember.

Uncompromising Monotheism

The *Shahadah* consists of two distinct parts. One is a negation and the second is an affirmation. It is interesting that the first part of the *Shahadah*, the part about believing in God, is phrased in a negating way. It doesn't just come out and say that God is our master; rather it goes a step further and makes the point that there is nothing worthy of our attention or allegiance *other* than God. There is no god but *the* God.

FROM THE SOURCE

According to Muhammad, God said, "I have never endowed My servants with a favor, without a group among them disbelieving in it and saying, 'Stars, it was due to the stars.'" Astrology is forbidden in Islamic Law as a false crutch upon which to interpret the world and events within it.

Islam is very expansive in its definition of false gods. Usually idols or statues come to mind when we think about man-made gods, but Muhammad made the point that anything that takes our attention away from our true purpose in life can be a false god. A belief in astrology, slavish adoration of some famous person, or veneration of paintings of people or animals are examples. Furthermore, Islam says that personal arrogance is grounds for having a false god. People who are so full of themselves that they walk the streets puffed up with pride should beware, the Qur'an says, because they've made *themselves* into false gods.

ASK THE IMAM

Islam forbids statues, paintings, and drawings of people and animals, equating them with potential idols. Abstract art and drawings, tapestries and fabric, nature scenes, cartoons, and dolls and figurines for children are generally exempted. A minority of very conservative Muslims even consider photographs forbidden, though this issue is hotly disputed among Muslim scholars.

As Muslims, when we affirm the first part of the *Shahadah*, we are saying that we want to dedicate ourselves to living for God alone and that we will not hold anyone or anything as worthy of veneration besides Him. It is a daily pillar of Islam and the first of the five rituals because it establishes the foundation upon which all other Islamic beliefs and practices are built. Billions of times each day people around the world declare that God is the One before Whom there are no others. That's quite a lot of public sentiment!

And Muhammad Is His Prophet

The second part of the *Shahadah* begins with an affirmation: "I declare that Muhammad is the Messenger of God." This part of the creed lays out the framework within which Islam says a person has to work to be truly obedient to God. The Qur'an, as you will recall, accepts that prophets were sent in the past to various nations. Jesus, Moses, Isaac, David, Abraham—all of them carried the same message from the same God, and they all taught a divinely revealed way of life. Anyone who followed them and their teachings and methods in their historical time would get to Heaven.

Islam also promotes the idea that the messages of these former prophets were lost, altered, or even fabricated by later followers. The Qur'an warns: "Woe to those who write the book with their own hands and then say, 'Here, this is from God,' to traffic with it for a miserable price. Woe to them for what they make and woe to them for what they fake." (Qur'an 2:79) So the mission of Muhammad was to restore the truth of God's authentic message so that people would once again have unimpeded access to God's true way of life.

By stating that Muhammad is God's last Messenger, we are pledging ourselves to practicing what he preached, doing what he did, and looking to him for our role model. Anyone who follows the model of a prophet previous to Muhammad is following a way that has been compromised, thus a common call in the Qur'an is for followers of previous revelation (especially Jews and Christians) to take a look at the last prophet's message to see the truth from their Lord in its unadulterated state. To be a true follower of Moses or Jesus, for example, is to recognize that God spoke to the world one last time and to enter into a way of life that is what their original prophets had taught. There is a special word to refer to a prophet's life example, and that is *Sunnah*, or Way of the Prophet. In his last official speech during his last pilgrimage to Mecca, Muhammad said, "I'm leaving two things behind for you. If you hold fast to them you will never go astray. They are the Qur'an and my Sunnah."

Muhammad is not considered divine in Islam. He is not a god. He is not sitting at the right hand of Allah meting out justice, nor is he a savior to whom Muslims can pray. "Muhammad is a man among men," says the Qur'an. Muslims revere him and love him for all of the sacrifices he went through in his struggles with the idol-worshippers of Arabia. He endured unimaginable hardships in order to bring God's last message to the world. He is also considered by Muslims to be the best model of a husband, father, leader, friend, guide, and politician.

He never ordered a palace to be built, even after Islam became triumphant in Arabia, nor did he ever amass any wealth. His total net worth when he died consisted of a reed bed and blanket, a bowl, and a shield that had been pawned. He lived an austere, almost Zen-like life all the way to the end. Western scholars and writers have begun to recognize his admirable qualities and comment on them. George Bernard Shaw wrote, "He must be called the Savior of Humanity. I believe that if a man like him were to assume the dictatorship of the modern world, he would succeed in solving its problems in a way that would bring it much needed peace and happiness." (*The Genuine Islam*, vol. 1, no. 8)

ASK THE IMAM

Muslims learn about their religion from only two basic sources, the Qur'an and the Prophet's *Sunnah*. The *Sunnah*, or Way of the Prophet, is contained in the books of hadiths. These books are the collected sayings and actions of the Prophet, categorized by topic, that were compiled in the first three centuries of the Islamic era.

Luckily for us, he lived at a time when the world was getting smaller and information could travel faster. His life and sayings have been documented by thousands of individuals who saw him, heard him, lived with him, traveled with him, and watched him from childhood to his assumption of his role as a prophet. Their writings provide a complete picture of who Muhammad was and what he was all about.

Expressions of Respect

Whenever Muslims hear the name of the Prophet Muhammad, they say the following phrase: *Salallahu alayhi wa sallam*, which translates as "the peace and blessings of God be upon him." Both the Qur'an and the Sunnah require us to say this to show our respect; if we don't, it is equated with being stingy. Many Muslim cultures have an entire corpus of music and poetry devoted to praising the Prophet. Muslims believe that whenever we wish peace upon the Prophet, an angel goes to Muhammad's grave and brings this news to his soul, which is resting there. (The souls of the departed remain in their graves in *Barzakh*.) On the Day of Judgment, God will accept the plea of Muhammad to save from Hellfire whomever he asks to be pardoned, up to a certain limit. Only a precious few will be granted the right to intercede on behalf of others on Judgment Day.

The Welcoming Tie

The *Shahadah*, our Declaration of Faith, negates false gods and affirms the way in which we must follow the path to God. The purpose of its frequent recitation is to remind us of those two principles.

The *Shahadah* is the defining statement of Islam. When a person desires to convert to Islam, all he or she need do is believe in what the *Shahadah* teaches and then recite it (or sign it if the converting person is mute) in front of as few as two witnesses. After this utterance, Muslims believe all the former sins of a convert are erased from their book of deeds. There are no lengthy years of study, as there are to convert to Judaism, nor is there a baptism ceremony, as in Christianity. Belief expressed in the heart and tongue is enough to get the spiritual ticket needed to be on the straight path to God.

The Least You Need to Know

- Islam has a unique set of practices called the Five Pillars of Islam, which encompass monotheism, prayer, fasting, charity, and pilgrimage.
- A Muslim must perform the five pillars, or it is counted as a sin.
- The Muslim Creed is called the *Shahadah,* or the Declaration of Faith. It consists of two parts: belief in God and acceptance of Muhammad as a prophet.
- Muhammad is not considered a god, a son of God, or even a savior in the classic Christian sense. He is a man who was chosen by God to deliver a message.
- Muslim conversion rituals consist of merely reciting the *Shahadah* in the presence of at least two witnesses.

Understanding Muslim Prayers

In This Chapter

- Discover the meaning of the famous Islamic call to prayer
- Learn about the purpose of Muslim worship
- Understand the process of the five daily prayers of Islam
- Unlock the mystery of what Muslims do when they pray

Regular prayer, known as *salat* in Arabic, is the second pillar of Islam. It is the ritual having the most direct impact on a Muslim's daily life. Prayer is often a contentious issue in our modern world. As much as people of faith promote its many benefits in public life, those who desire a well-defined separation of church and state often strive to have laws enacted that curtail its practice in public situations. Both sides have reasons for their actions; as Muslims continue to enter mainstream life in the West, they, too, are now increasingly being asked to take sides in this debate. This presents an odd situation in that Islam commands its followers to pray five times each day but then discourages them from participating in the prayers of non-Muslims if they mention topics contrary to Islamic teachings. Is prayer in Islam a public or a private act? The answer is that it is both.

The entire philosophy of prayer in Islam is that it is a way for the individual to elevate his or her mind to seek God. It also has the side benefit of curbing the desire to hearken to immoral inclinations. Images of Muslims lined up solemnly in rows are common staples of news magazines, and many in the West have expressed respect for the group discipline that this activity promotes. Public observances thus serve to reinforce within the community the importance of regular prayer and cooperative action. In this chapter, I explore this ritual and its importance. In addition, I walk with you, step-by-step, through every stage of the Islamic way of prayer so that you can gain an understanding of what it's all about and why this practice won't easily fit into the current debate about prayer in the modern Western world.

When Do Muslims Pray?

Muslims pray five times each day. Each of the five daily prayers is said within a specific range of time during the day. There are no exemptions to the religious requirement to perform prayers except for children under puberty, women during their menses, the unconscious, the incapacitated, and the mentally challenged. The official prayer times and their names are as follows:

- **Fajr**   From first light to just before sunrise

- **Zuhr**   Just after noontime

- **'Asr**   Late afternoon

- **Maghrib**   Just after sunset

- **'Isha**   Any time at night

Because the seasons change and the days get longer or shorter throughout the year, the times we pray will move a bit each month. In the summer, our first prayer may start at 4:30 A.M. and our last prayer may be at nearly 10:00 at night! In the winter, our range of prayer may be from 7:30 A.M. to 6:30 P.M. The time for each prayer begins according to the position of the sun (or lack thereof) and is valid until the next prayer time begins, so there is a lot of leeway and flexibility on the exact moment to make the *salat*. These fixed timings have been laid out in the Qur'an, and no prayer may be said before the official time begins. Any prayer said when the prayer time is over is considered a late prayer and is marked as such by the angels who record our deeds.

The Muslim Call to Prayer

Islam requires prayer to be performed at fixed times, yet in premodern days clocks hadn't yet been invented. People told time by the position of the sun. In the first Islamic community in Arabia, some way had to be found to let people know that the prayer time had come. Moreover, because Islam taught that prayer in congregation was better in the sight of God than prayer alone, people needed to be informed when the congregation was forming in the mosque. Yet another reason for notifying people is that Muslim men over the age of puberty are required to attend a special service on Friday afternoon in which they hear a sermon. This is called *Salatul-Jumu'ah* (the Gathering Prayer).

Several ideas were bandied about by Muhammad's followers: bells like those used in churches, horns like those in synagogues, drums, and so on. But Muhammad did not approve of any of them. He prayed for guidance from God on this issue, and the answer came in a unique way. A companion came to the Prophet a few days later and said that in his dreams he saw a man calling out phrases in a loud voice. He was asking people to come to prayer. Muhammad listened to the man's words and declared that this dream came from God. He ordered the man to teach the words to a Muslim convert named Bilal, who had a beautiful voice. (Bilal was an African slave who was freed from his idolatrous master by the Muslims.) Bilal then stood atop a wall of the mosque in Medina (the former city name of Yathrib had been dropped) and called out loudly the following words:

> *Allahu Akbar, Allahu Akbar.*
>
> *Allahu Akbar, Allahu Akbar.*
>
> *Ashahadu an la ilaha ill Allah.*
>
> *Ashahadu an la ilaha ill Allah.*
>
> *Ashahadu anna Muhammadar Rasulullah.*
>
> *Ashahadu anna Muhammadar Rasulullah.*
>
> *Haya alas Salah. Haya alas Salah.*
>
> *Haya alal Falah. Haya alal Falah.*
>
> *Allahu Akbar, Allahu Akbar.*
>
> *La ilaha ill Allah.*

The meaning is as follows:

> God is greater, God is greater.
>
> God is greater, God is greater.
>
> I declare there is no god but God.

I declare there is no god but God.

I declare Muhammad is the Messenger of God.

I declare Muhammad is the Messenger of God.

Rush to prayer. Rush to prayer.

Rush to success. Rush to success.

God is greater, God is greater.

There is no god but God.

A person who calls the *azan* is termed a *muazzin*. It is not a special office or holy position. Any male can perform it, but Muslims usually appoint the person who has the nicest and loudest voice to do it. No trip to a Muslim country is complete until you've been awakened in the early morning to the sounds of the *azan* floating over the landscape.

> **DEFINITION**
>
> **Allahu Akbar** is actually an incomplete sentence in Arabic. Literally it means, "God is greater than …" The logical question becomes, "Greater than what?" The implication of leaving it as an unfinished sentence is that no matter how you complete it, God is greater than that, too.

Humble Pie

The purpose of *salat* is to present ourselves before God as humble servants. *Salat* is performed in a set manner, and the basic rules are the same for Muslims all over the world. The *salat* procedure combines a set of ritualistic movements with memorized passages that are said at specific times. While learning the physical aspects of the prayer is simple, learning by heart the words we must say is a little more challenging. Even more challenging than that is the final goal of *salat*—producing such a meditative state that no distractions are able to take our focus from God.

Why do Islamic prayers combine physical movements with memorized passages and assorted supplications? The answer lies in the makeup of our human selves. In the old days, when a king or noble walked by, the required response was to bow and show one's deference to the power inherent in the office the person represented. We submit physically as a sign of what is in our heart. If we stand stiff-necked and pray merely by saying whatever comes into our mind (and maybe getting emotional along the way), then the heart is humbled to a degree but the body betrays a lack of true deference. The body is left behind. Think about it: if you really believe in the power of God, then to bow in submission is no strange or demeaning thing.

Likewise, if our prayer is nothing more than whatever words we feel like saying at the moment, then one prayer would be no better than another. There would be no structure, no dignified way to say to God that we are obedient to Him, rather than a rabble of babbling voices. Islam says that all three of our components (mind, heart, and body) must be unified in prayer for it to be truly meaningful. First, we humble our hearts out of love for God. Then, we recite prayers that God gave us and concentrate on their meanings so we can learn how to remember God throughout our lives. Finally, we bring it all together by bowing down low so we feel with our physical senses what true humbleness means.

FROM THE SOURCE

Muhammad once said: "Your Lord delights at a shepherd who, on the peak of a mountain crag, gives the call to prayer and prays. Then Allah says, 'Look at this servant of Mine. He gives the call to prayer and performs the prayers; he is in awe of Me. I will forgive My servant [all his sins] and admit him to Paradise.'"

Each of the five daily prayers is performed in a similar way. The only difference between them is the total number of segments in each. The basic procedure to each prayer consists of standing and reciting a chapter from the Qur'an, bowing at the waist and glorifying God, and then prostrating twice on the ground while extolling God's power. This complete segment is called a *Ra'kah*, or unit of prayer. The early morning prayer consists of two units like this, whereas the two afternoon prayers and the night prayer consist of four units. The sunset prayer has three units. The varying number of units serves to give variety to our daily schedule so that we have to keep ourselves aware of what we're doing and also the varying lengths are fitted to the amount of time we may have at different points throughout the day to spend in prayer without it becoming a burden.

The Prayer Described

Let me walk you through a complete prayer procedure modeled on the early morning *Salatul-Fajr*. Try to put yourself into the mind-set of a Muslim, and you will see how this ritual can be very powerful as a source of spiritual rejuvenation and contentment. Let's begin.

After you have met the seven preparatory requirements for prayer, such as ablution and facing Mecca, begin your prayer by raising your hands to the side of your head and saying, in Arabic, *"Allahu Akbar,"* or *"God is greater."* (For the duration of this descriptive narrative I will only give the English meaning of what is said in the prayers.) From that moment onward, you are considered to be cut off from the world. All your attention and focus must be on God. You are presenting yourself to Him and should show proper deference. If you laugh, talk to someone, look around, or do anything similar, then your prayer is broken and you must start again. You must ignore everything that happens around you until you are finished. (Emergencies such as helping an injured person or avoiding imminent danger are valid excuses to interrupt prayer.)

ASK THE IMAM

Islamic prayers are said in Arabic exclusively so that all Muslims can be unified in their language of worship, in much the same way that Catholicism used to require Latin services. Muhammad even taught non-Arab converts to say the prayers in Arabic. Supplications, however, can be made in any language.

Next, fold your hands over your lower chest with the right hand over the left and recite the first chapter of the Holy Qur'an, which for Muslims is sort of like the *Lord's Prayer*. It is a beautiful summary of the entire message of Islam and reads as follows:

> In the Name of God, the Compassionate Source of All Mercy. All Praise be to God, the Lord of all the worlds, the Compassionate Source of All Mercy and Master of the Day of Judgment. You alone do we serve and it is to You alone that we look for help. Guide us on the Straight Path; the path of those who have earned Your favor, not the path of those who have earned Your anger, nor of those who have gone astray. (Qur'an 1:1–7)

Following this you say "Ameen," or "Let it be so." Then you must recite one more portion of the Qur'an, of your own choosing. It can be as few as three verses. (Muslims are encouraged to learn at least some of the Qur'an by heart for use in prayer.) Say, "God is greater" once again and bow forward at the waist, resting your hands on your knees. Repeat three times, *"Glory to my Lord, the Greatest."*

Then you say, *"God hears those who praise Him,"* and stand back upright with your arms at your sides. After another *"God is greater,"* you get down on your hands and knees and bow your forehead to the ground. Say three times, *"Glory to My Lord, Most High."*

Repeat, *"God is greater"* and rise to a sitting position. Declare that God is greater again and then bow on your forehead once more, repeating what you said the first time. This ends one unit of prayer. From here you say, *"God is greater"* one last time and then stand up again, fold your hands in front, and begin the whole process over.

The only difference in the second and final unit of movements is that after you recite the opening chapter of the Qur'an, you must choose a different second passage to recite afterward. When you finish with your second and final prostration, you rise to a sitting position and say two short benedictions. The first one extols the beauty of righteousness and faith while the second one is a heartfelt plea for God to bless the noble efforts of both Muhammad and Abraham. Following this you may slip in a supplication of your choice if you wish. Then you end your prayer by turning your face first to the right and then the left, wishing peace upon all those on either side of you by saying, "Peace be upon you and the mercy of God." (Even if there is no one at your side, the angels are there.) This is what Muslims do and say when they pray.

FROM THE SOURCE

When the Prophet Muhammad uttered the salutation at the end of the prayer, he would say: "O Allah, forgive me my former and latter sins, what I have kept secret and what I have done openly, and what I have done extravagantly; and what You know better than I do. You are the Advancer and the Delayer. There is no god but You."

If a Muslim is praying in a group with other Muslims, then one of them (usually the most knowledgeable) will act as an *Imam*, or prayer leader. The Imam will stand in front of everyone while the rest of the people will form straight rows behind him (or her if the congregation is made up of only women and minors), leaving enough space between each row to bow down. The Imam will recite the passages of the Qur'an out loud while the participants will follow along silently. When it is time for physical movement, the Imam does it first and the rest follow.

Men and women line up in separate rows with all the older men filling the first rows. Then minor-age children make their own rows in the middle, and finally the oldest women fill up the rearmost rows. If any men are present, a male is always chosen for the Imam. Why don't men and women mix all together in the rows? Given the nature of how we pray with all the bowing and prostrating, many men (and women) might have a hard time concentrating on their prayers if the opposite sex were prostrating just ahead of them. That is why we separate the men and the women in congregational prayer. It has nothing to do with any form of discrimination or symbolic assignment of status. Muhammad, himself, said that there is no decrease in reward for women in the back rows. Although some Muslim cultures take this separation idea to the extreme, such as segregating dinner parties and the like, traditional Islam as it was practiced in its first few centuries was much more progressive on this issue of men and women interacting (in a formal way) in society and community life.

The Least You Need to Know

- Muslims have to pray five times every day at predetermined times.
- The Islamic prayer consists of ritual bowing and the reciting of prayers and glorifications to God in structured segments.
- Muslims gather on Friday afternoons for their congregational religious service, which is mandatory for men and optional for women and minors.
- Muslim students and employees need a few minutes every afternoon to perform their obligation of prayer.

Elevating the Soul

In This Chapter

- Learn about the third pillar of Islam, the practice of *zakat*
- Discover how wealth is regarded in Islam
- Learn about fasting, the fourth pillar of Islam, and the month-long fasting ritual of Ramadan
- Find out what a Muslim learns from charity and fasting

Avarice and gluttony are counted among the Seven Deadly Sins in Catholicism. The effects of these two vices have far-reaching consequences not only for the individual but for society as well. The green-eyed monster, greed, causes envy and hatred by pitting the haves against the have-nots. Those of means become loath to part with their money, while the poor become jealous and spiteful over their woeful condition. The eternal struggle pitting the classes against each other (over the control of resources and wealth) has spawned revolutions and created new ideologies such as socialism and communism. In capitalist nations, the problem of social and economic justice is only partially addressed by scant welfare and social programs whose existence is always begrudged and under constant assault.

Personal gluttony, as expressed in the uncontrolled urge to use and consume for pleasure, engage in sex and other diversions, and take harmful drugs and alcohol, has the disastrous result of causing ill health, addiction, lethargy, family discord, criminal activities, and feelings of hopelessness in its victims. Governments spend billions of dollars each year trying to curb people's excessive appetites and urges. But these programs often don't address the root causes of overindulgence and thus usually return poor results, leaving people more disheartened than before. The term used to describe this backsliding and failure to make long-lasting life changes is *relapse*.

Islam takes these two ailments, greed and gluttony, and considers them in a new light. The problem is not that all our self-help programs are doomed to fail in the face of human intransigence; rather, it is that the root cause of our shortcomings in the first place is often unaddressed: We have forgotten why we are alive. We are not eternally defective as a species or naturally inclined to sin. We are merely forgetful of what life is about, and *Shaytan* uses our desire for pleasure to accentuate this. So to attack this twin-headed beast, Islam prescribes a unique antidote that emphasizes personal reform along with physical action. We can strive for success and even accumulate money, but we are frequently reminded that only faith and good deeds get us into heaven, and we will die one day sooner than we think. Next, we are required as Muslims to pay a portion of our wealth each year like a tax for the benefit of the poor and needy. Islam also says that we can eat and drink and procreate—but a month-long fast from those things will be required of us every year in order to teach us that we have mastery over our desires and not vice versa. We learn to moderate our desires and urges, then, to reach a new level of self-discipline. In this chapter, I focus on the third and fourth pillars of the Five Pillars of Islam and how Muslims use them to avoid the traps of greed and gluttony.

The Burden of Wealth

"The rich get richer, and the poor get poorer" is accepted common wisdom. Throughout human history there have always been those who had it a little better than everyone else: finer food, nicer quarters, more profitable businesses, and higher-class lifestyles. These are the stuff of everyone's dreams. But every dream has the potential to become a nightmare and everyone has the potential to fall into misfortune. For every person who lives well, someone else has to make do with much less. Some people even live in desperate, pitiful conditions with no way out and nowhere to turn. There is no worse feeling than seeing one's own children starving or relatives in grave sickness and knowing there is nothing you can do to help them. In such cases, the poor may appeal to the rich for help, and deliverance may come from kind-hearted benefactors. However, another outcome is equally possible: that the wealthy may turn their faces away and choose not to see. It is when the rich fail to remember their blessed position with regard to the fortunes of others that the sins of greed and miserliness come in.

One of the hallmarks of any community is the way in which it treats its weaker members. The Qur'an explains that there are always those who are stronger and wealthier, and that their test in life lies in what they will do with their accentuated capabilities.

Likewise, we are taught that the poor and weak are also given their condition as a test and are judged in how they manage their spiritual state and whether they use their God-given talents to at least try to better themselves. The two positions can even be reversed, with a wealthy person suddenly losing it all or a poor soul gaining everything in an instant. (Eddie Murphy and Dan Aykroyd portrayed two such characters in the movie *Trading Places*.) The Qur'an puts it this way: "We alternate these days of varying fortunes among mankind so that Allah may highlight the true believers and take witnesses to the truth from among you." (Qur'an 3:40)

Islam commands its followers to give up a portion of their annual savings for the benefit of the poor. An Islamic government even has the task of imposing this tax on its citizens and using the collected funds for welfare and social programs for the less fortunate. The Qur'an tells Muslims to give this mandated charity with a friendly, jovial spirit, recognizing that all prosperity ultimately comes from God's favor and grace. No matter how much we may boast that we are self-made successes, the Qur'an reminds us, it was really God who created all the conditions that resulted in our triumphs. We pay God back by doing His work in the world. And perhaps the greatest work we can do in His Name is alleviating the suffering of others. That is what the third pillar of Islam, *zakat*, or the Islamic duty of charity, is for.

DEFINITION

Zakat is usually translated as *charity*. The word *zakat*, however, literally means to purify. How is charity related to purity? Quite simply, the material world has the potential to distract us from our primary mission: to surrender ourselves to God. Therefore, when we are made to let go of some of our worldly possessions, we learn to force ourselves to let go of some of our greed.

Bah! Humbug!

"Allah has bought from the believers their lives and wealth and in exchange will give them Paradise," states the Qur'an. For Muslims, both our lives and our money are given in pledge to God. When we declare that we believe in Him and seek to follow His will, it follows that we recognize our responsibility to our Lord. Sometimes God requires sacrifice on our part in the great plan He has for the universe. Men and women sometimes have to struggle and die for a just cause. In the same way, there are times when resources are needed to do justice.

That's how Islam looks at wealth: as a proof of faith (or lack of it). What will you do with what you have received, especially when you are asked to give some of it up? Will greed overtake your heart and cause you to sneer at the plight of the less fortunate? How can we learn that wealth has no permanent value in the great test of life that will lead ultimately to the Day of Judgment? Islam requires its followers to give in charity to force them to learn this lesson. Those who hesitate or refuse to pay *zakat* provide evidence from their own actions that they are insincere and focused only on the things of this world. Imam Abu Hamid Al Ghazali, a great Islamic scholar of the eleventh century, explained this concept in his monumental work, *Ihya Uloomuddin:*

> Worldly goods are an object of love in everybody's eyes, being the means by which they enjoy the benefits of this world; because of them they become attached to life and shy away from death, even though death leads to meeting the Beloved [God]. The truth of our claim to love God is therefore put to the test, and we are asked to give up wealth which is the darling apple of our eye.

If we cling to our wealth with gnarled fingers, such as Ebeneezer Scrooge did in Charles Dickens's *A Christmas Carol,* then we are saying that this life is all we believe in. The Qur'an promises eternal paradise to those who make sacrifices in this life, and one of the sacrifices Islam expects of us is to use our resources for the benefit of the needy and helpless. Because Muslims believe that God is the Creator and True Owner of everything, whatever is placed in our hands throughout our lives is considered to be like a trust. We can't take it with us, and the Qur'an provides a very blunt explanation of the folly of those who look only upon the transitory materials of this world:

> Do any of you wish to have a farm with date-palms, vines and streams and all kinds of fruit, but then to be stricken with old age while your children are still small? [Do you want] your prime lands to be caught in a tornado followed by a fire and have it all burnt up? This is how Allah makes signs clear to you so you may consider. (Qur'an 2:266)

Whatever is in your hand now, Islam reminds us, will be gone very shortly. Financial empires and hard-earned fortunes may outlive our deaths but only for a few days or years. In this regard, Islam is very similar to Taoism and Buddhism with its emphasis on transcending the world. There is an entire corpus of literature, backed up by innumerable Qur'anic verses and hadiths on this subject (and Sufism, an Islamic offshoot, especially emphasizes this part of Islam). Though Islam does not necessarily advocate living the life of a poor hermit, nor does it call wealth a sin, at the same time it challenges people to let go of some of their love of material possessions so that they can become more willing to help those who are less fortunate. When Prophet Muhammad passed away, his personal possessions consisted of only a reed bed and blanket, a bowl, and a shield that he had pawned to a Jewish merchant.

Who Must Pay *Zakat?*

Zakat, as a religious duty, is due from anyone who meets the following requirements:

- The person must have a minimum amount of savings or assets that have been held for at least one year. The value of three ounces of gold is given as the usual figure above which *zakat* is due. In today's terms it would be a minimum of about $1,000. Business assets, cars, farm animals, cash, and even jewelry are also *zakatable*.

- The man or woman must be past the age of puberty and of sane mind. There is no *zakat* due from children or the mentally challenged.

- All yearly expenses must be paid, including any debts.

If all conditions are met, then *zakat* in the amount of 2½ percent of your average annual wealth should be paid to either a government agency designed to collect it or a local mosque or charitable organization for distribution to those who deserve it. This is welfare Islamic style, and because the rate is constant, the wealthy will pay a larger share of money into the fund than the poor will. It is the perfect system for redistributing the wealth!

The Fast of Ramadan

The fourth pillar of Islam is known as *Saum,* or fasting. During the month of Ramadan, which is the ninth month of the Islamic lunar calendar, Muslims are required to observe a strict fast from dawn until dusk. Because a lunar month has about 30 days in it, what purpose is there in this long and arduous practice? As you will see, the benefits achieved are truly life-changing.

From the very beginning of time, people have been involved with the great struggle to master their bodies and emotions. The urge to eat is one of the most powerful motivations anyone must face. Many people fail and overeat or consume unhealthy foods. Other substances can be abused by our penchant for pleasure: Drugs, alcohol, and cigarettes can pull us down just as easily as too many tubs of our favorite ice cream. Sexual addiction is another unique problem that can drive people to commit excesses and cause harm to themselves and others. The rise in AIDS, teen pregnancy, rampant promiscuity, and prostitution has reached the level of national policy issues, and the problem seems to get worse every year.

Reform programs such as diet fads, cold turkey denial, counseling, and alcohol and drug treatment programs are often unsuccessful, leading people to relapse into their self-destructive overindulgence. Merely giving these vices up for a short period won't solve the problem. Is there no way out of personal gluttony? The answer lies not in watching our weight with new pills or eating plans or in wearing a nicotine patch, but in the education of our soul and in curbing its desires from within.

Islam's cure starts with defining the problem as a spiritual identity crisis. When we forget that God exists and is watching us, when we ignore our *fitrah*, or inner compulsion to seek God (as explained in Chapter 2), when we fail to live according to God's good laws and forget the advice of the prophets, then we can fall prey to any self-destructive impulse. The solution, then, must begin with strengthening the soul and then bringing the body along in step.

Islam carries with it a fasting component for this reason. We can become better *enlightened* only when we rise above the flesh and recognize the force of our spirit, our very human will. The Qur'an explains the purpose of fasting in this way: "You who believe! Fasting is prescribed for you, as it was prescribed for those before you, so you can gain more spiritual awareness." (Qur'an 2:183) Because the Qur'an has given fasting in Ramadan the status of a religious duty, whose neglect is sinful, the conscientious person resolves to complete the fasting period. It is through this action that the real transformation takes place.

Welcoming Ramadan

When the new moon is sighted, signaling the beginning of the month of Ramadan, Muslims gather and say this prayer: "God is Greater, God is Greater, God is Greater. Praise be to God Who created me and you and Who decreed for you the phases [of the moon] and made you a sign for the universe." Then a short supplication is quietly said in which we dedicate ourselves to fasting in this month.

There are no special preparations to begin the month of Ramadan. Muslims understand that it is going to be a month of intense religious devotion and a time of self-denial: no food, drink, sex, profanity, fighting, or lying allowed from first light to sundown. The main components of the month will consist of two meals: one before dawn and one after sunset. There is also a special prayer service every night in the mosque.

Wake Up! It's Time for Sahoor

Now imagine waking up, long before the first light of the sun has risen over the darkened sky, and taking a small meal, called a *sahoor*, in silence. When the hint of light approaches, the meal has to end and then you pray the morning prayer and read a chapter or two of the Qur'an. During the daylight hours, you must abstain from all food, liquids, inhaled substances, sexual activity, and nutritionally related medicine or any nonessential oral medicine.

In addition, all normally undesirable behaviors are forbidden, with the threat that God won't accept your fasting if you engage in them. No fighting, cursing, arguing, lying, gossiping, or other sins are to be indulged in. Of course, a Muslim must naturally avoid such sins anyway, but sometimes people fall into error if they haven't been reminded of the importance of their actions for a while. Fasting for a month from these vices is the best corrective. If God doesn't accept your fasting, you may not go to heaven no matter what other good deeds you did. There's an incentive for you!

Now you are expected to carry on with your normal day. You have to go to work, take care of the kids, do the lawn work, and anything else that comes up. The difference is that by about 2:00 P.M., time seems to move painfully slow for you. You fight the urge to get that cola, and snacking is out of the question. You also become hyperaware of your behavior and want to avoid committing any sin as much as humanly possible. Doing good deeds is also occupying a prime place in your thinking because in this month your angels record each good deed as doubled or tripled or more.

When the sun finally declines completely past the horizon, the period of fasting is over. You waited the last couple of hours in your home reading the Qur'an alone or with your family and making supplications and *dhikr*. When the last sliver of the sun has fallen past the horizon, the *Muazzin's* call brings a rush of joy to the house. You thank God for His mercy in allowing you to complete the day's fast, and now you're allowed to take a small snack, called an *iftar*, before going to pray the sunset prayer.

Families usually join together for *iftar*. When the prayer is finished, you celebrate the end of the day with a joyous dinner at home or in the mosque, where you gratefully partake of food and gain a new appreciation for the value of eating and drinking.

After the last regularly scheduled prayer of the day, you might go to the mosque and join in as the congregation prays the special Ramadan prayer known as Salah al-Tarawih. Each night the Imam will stand with the other worshippers in prayer and read one thirtieth of the Qur'an aloud until the end of the month when the reading is complete. Then the celebration of the Festival of Fast Breaking, or Eid ul Fitr, will engulf the hearts and minds of the community with laughter, joy, and a sense of accomplishment. The holiday begins with the 'Eid Prayer and sermon on the morning after Ramadan ends and lasts two days, with dinner parties, family outings, fairs, carnivals, and great celebrations.

The Month of Training

What are some of the lessons learned by participating in the Ramadan fast? You would be surprised at the variety. The month of Ramadan provides a sort of spiritual and moral "boot camp." We know that fasting in Ramadan is a duty from God and that any sins may spoil our record of fasting, so we take great pains to be on our best behavior. This intense modification of our habits is designed to help us avoid such sins throughout the rest of the year.

The Blessed Prophet once remarked, "Whoever doesn't give up lying and acting on lies during fasting, then God has no need of him giving up food and drink." On another occasion he warned, "There are many people who get nothing from fasting except hunger and thirst." Clearly, the moral dimension is as important as the physical aspects of fasting.

The lessons learned during Ramadan are many. We learn what it means to be hungry, so we feel more compassion for the poor. We understand how close we are to leaving this world at any moment and how much we depend on food and liquids. We learn to control our animal urges and passions, and we clear our minds and thoughts for serious remembrance of God. We restrain our anger, and we train our habits toward prayer, forgiveness, self-sacrifice, and good behavior.

DEFINITION

Muslims greet each other on their 'Eid festival with the words, '*Eid Mubarak!* which means, "A Blessed 'Eid to you!" Gift-giving is common, especially for children, and cards are exchanged.

The Least You Need to Know

- Greed and gluttony are considered conditions of the soul and can be cured only with a combination of spiritual advice and a program of action.
- *Zakat,* the third pillar of Islam, is a yearly charity tax on every Muslim that amounts to 2½ percent of all the person's annually valued assets.
- Ramadan is the name of the month in which Muslims fast from food and drink from first light until sunset.
- *Saum* or fasting, the fourth pillar of Islam, teaches Muslims to control their desires and urges for worldly satisfaction and to feel empathy for the poor. The reward for successful completion is forgiveness of the individual's sins.

Gathering in Mecca

In This Chapter

- Learn about the *Hajj,* the annual Muslim pilgrimage to Mecca and the fifth pillar of Islam
- Discover what Muslims believe about Abraham and his sons, Isaac and Ishmael
- Know all of the rituals of the *Hajj*

Throughout the centuries people have held certain places in great esteem. Art lovers adore Paris and flock to its galleries in droves to pay homage to the artists of the past and present. Mountain climbers head for Nepal and its soaring peaks, and aspiring students dream of going to Yale, Harvard, or Oxford. People seeking more spiritually significant experiences usually travel to religious sites. Of all the religious gatherings in the world, though, there is one that stands out for the sheer magnitude of its size and scope. This is the Islamic pilgrimage, or *Hajj.* It is the largest annual spiritual get-together in the world, with over two million people descending upon a desert oasis city once a year for about a week.

Mecca, the birthplace of Muhammad and home to a shrine with roots going back to the Prophet Abraham, is the center of attention for more than a billion Muslims around the globe. Although every Muslim desires to make this once-in-a-lifetime journey, few non-Muslims know anything about this arduous and self-renewing ritual of Islam. In this chapter, I help you discover the significance of the *Hajj* and what Muslims hope to achieve by going there. By religious law, no one is allowed in Mecca except followers of the Prophet Muhammad, so prepare to enter a world few outside of Islam have ever seen.

Introducing the *Hajj* Ritual

For over 14 centuries people from all over the globe have undertaken a journey to the Arabian Peninsula for the sake of obeying God. From every nation and every land, using every mode of transportation, Muslim men and women have set their sights on the city of Mecca (sometimes spelled Makkah) in what is today Saudi Arabia. They come to worship God, to renew their faith, to honor God's last prophet, and to look for the meaning of life in a land devoid of an abundance of life. This is the fifth pillar of Islam, known as the *Hajj*.

ASK THE IMAM

Mecca is located along a corridor of semi-arid land hugging the western coastal region of Arabia and extending for hundreds of miles to the north and south. The region, whose name is *the Hijaz*, receives some annual rainfall but not enough to sustain more than limited agriculture such as date palm or scattered grain production. The summers can be brutally hot, though sporadic rains generally come in the autumn through spring.

The Origin of a Holy Place

The main feature of the city of Mecca is a curious, box-shape building in the center of town called the *Ka'bah*, or Cube. It is a religious shrine made of bricks and covered by a heavy black cloth embroidered with gold thread. It stands about 50 feet high and measures about 40 feet on each side, with two sides being slightly longer than the other pair. Surrounding it is a large pillared building with tall minarets called the Masjid al Haram. Four thousand years ago, the valley of Mecca, then called *Baca*, was a dry and uninhabited place. That is, until one day when a man traveling in a small caravan brought his wife and young son there and told them that this wasteland was to be their new home.

The man's name was Abraham, and he was instructed by God to bring his second wife, Hagar, and their son, Ishmael, to Arabia from Palestine. This may have been to protect them from any potential conflicts with Abraham's first wife, Sarah, who wanted her child, Isaac, to be the next leader of the tribe after Abraham passed away. Besides being the second wife, Hagar had the unenviable position of having been Sarah's servant before her status was elevated to that of a co-wife. If Abraham had to choose whom to move, guess who had to go!

Muslims believe that God instructed the Prophet Abraham to take Hagar and her son to the wilderness of Arabia and leave them there. He obeyed his Lord and left them with only limited supplies of food and water. Then he made the two-week journey back to Palestine, leaving his little family behind and trusting in God that they would be safe. Hagar and Ishmael pitched a tent and waited. Their supplies quickly ran out, however, and within a few days the mother and son were beginning to suffer the effects of dehydration and hunger. In her desperation, Hagar ran up and down two hills trying to spot any help in the distance, but there was none. Finally, she collapsed next to Ishmael in the center of the valley and prayed to God for deliverance.

DISPELLING THE MYTH

Hagar was a legitimate wife of Abraham, and her son, Ishmael, was his first heir. Although traditional Judeo-Christian thinking favors Isaac, Jewish law makes no distinction regarding the mother of the first-born son. The Bible itself calls Hagar Abraham's *wife* (Genesis 16:3) and thus Muslims would assert that both sons of Abraham were to be blessed through the ages.

The boy struck his foot on the ground, and the action caused a water-spring near the surface to gush forth. The water was cool and sweet. Hagar and Ishmael were saved! With their water supply secure, they were able to trade water with wandering nomads for food and other needs. In time, the Prophet Abraham came back from Palestine to check up on his family in Baca and was amazed to see them the masters of a very profitable well. Abraham built a shrine to God to celebrate the deliverance of his family, and then returned northward to his first wife, and her son Isaac. In time Bedouin nomads settled in the valley and the town of Mecca was born!

After many more centuries had passed, Mecca became a vibrant city, not only because of its reliable water source, but also because of its rising position as a stop on the international caravan route from Yemen and India through to Syria and Europe. But Abraham's religion was not to survive there intact. Gradually, people began to develop false ideas about spirits and a plurality of gods. Finally, after many centuries of accumulated tribal folklore and custom, the shrine of Abraham was turned into a house to store idols and statues, which people worshipped instead of the one, unseen God. It would be many years before the right prophet arose to clean up those false ideas and restore the *Ka'bah* to the worship of the one true God. That prophet, who would be a descendant of the Prophet Abraham through his son Ishmael, was named Muhammad.

> **DEFINITION**
>
> The main religious shrine in Mecca known as the *Ka'bah,* although it is often referred to as *Baytullah,* meaning the House of God. Muslims don't believe God lives in the *Ka'bah,* however; it is merely the focal point of religious devotion.

Why Do Muslims Go to Mecca?

Every year, thousands of eager Muslims from every country anticipate making the *Hajj.* For many, it is the greatest journey they will ever make and the one goal they've patiently waited for all of their lives. But before performing this important act of service to God, Muslims must have all of their debts paid and all of their worldly affairs put in order. (You never know what will happen to you tomorrow, so it is best to prepare today.) In the past, it was more difficult to get to Mecca, with the journey taking anywhere from months to years, but today it's really quite speedy, and most people spend less than two weeks on their entire trip (although the official *Hajj* is only three days, there are optional holy rites before and afterward—*and don't forget the shopping and sightseeing when you're done*).

The purpose of the *Hajj* is twofold: to honor the faith and life of the Prophet Abraham and to come together as a community to renew our commitment to God's way of life and to learn the stark reality about the shortness of our lives and our accountability to Him. (Mecca is not considered holy because Prophet Muhammad was born and raised there.) It is not an easy task, though, for Mecca is a hot, dry place for most of the year and the sun is harsh and unforgiving. In addition, some of the rituals performed during the *Hajj* require a fair amount of physical exertion. Add to this the fact that now almost two million people converge on this one small town for about a week each year and you have quite a recipe for hardship and struggle.

> **DEFINITION**
>
> A person who makes the *Hajj* is called a *Hajji.* People often add *Al Hajj* (an alumnus of the *Hajj*) as a title to their first name in order to show they have completed it.

But the *Hajj* comes with its abundant rewards, making whatever we have to endure well worth it. The first reward is total forgiveness for all our sins. Muhammad said that a perfectly done *Hajj* permits us to enter into Paradise (assuming we maintain our faith for the rest of our lives). We also get the chance to follow in the footsteps of

Abraham, whom Muslims revere as the *Friend of God*. By participating in the rituals initiated by Abraham, Muslims feel as though they are with him in spirit. Another benefit is to see the city where the Prophet Muhammad was born. Muslims love him and respect him, and to see the streets he walked on is akin to Christians visiting Jerusalem or Bethlehem and feeling the presence of Jesus. The sense of immediacy is quite satisfying. Finally, the *Hajjis* get the chance to meet Muslims from all over the world; every race and culture is represented, and people's bonds of universal brotherhood are strengthened.

The *Hajj* had such a profound effect on Malcolm X that he renounced racism against whites, even though racism was a cardinal teaching of the patently misnamed Nation of Islam—a skewed organization that mixed a few scant pieces of Islam and Christianity with racial exclusivity. One of the factors in his decision was his experience in Mecca, where he was walking with, sitting with, and living with white Muslims who taught him, through their example, that the Islamic teaching of equality was better than the Nation of Islam's narrow view of whites as devils. When he returned to the United States, Malcolm X changed his name to Al Hajj Malik Shabbaz and left the Nation of Islam.

The Rituals of the *Hajj*

Muslims can perform two types of pilgrimages. The smaller pilgrimage, which can be done anytime throughout the year, is called an *'Umrah*. It doesn't count toward the once-in-a-lifetime pilgrimage, however. Rather, it is an act of piety performed to get extra merit. Many Muslim families make the decision to go for *'Umrah* rather than taking a vacation at their favorite resort.

The main pilgrimage, or *Hajj*, must be performed during the second week of the Islamic month called *Dhul Hijjah*. This is the pilgrimage called for in the Qur'an as a duty upon all believers who can afford it. Most people combine an *'Umrah* with the main *Hajj*, doing them back-to-back in a week, and this is the method I will be describing shortly. Regardless of the type of pilgrimage one chooses, however, certain restrictions are placed upon those who undertake this journey for God. These restrictions serve to create uniformity in practice among untold thousands of people and also to emphasize that pilgrimage is no vacation. You're here to worship God, so you have some rules to follow.

All male pilgrims must wear two white garments that are called the *Ihram* (restricting clothes). Stitching is not allowed in the cloth, nor can any straps be used to join the two pieces together. The two garments go on sort of like a toga. Women are allowed to wear whatever clothes they wish.

On to Mecca!

The *Hajj* begins when a person arrives at a set point some miles outside of Mecca called a *miqat*. This point is equivalent to an entry station and marks the border after which a person on Hajj must abide by pilgrimage restrictions. Here the pilgrims bathe and the men change from their normal clothes into their *Ihram* garments and make the intention to do the *Hajj*. A bus then takes the pilgrims into Mecca itself, where they will approach the giant complex within which is the *Masjid al Haram*. This is the huge building surrounding the holy places that is ringed with columns and minarets. In the center of the complex, in an open courtyard stands, on holy ground, the *Ka'bah*, covered in a black cloth called the *Kiswah* and embroidered with verses from the Qur'an. All along the *Hajj* journey, the pilgrims chant a special passage over and over until sunset to remind themselves why they are there. The passage should be repeated often with an earnest heart. It is recited as follows: *Labayk! Allahumma labayk. Labayk la sharika laka labayk. Innal hamda wan ni'mata laka wal mulk. La sharika lak.* This translates as: "Here I am at Your service. O God, here I am at Your service. Here I am at Your service, there is no partner with You. Here I am at Your service. All praise and all blessings belong to You. All dominion is Yours and You have no partner."

Nothing Like Being There

Now let's join with the pilgrims for a moment and look at the *Hajj* through the eyes of someone performing it. When the awe-inspiring sight of the *Ka'bah* presents itself before us, we join the throngs of pilgrims and walk around it counterclockwise in a great knot of people seven times, pointing toward it and repeating our chanting as we move. This is called the *Tawaf*, or Encircling. Imagine two million people all in the same place doing what we are doing! (The *Hajj* is the largest annual religious gathering in the world.)

Muhammad Asad, a Jewish convert to Islam, described his first impression of the *Ka'bah* in the following words.

> And there I stood before the Temple of Abraham and gazed at the marvel without thinking (for thoughts and reflections came only much later), and out of some hidden, smiling kernel within me there slowly grew an elation like a song.

Smooth marble slabs, with sunlight reflections dancing upon them, covered the ground in a wide circle around the *Ka'bah*, and over these marble slabs walked many people, men and women, round and round the black-draped House of God. Among them were some who wept, some who loudly called to God in prayer, and many who had no words and no tears but could only walk with lowered heads.

–From *The Road to Mecca*

Many people who have returned from the *Hajj* have described their first meeting with the Holy Shrine in similar terms, and any pilgrim, of any faith, can attest to the power of being in a place of holy sanctuary. Continuing onward, then, when we have finally completed seven rounds, we make our way to the *Maqami Ibrahim*, or Station of Abraham. Here we offer a prayer by the spot where Abraham was purported to have stood while invoking God's blessings upon the pilgrimage shrine. Next we pay a visit to the fountain that saved Hagar and Ishmael from perishing. The *Well of Zam Zam*, as it is called, has never failed since their time. We drink the water reverently and taste its heavy mineral content. Muhammad said that it is water that can improve one's health dramatically. (Yes, they bottle it and sell it all over the world!)

From there we move to a long, covered walkway running between the two hills between which Hagar, in her desperation, ran back and forth. We, too, will walk between those two hills to commemorate her frantic search—but we will walk on a giant tiled path completing seven circuits. The rest of the day we will spend in prayer, study, and reflection. This completes the *'Umrah* portion of our combined *Hajj*, and the next day, which is the eighth day of the month, our compulsory rituals will begin. All during the *Hajj*, pilgrims are expected to ponder the meaning of their lives and what they have done in the world thus far. The harsh landscape of brown dirt, stunted trees, and black rocks helps to clear a person's thoughts with its absence of flashiness and comfort. (If you've ever been to Arizona or New Mexico, that's what western Arabia looks like.)

ASK THE IMAM

Men and women follow the exact same rituals on the *Hajj*. They also pray together in mixed groups, side-by-side, unlike any other time. This is done for the sake of practicality: with millions of people to line up, it is impossible to form separate male and female rows.

The next day, we travel to a barren plain named *Mina* where we spend the day in the open air, praising God and taking stock of our soul. We pass the night in tents and the next morning begin perhaps the hardest part of the journey. (Keep in mind that the temperature during the day is often over 100°F.) Next, we pilgrims will move to a wide, open plain, a few miles outside Mecca, called the *Plain of Arafah*. It is literally a huge, barren wasteland that signifies what it will be like on the Day of Judgment when all people will be lined up and sweltering in the heat. We remain there the whole day until night falls and then travel to another place called *Muzdalifah*.

While camping there for the night in open tents with the desert wind blowing softly over our campfires, we will join with the other pilgrims in gathering together a set number of small stones that are just the right size for throwing. In the morning we stand together and praise God and then travel back to Mina where we approach a large, round, roofless enclosure, inside of which are several tall stone pillars. All of us gather around the low wall and throw our stones at the pillars, which represent *Shaytan*, who had tried to dissuade Abraham from sacrificing his son. This exercise is an affirmation that, although *Shaytan* is real, we can fight against him if we are determined, even as Abraham did.

After we have "stoned the Devil," it is time to re-create the test of loyalty that God required of Abraham. God's purpose was not to require Abraham to sacrifice his son but to make Abraham decide whether he loved God more than anything else. Even as an animal was sacrificed instead of Abraham's son, we do the same by offering a sacrifice on a plain about a mile outside the city of Mecca. The sacrificial animals—usually goats, camels, cows, or sheep—are brought for the pilgrims to slaughter. Because there are so many pilgrims, each group of 5 to 10 people will have one animal.

While it may seem bizarre by today's standards to sacrifice animals during religious rituals, we have to look deeper into why it's being done and how. The idea behind the sacrifice is that we are willing to give up what we love for God's sake, just as Abraham was willing to do that. Further still, Islam has very strict rules about how to slaughter an animal. The knife must be sharp, and a swift cut to the jugular vein is all that is allowed. In addition, no one is permitted to slaughter an animal in the presence of another animal. The animal feels no pain, nor is it made to feel scared. This is essentially similar to Jewish kosher regulations.

Unlike the Old Testament of the Bible, which calls for sacrificial animals being burnt on altars, Islam has no such practice. The meat from the slaughtered animals is used to feed the pilgrims, and the majority is distributed to the poor. Nothing is wasted.

The meat is processed at a nearby canning factory, and the cans of food are sent to the poor and to refugees all over the world. So looked at from another angle, the rite of sacrifice during the Islamic pilgrimage is another way to help those in need. Where do you think all the meat used in hamburgers and fried chicken comes from? Industry slaughterhouses in the West kill thousands of animals each day in very painful ways *and* in the presence of other animals. Islam is much more humane in its practice and adds a religious dimension once a year besides.

Crew Cut, Anyone?

The official *Hajj* ends on the tenth day of the month, and this is also the day in which Muslims throughout the world celebrate their second main holiday, *'Eid ul Adha.* Muslims are encouraged to make a sacrifice on this day wherever they live and distribute the meat to the poor and needy. As for the *Hajji,* their next step is for men to shave off their hair, signifying their rebirth into true faith. Women don't shave their hair but merely cut a lock. At this point, the pilgrims are released from most of their *Hajj* restrictions, and they can return to Mecca for another *circuit* around the *Ka'bah.* The next few days of religious ritual are optional and are spent in *stoning* the *Satan-pillars* again, visiting various sites around the city, praying, making supplication, and studying the Qur'an.

ASK THE IMAM

There is a black stone about the size of a basketball set in a frame in one corner of the *Ka'bah.* It is a meteorite used by Abraham as part of his original shrine. Muslims point to, or kiss, this stone while circling the *Ka'bah* to express their love for Abraham. It is not considered magical or supernatural in nature.

The Least You Need to Know

- Every Muslim who can afford it and who is physically able must make a pilgrimage to Mecca at least once in his or her life.
- Only Muslims are allowed to enter Mecca.
- The *Hajj* ritual consists of a series of activities each designed to teach the pilgrim a different lesson or to commemorate an event from Abraham's life. The main idea behind the *Hajj* is to learn how to let go of what we love in place of God.

- The *Hajj* is the largest religious gathering in the world and is covered by major news networks every year.
- The main religious site in Mecca is the *Ka'bah*. It is a cube-shape building whose foundation, Muslims believe, was originally constructed by Abraham.

Uncovering the Real Story About *Jihad*

In This Chapter

- Find out why the media often associates Muslims with violence
- Understand the Islamic view of war and conflict and how it relates to modern times
- Learn about the true nature of *jihad,* which is not what you might have thought
- Discover social activism's place in Islam

Perhaps no other term from the world of Islam is as misunderstood in the West as *jihad.* Its very mention conjures up images of swarthy brown terrorists in ragged turbans and robes, Kalashnikov rifles slung over their shoulders, ready to mow down anyone who isn't a believer. It would be easy to believe that these pictures define the term *jihad.* Nightly news reports perhaps unwittingly deliver the wrong kind of message with almost daily stories of one *Islamic* group or another either named *Something-Jihad* or calling for a *jihad* against America, *the Great Satan.* Chanting crowds of flag-burning Third Worlders are often queued to seal the impression that Muslims are a bunch of unruly fanatics.

Just what is a *jihad,* though, and are all the images and events associated with it a valid comparison with actual Islamic teachings? Is there any relationship between events throughout the world and the proper application of religious values? No one would deny that we live in a world filled with injustice. Are Westerners giving a fair hearing to the grievances of the world's poor and downtrodden, who might just be using religion as a veneer over a real political injustice? These are the questions I attempt to answer in this chapter. Although some of the concepts may be controversial, it must be remembered that there are many sides to any issue, and whenever conflict or injustice is perceived, passions will run very high.

What Is *Jihad?*

The word *jihad* literally means to struggle or strive or to work for something with determination. Although Westerners often assume it means holy war, that is not a correct translation of the Arabic term. The Arabic word for war is actually *harb*, and the word for fighting is *qital*, and neither is construed to be holy or religiously mandated. This is important to know because "making *jihad*" is any action done to further the cause of God no matter how great or small. Providing missionary services in a tough place, going to a far land to study, or even just donating money when it's a hardship can be a type of *jihad*. On the personal level, just trying to curb your undue desires for the forbidden pleasures of this world is considered a type of *jihad*.

DEFINITION

Jihad in Arabic means to struggle or strive for something. It does not mean a holy war, as English dictionaries often mislabel it.

However, the word *jihad* is most often associated with the act of physically confronting evil and wrongdoing; hence, it can be applied to the act of fighting as well. But the goal of a physical *jihad* is not to have a big war, gain riches, or kill people; it is to further the cause of Allah and to create justice on Earth. Then, when the evil is removed, or the other side wants peace, Muslims are to make peace as well.

FROM THE SOURCE

Muhammad said the following to some soldiers after they had left the battlefield victorious one day: "You have left the lesser *jihad,* now you are coming to the greater *jihad.* The struggle against yourself."

The Qur'an explains for us the reasons why fighting is sometimes a part of *jihad*:

> Let those fight in the Cause of God who sell the life of this world for the next life. To the one who fights in the Cause of God, whether he is killed or achieves victory, We shall soon give him a great reward. And why shouldn't you fight in the Cause of God and of those who, being weak, are mistreated; the men, women and children whose only cry is, "Our Lord! Save us from this land whose people are oppressors and bring to us from You someone who will protect us and bring to us from You someone who will help." Those who believe fight in the Cause of God, and those who reject faith fight in the cause of evil. So fight against the friends of Shaytan. (Qur'an 4:74–76)

Islamic civilization is not a society of vigilantes. It's a religion that teaches the rule of law. It's not up to anyone who feels like it to declare a military *jihad*. Although it seems everyone and their uncle is waving the term around these days, only an established Islamic government or a recognized worldwide leader of Islam has the authority to declare a jihad. Neither one exists in the Muslim world right now. Instead, what you have is a large number of small groups, each claiming to uphold the mantle of authenticity. What is interesting to note, however, is that most of these groups arose in response to either a totalitarian regime or a specific attack or invasion from outside their country. Hamas did not exist before Israel was established, Al Qaeda developed from groups that arose during the Soviet invasion of Afghanistan, and the Moro rebels in the southern Philippines grew as a response to colonialism from the Christian north of their nation. Thus, again we see political grievances being cloaked in the guise of religion. Just as Christians have used their religion as a cover for political agendas, so, too, do some Muslims. The key for the thinking person is to not blame the religion for what some people do. All religions teach good things, but not all who claim to follow their religion (or secular ideas) are good.

Jihad is one of the most misused words in the world today. It means to struggle in God's way. Obviously, planting bombs to harm civilians, flying planes into buildings, murdering captives, or kidnapping tourists for ransom is not part of a Godly campaign for truth and justice. Muslims around the world are just as horrified as anyone else when a terrorist crime is perpetrated. We are doubly outraged when people try to attach a religious reason to their dastardly act, no matter which religion is being invoked. If someone does something in a way other than what God ordained, then it is a crime that the individual will have to answer for on the Day of Judgment.

Social Activism in Islam

There are many levels of *jihad*. An important part of our daily life as Muslims is to strive (or "make *jihad*") to improve society. Judaism has its concept of *Tikun Olam*, or perfecting the world, and many other religions have a similar idea. The key phrase guiding Muslims in social improvement campaigns comes from the Qur'an, which says that Muslims must "encourage the good while forbidding evil." Thus, Muslims must be active in the social affairs of any community they live in.

Examples of activities that a Muslim must oppose, or struggle against, are …

- The selling of alcohol, pornography, and drugs.
- Littering and pollution.

- Public disputes that turn chaotic.

- Gossip or slander in the media.

- Corruption in government.

- Pedophilia or spousal abuse.

- Cruelty to animals.

FROM THE SOURCE

Whoever recommends and helps in a good cause becomes a partner in it. And whoever recommends and helps in an evil cause shares in its burdens and Allah has power over all things. (Qur'an 4:85)

These and many other vices are mentioned in Islam as sources of discord and injustice that must be opposed. What are the ways allowed by Islam to change things? An important saying of the Prophet Muhammad with regard to stopping vice is that if you see an evil deed you should try to correct it with your hand or your tongue, or at least feel bad about it in your heart if you think you can do nothing about it.

Islam is a proactive way of life, meaning we are taught to get involved and take action in the defense and promotion of social justice. What sorts of things should we try to encourage in our societies? Free medical care, aid to the poor and orphans, better schools, accountability in government, clean water and air, humane treatment of animals, and assistance for the elderly and handicapped are good things to start with. All of these have a good track record in classical Islamic civilization, where there was often government supported health care and schools.

We will never have a perfect world. This life is not the place for perfection. But we can employ our hands, words, and feelings toward making it a better place than how we found it. This is the purpose of encouraging the right and forbidding the wrong in Islam. A person can't feel personally pious yet ignore the decline of morals in his or her own community.

The Myth of the Holy War

I turned on the evening news to see what was happening in the world. The first report was about a terrorist group named the *Islamic Jihad Brigade*, which was threatening to plant bombs on planes. The second report was about *Muslim extremist* groups declaring a *jihad* against America. The final report was about *Islamic terrorism* against Israel and the new wave of suicide bombers. Any reasonable person might conclude that with the demise of the Soviet Union the next great enemy of freedom-loving people everywhere is Islam. This is an unfortunate conclusion because Islam is not the enemy of the West nor of the Judeo-Christian tradition. On the contrary, Islam is a cousin to the West, and its core values have more in common with modern international norms than most people realize. Why is there such a horrible misperception, then?

As is the case with many ancient prejudices and fears, history and its many twists and turns is the primary culprit for this misunderstanding about Islam. Europe's first encounter with Islam was through the eyes of the Byzantine Empire, which initiated hostilities against Muslims since Muhammad's time. This set the stage for an ongoing condition of hostility, which at times simmered down into a type of cold war. As Byzantine power waned in the eighth and ninth centuries, Muslim armies continued to bite off more and more territory. The Muslim advance stalled for a time, however, due to pressure from the invading Mongols in the thirteenth century, but with the conversion of the Turks to Islam a renewed campaign against the Byzantines was initiated.

So how did Western Europe get dragged into conflict with the Muslim world? Basically, with the increasing growth of Muslim power in the East, the Catholic Church felt its interests in Jerusalem and elsewhere were being threatened. The Church also felt that a unified Western alliance against Islam (under the leadership of the Pope) would reinforce Church influence and hegemony among the rebellious kings of Europe and possibly bring the Orthodox Byzantines back under Rome's authority. Thus the era of the Crusades was launched in the year 1098 C.E., and this event introduced the concept among Westerners that the Muslim world, and thus Islam, was their common foe. The forces of propaganda were quick to follow.

For most of the Middle Ages, Europeans painted an image of Islam that was designed to provoke fear and loathing in the minds of the populace, especially when the rulers were attempting to drum up support for the various Crusades that issued from Europe from time to time until the year 1291. The *Saracens* and the *Turks* (two derogatory European terms for Muslims) were viewed as minions of the Devil whose only desire was to enslave and bring on the worship of Satan. In his book *The Life of Mohammed*, Emile Deir Mongem writes:

> When the war blazed up between Islam and Christianity … each side misunderstood the other one. It should be admitted, however, that the basic misunderstanding was more on the part of westerners than the easterners …. argumentative debaters overloaded Islam with vices, degradation, and abasement without taking the trouble to study it …

—Afif Tabbarah, *The Spirit of Islam* (publisher, 1978)

DISPELLING THE MYTH

The late Osama bin Laden, along with many of his top henchmen, made it an ongoing habit to issue *fatwas,* or religious verdicts, in which they declared all kinds of vengeful threats against anyone, no matter how innocent. This type of blanket condemnation is so out-of-bounds according to the dictates of traditional Islamic legal theory that even the Taliban issued a public statement in 2000 that bin Laden was not qualified to issue religious verdicts. Obviously, no Muslim government or recognized Islamic organization paid any attention to the ravings of the bin Laden crew.

The nineteenth-century orientalist Count Henri de Castri goes even further when he comments on the practice of "mercenary poets" and paid storytellers who traveled Europe inciting hatred and misinformation against Islam. "Out of total ignorance of Islam, these songs were charged with hatred against Moslems … and inculcated such mistaken views in the minds of Christians, even to our present day. Every singer used to consider Moslems as polytheists, disbelievers, and disobedient idolaters." The campaign of anti-Islamic slander was so successful that to this day some textbooks in European and American schools refer to Muhammad as having epilepsy, the Qur'an as being copied from the Bible, Muslim armies as forcing conversions on people (by the sword), and Islam as being against science and learning. All of these things are quite untrue, and enlightened Western authors from Arnold Toynbee and Bertrand Russell to Yvonne Haddad and John Esposito have been dispelling these myths in book after book for decades; nevertheless, the message hasn't reached the masses, who still believe numerous false myths concerning Islam.

When Europeans succeeded in occupying virtually the entire Muslim world during the era of Colonialism, they considered their victory over Islam complete. The occupiers closed Islamic schools and colleges all over the Muslim world, arrested and killed religious leaders, disenfranchised the population, and installed as rulers Western-educated natives who were completely dependent on their European masters. But with the end of Colonialism in the mid-1960s, European fears about the return of Islamic power have caused another round of hysteria to grip the Western world.

Virtually all Muslims now feel that the modern Western media have taken on the role of the mercenary poets of the past: presenting an overly negative view of Islam or unfairly connecting violent events with it. They feel that political or regional conflicts are seen only through the eyes of religion, and Islam is blamed for anything and everything that happens. (You don't have to agree with this sentiment, but just understand that it's widespread.) This is unfortunate, because the roots of nearly every conflict in the Muslim world, whether it is the breakup of the former Yugoslavia and its wars, the anti-Muslim riots perpetuated by Hindus in India, the friction between Christians and Muslims in Nigeria, the Arab-Israeli conflict, or the existence of rebel groups in places as far flung as the Philippines or Chechnya, are directly related to the past meddling of outsiders in those lands.

Islam on War

What is the position of Islam on war and conflict? Peace on Earth is, of course, the ideal that the world of Islam works toward, and war is abhorred as the last, worst option. However, there are times when there is no alternative but to fight. Every society has its own views about a just war. What do Muslims believe is worth fighting for? According to Islamic Law, an armed struggle can be initiated only for the following three reasons:

- To defend your community or nation from aggressors

- To liberate people living under oppressive regimes

- To remove any government that will not allow the free practice of Islam within its borders

The first two reasons are easy to understand. The third would be necessary if, for example, a country forbade the practice of Islam or its preaching. Obviously from the Qur'an's perspective, such a country is attempting to stop God's religion from being preached. Interestingly enough, Islam does not give people the right to declare a war vigilante style. A group of disgruntled people in country X, for example, doesn't have the sanction to start an armed struggle in the name of Islam, even if they have legitimate grievances. The power to declare war rests only with the properly chosen authorities in an Islamic state (elected by the majority, confirmed and accountable). The leader of the entire Muslim community is the only one who can ask Muslims to enlist in the army and fight in a just war, not someone with a big name or an inflated sense of importance.

DISPELLING THE MYTH

Muslims who are living in non-Muslim societies are bound by Islamic Law to live peacefully with their neighbors so long as no injustice is being done to anyone. Crime and vice must be opposed regardless.

At the same time, an individual Muslim is not authorized by Islamic Law to tell people to go and fight, because the main principle of Islamic governance is mutual consultation, known as *Shura*. Nobody can make a big decision without legitimate representatives discussing it first. Muhammad also used to consult with leaders of the community before deciding matters of war and peace. So looked at in this light, we can see that most of the groups of Muslim background engaging in armed struggle around the world have no more legitimacy in the eyes of traditional Islam than the Crusaders had when they invaded and sacked the city of Constantinople, which was a *Christian* city!

Muslims are actually divided about supporting most of these militant groups for this very reason. They often support the *objectives* but feel queasy about the *methods* and the exclusive claim to authority of the participants. The worldwide Muslim community is in somewhat of an awkward position because there is currently no traditional Islamic government functioning today. So there is no official agency to police the activities of would-be vigilantes or at least provide an authoritative ruling on the legality of their actions.

Islam and Terrorism

What does Islam say about terrorism? The first thing that must be considered is that, no matter what they say, religion is often not in the forefront of any terrorist's mind. They feel that they have been wronged and they are looking for revenge. This is what causes some people to go over the edge into extremism in the first place. And so it follows that if some extremists with Muslim-sounding names shout, "Allah is Great," or give their clandestine groups names that refer to Islamic themes, it is oftentimes more of a veneer to gain the support of others than a sincere orientation they follow for themselves. Adolf Hitler and the Nazis sometimes used references to Christianity to justify hostility to the Jews. Slave owners in America repeatedly justified slavery with the excuse that they were saving the souls of the Africans, and Hindu fundamentalists in India claim that their attacks on Islam are designed to bring Indian Muslims back to their true religion: Hinduism. So as you can see, people misuse religion quite often, and Islam is misused as much as any other faith.

The Rules of War

The rules for the conduct of war in Islam forbid the killing of noncombatants. The Prophet Muhammad never allowed any Muslim soldier to harm women, children, or the innocent. The trouble with bombing a bus or marketplace is that soldiers are not the ones who are killed. Thus, the people who engage in this type of attack are going against the teachings of Islam. According to the Qur'an, "If you kill a life unjustly it is as if you killed all life." (Qur'an 5:32) Suicide bombers are also guilty of ignoring Islamic teachings, because suicide is forbidden in Islam. The Prophet Muhammad said, "Whoever kills himself with a weapon will have that weapon in his hand, and will kill himself forever in the fire of Hell," and yet this is exactly what these people do when they detonate bombs strapped to their bodies. Are there some religious leaders in that part of the world who condone these actions? Yes, there are, but remember that they, too, have been shaped by the same sense of injustice as the rest of the people there. Muslim scholars in other parts of the world condemn these actions as being against the letter and the spirit of the religion.

DISPELLING THE MYTH

Hiraba is the Arabic word used by Muslims in the medieval period to refer to the crime of terrorism. Ibn Hazm, a famed thirteenth-century Muslim theologian, defined *hiraba* as: "One who puts people in fear on the road, with or without a weapon, at night or day, in urban areas or in open spaces, in the palace of a caliph or a mosque, with or without accomplices, in the desert or in the village, in a large or small city, with one or more people … making people fear that they'll be killed, or robbed, or raped … whether the attackers are one or many." So as you can see, terrorism really is forbidden in Islam and previous generations of Muslims considered it criminal!

So we can say that there is no such thing as terrorism allowed in Islam and that people who are attempting to get revenge for injustices done to them are mislabeling their fights as religious in nature. Muslims all over the world affirm this thesis, though it seems sometimes that the only people who are featured in the Western media are those who engage in spectacular acts of savagery and mayhem, such as the insurgents in Iraq who are, as of this writing, engaged in a struggle with American occupation forces. Their struggle is for regaining their independence; it is not about teaching people about religious or moral values.

Harming innocents is forbidden in Islam, so those who engage in activities designed to kill as many people as possible cannot rightly call upon religion to justify their actions. Be that as it may, as I noted above there are some misguided Muslims with legitimate grievances who seem to do everything in the world to make themselves, and Islam, look bad in their pursuit of redress. They say they are *doing jihad*; however, in reality they often break all the rules for carrying out one. Even as Christianity and Judaism have sometimes been wrongfully used to justify the actions of extremists, a small minority of Muslims is doing the same with Islam. The overwhelming majority of Muslims do not support, condone, or engage in such reprehensible acts.

The Least You Need to Know

- Stereotypes of Islam as a violent religion began in the Middle Ages and have persisted into modern times.
- *Jihad* does not mean holy war. It means any exertion in the cause of God.
- *Jihad* is the term usually used to describe a war fought for God's sake; however, even going to school can be a kind of *jihad.*
- Any war for conquest or glory is forbidden in Islam.
- Terrorism is forbidden in Islam, and the actions of people who engage in it and use Islamic slogans are not sanctioned by Islamic teachings.
- Islam has a strong tradition of social activism, and the Qur'an calls on Muslims to oppose vice by working for the welfare of their fellow human beings. Such a struggle is also considered a *jihad.*

Islam and Other Religions

In a multireligious world there are bound to be numerous bumps on the road as each religion interacts with another. Islam, as taught by the Prophet Muhammad in the seventh century, existed in a land where idolatry, Christianity, Judaism, Zoroastrianism, and mysticism coexisted. As a result there is a clear track record of relations among all the faiths from Islam's earliest days. This helps Muslims understand multiculturalism and differing religious beliefs and makes us tolerant and accepting of other people's deeply felt convictions.

Although idolatry is generally frowned upon in the Qur'an, Judaism and Christianity have a special status in Islam. Muslims call the followers of each of these two great monotheistic religions "People of the Book." This is a respectful reference to our belief that in the past God revealed His message to prophets whose later followers crafted those two religions. The Prophet Muhammad had both Jewish and Christian acquaintances and always taught Muslims to be respectful and upright toward the sincere adherents of these faiths. In this part, I explore the relationship between Islam, Christianity, and Judaism in great detail.

It's All in the Prophets

In This Chapter

- Learn what Islam says about prophets and revelation from God
- Find out how Islam describes the major biblical prophets
- Discover how Islam views other religions
- Understand how Muslims view the Bible

Islam is a faith whose legitimacy lies in the idea that all true religion is part of a historical cycle. Islam asserts that it is nothing less than a continuation of the message given to previous prophets. All prophets taught the same core beliefs, declares the Qur'an, and thus the followers of previously revealed religions must be respected on a certain level. Furthermore, the Qur'an contains the stories of many prophets that are also mentioned in the Bible. These stories, however, are not told in the same manner, and important differences do exist.

Jews and Christians are often mentioned in the Qur'an as people who have received God's guidance in the past. The trials, triumphs, and perceived failures of both of those communities are presented as lessons for Muslims to learn from. In this chapter, I will be highlighting what Islam teaches about prophets and the messages they received from God. Islam teaches that every nation received a prophet from God, and a complementary component of this ideology is that all people are equal, regardless of race or color, and are endowed with a standard foundation of human rights that must be respected. As you will see, this intertwining of prophetic history and humanistic values creates a very interesting worldview for the practitioner of Islam.

All Prophets Are Brothers

Any student of world religions soon comes upon a startling discovery: The precepts, beliefs, and practices of all the major religions have an identifiable commonality to them. Judaism teaches its practitioners to pray, as does Hinduism. Islam asks its followers not to harm animals senselessly, as does Buddhism. Christianity orders its adherents to show compassion toward the sick, and so does Zoroastrianism. When a person realizes the incredible similarities in all religions, what should he or she do about it? Would it be prudent then to say that all religions are equal? Islam would answer in the negative, but before I discuss that, let's look at what a few modern researchers have theorized about religion and its origins.

Many thinkers have tried to assert that religion is nothing more than a man-made system for keeping social cohesion. Authorities from diverse disciplines such as Sigmund Freud (psychology), Margaret Mead (anthropology), and Carl Sagan (astronomy) have echoed this view. Under this theory, when emerging human communities needed a way to get people to cooperate, they began calling upon nonexistent gods and spirits that could punish the recalcitrant members of the group if they didn't comply. Other researchers have even postulated that religion was the invention of people who were frightened of the world around them and needed to feel that they had allies in a world full of supernatural phenomena. They cite the proliferation of anthropomorphic gods such as the many river gods, mountain gods, or animal gods found throughout the world.

Although these arguments are interesting and with some merit, at the same time they fail to answer certain fundamental issues that Muslims would assert are evidence for the existence of a higher power. The first issue revolves around the human mind. Recent studies into human psychology have found that people who practice some form of religion are generally more peaceful and freer from worry. They even tend to live longer! If faith increases longevity, well-being, and the general mental condition, then there must be some component in our makeup that either requires it or thrives upon it.

Second, mere mechanical processes cannot explain the existence of a universally accepted standard of right and wrong. Morality and evil are purely human concepts. One doesn't find an emphasis on virtue in the animal kingdom. If the Darwinian survival of the fittest is the way in which life continually develops, then *morality* and *compassion* would actually hold back the strongest from acquiring ever-greater resources and the best mating opportunities. But the very fact that religion has laid a foundation for personal conduct that goes against the basic principles of natural selection is proof that there must be a unique source for our belief in the concept of right and wrong. Muslims would say that God placed a *fitrah*, or natural inclination within us, as part of our innate constitution. In other words, we were born with a conscience.

The third issue concerns the main features of religion itself. Every religion on Earth has a set of very similar precepts. Whether it is a local tribal religion or a widespread tradition, the core values seem consistent, giving rise to the theory that all religion is, in fact, from a singular source. All religions teach that stealing, adultery, lying, cheating, and murder are wrong. Each also has some form of self-denial rituals to teach enlightenment, prayer methods for communicating with the higher power, and either an oral or a written tradition that is passed on through the generations. The evidence would suggest that the scattered peoples of the world had a single source for most of what they believe.

FROM THE SOURCE

We raised in every nation a Messenger, saying: "Serve God and keep away from falsehood." After that, God guided some of them while deviation proved true against the others. So travel through the earth and see what was the end of those who denied Our Message. (Qur'an 16:36)

There are other issues that could be explored, but my main focus here is on the multitude of related ideas and the continuity of concepts found in world religions collectively. But there are, to be fair, many major differences among religions as well. This brings me to the question: Why are there so many religions in the world that are similar and different at the same time? What does Islam say about this phenomenon? Islam's answer is straightforward and clear: All revealed religions began with a true prophet from God. People's alterations over time have caused the introduction of varied practices and rituals that may not have any relationship to what their ancient prophet actually taught.

Will the Real Prophet Please Stand Up?

Everything in the material world has a beginning. Likewise, every religion has a main figure who first started to teach it. Islam calls such people prophets and messengers. Whereas some would assert that these people made up their own religious beliefs and promulgated them, Islam would say that all of those founders were really just relaying a message from the same source: God.

The Qur'an puts it this way:

> O Muhammad, We have sent revelations to you just as We sent them to
> Noah and the Prophets who came after him; We also sent revelations to
> Abraham, Ishmael, Isaac, Jacob, his descendants, and to Jesus, Job, Jonah,
> Aaron and Solomon. We revealed the Psalms to David. Revelations were
> also sent to those Messengers whom We have already mentioned to you
> and to those whose name We have not mentioned to you, and God spoke
> to Moses directly. All these Messengers conveyed good news to mankind
> and admonished them so that, after conveying the message through the
> Messengers, people would have no excuse to plead against God. Indeed, God
> is the Mighty, the Wise. (Qur'an 4:163–165)

So Islam accepts all true prophets from God whether He told us their name in the
Qur'an or not. Muslims are asked to be tolerant of the religions of other people for
this very reason. Upon learning of a different religion, our basic attitude is one of
inquiry, not prejudice. Who was its prophet? Was he an authentic prophet from God
or a charlatan? What does this other religion have in common with Islam?

Islam recognizes that there is a great diversity of religious expression in the world.
To set up every religion as equal with its peers and then to judge them would not be
fair. Are there concocted religions? Undoubtedly there are, but at the same time there
are other spiritual traditions whose origins are harder to explain. What has sustained
Judaism or Buddhism or any of the other major religions for thousands of years? Each
religion must be judged on its own merits, not on the sophistication, excesses, or
shortcomings of others.

When Muslims try to identify a potential prophet in a religion they have just
encountered, they must first ask several questions. The first question is this: Was the
religion founded between the time of Adam and Muhammad? This is an important
question because the Qur'an calls Muhammad the seal and last Prophet to the world.
If the religion was founded after the time of Muhammad, then Islam says it is a false
religion. To be even more accurate, we find that Prophet Muhammad said, "There
were no Prophets sent to the world between Jesus and I." By this stricter definition,
any religion, other than Islam, can be preliminarily true only if its founder lived
before the removal of Jesus from the world. So the cutoff date for a religion's validity
is about 33 C.E., with Islam coming later (in 610 C.E.).

The second question is what did that founding person teach? This is where a little
deeper investigation is necessary. Through the use of whatever old records are

available, a survey of current practices and their consistency can be conducted. Finally, a thorough comparison with other related religions can help to sweep away centuries of accretions, exposing a more accurate picture of what the ancient ideals were. For example, Buddhism as it is practiced in China is a synthesis of the core principles of Buddhism with folklore, ancestor worship, superstition, and popular myth. When you strip away the baggage, however, you find a religious message not all that dissimilar from Islam. Some Muslim scholars, who have undertaken such a survey, are of the opinion that Buddha might even have been a prophet of God whose teachings became altered through the centuries.

Other Muslim scholars have attempted to show that Socrates, Lao-Tzu, Hammurabi, and Zoroaster were prophets of God acceptable to Islam. While these theories cannot really be proven with available data, it is interesting to get a peek into how the world of Islam tries to make sense of and integrate the founders of other religions into its own milieu. None of this influences Islamic teachings, however, which are forever enshrined in the Qur'an and in the sayings of Muhammad. This process does serve to accentuate the strain of tolerance inherent in Islamic philosophy, though. If all true religion is from God, then all prophets must be brothers. How can a Muslim discriminate against a follower of another religion?

Introducing the Prophets in Islam

When God banished Adam and Eve from the garden, He said that people would live in hatred and rivalry on the Earth. *Shaytan*, along with our animal desires, would factor greatly in that prophecy. According to Islam, Adam was the first prophet in the world. He has this title because he taught his descendants to love God and loathe the influences of the Devil. As generations marched by, and *Shaytan* attempted to corrupt them, God raised up new prophets to teach people the right way to live again.

In those remote times, the major sins of men and women were not that they disbelieved in God, but that they fell prey to anger and hatred and false ideas. The Qur'an says, "All People were once a single nation; later on they became divided after inventing different lifestyles." (Qur'an 10:19)

The greatest triumph of *Shaytan*, however, was in eventually goading people into worshipping idols instead of God. By working to get people to reject the guidance of God completely, *Shaytan* hoped to counteract the prophecy God gave to Adam and Eve that He would send prophets to guide their descendants. According to Islam, *Shaytan* thought if no one believed in God, no one would listen to His prophets.

How and when did he succeed in doing this? The Prophet Muhammad explained that in the generations prior to the Prophet Noah, there lived five great heroes whose deeds and reputations were known far and wide. When they died, the next generation decided to erect statues of those men to honor them. A few decades later, *Shaytan* implanted the idea into people's thoughts that their fathers actually worshipped these statues and thus veneration of false gods began. This is the Islamic explanation for the origin of idolatry.

From then on, the struggle between God's prophets and the misguided notions of people would be a conflict wrought with violence and great confusion. But God never sent any angels or supernatural creatures to Earth to show people that His power was real. The test would be compromised if God showed His hand too early. Islam teaches that all prophets were plain human beings with no magical qualities or abilities in themselves. The Qur'an explains it this way: "We didn't send any Messengers before you except that they were people whom We inspired. They lived in human communities." (Qur'an 12:109)

Sometimes God would grant miracles to these prophets to give the faithless people a chance to reflect. Many of the miracles mentioned as gifts to the prophets in the Bible are also mentioned in the Qur'an. Moses had a staff that turned into a snake. Jesus could heal people. Solomon, according to the Qur'an, could control the *jinns* and understand the languages of animals. But the usual reaction of people to these miracles was often skepticism. People generally didn't believe in what their prophets brought. On one level this attitude is understandable; after all, if a man came to you and said he was a prophet, would you believe him? Probably not.

The Qur'an even comments on people's usual reactions to one of their own claiming prophethood:

> Do people find it incredible that We send Our inspiration to a man from among themselves? That he should warn humanity [of the danger of evil] and give good news to the believers that they are held in high esteem in truth before their Lord. The Truth-Hiders just say, "This [revelation he brings] is evidently clear sorcery!" (Qur'an 10:2)

ASK THE IMAM

Muhammad performed several miracles during his ministry. Although they were not as numerous as the miracles granted to Jesus, Muhammad is credited with healing and other such miraculous acts. He always asserted, however, that his greatest miracle was the Qur'an itself.

However, prophets were no ordinary men. They had logic and reasoning that could not be explained or denied if given a fair hearing. What would cause people to oppose someone like that? Love for material wealth, sin, or decadence could be definitive factors, for along with bringing a spiritual message, the Qur'an notes that the prophets also brought a message of social reform and personal accountability for one's own behavior. People were asked to change their lives but were prone to resist.

The basic theme in Qur'anic stories is that people just won't listen, no matter what signs are given them. They have become focused on gods of their own making and don't want to change their lifestyles. They're even willing to resort to violence to protect their unjust ways. The Qur'an charges that "… if you were to dig a tunnel in the earth or raise a ladder into the sky and bring them a sign [they still wouldn't be convinced]." In another place it quotes people as doubting miracles and prophecies by saying, "It's nothing more than magic." For all his many miracles, even Jesus' disciples doubted him sometimes.

Looking at the Characteristics of the Prophets

Many Western scholars have a misconception about the mission of prophets in Islam. They often write that in Islam a prophet is not allowed to fail, so the Qur'an paints a rosy picture of success for God's messengers. This is simply not true. The Qur'an contains several references to prophets who failed to convince their people and even to prophets who were killed by their own communities. It's not that a prophet cannot fail; rather, sometimes people are so obstinate that no amount of convincing will get them to leave their evil ways. The excuse that the Qur'an records as having the least merit but the greatest use is, "We found our parents doing it, so we will do it, too." Then the Qur'an adds, "What! Even though they had no sense or guidance!"

The Qur'an contains many different types of prophetic stories. There are stories of prophets who convinced the poor to follow them but who were attacked by the rich. Other prophets are presented as rulers or kings who worked to guide their nation, whereas others are portrayed as men with struggles in their soul and doubts about what they were doing. It is interesting to note here that the Qur'an often uses these different themes to convince people that Muhammad is also an authentic prophet and is undergoing some of the same trials that previous prophets went through.

Are there any qualities that would make God choose a person to be a prophet? You bet there are. In general, people who were given a revelation from God were moral individuals who sought out God with earnest hearts. The Prophet Abraham is portrayed in the Qur'an as searching for God amid an idolatrous society even from childhood. His own father was a maker of idols, so Abraham grew up seeing his dad carving faces in stone and thus understood from an early age that the idols were man-made in the worst sense.

One beautiful passage of the Qur'an has Abraham seeing the stars and praying to them as gods. When they set in the late night, he realizes that they were just heavenly bodies, so he turns to the moon next and finally to the morning sun, thinking each must have been God. When they each set in turn, he realizes that God cannot be found in natural phenomena. A heavenly body is no more a god than a carved idol. Later God revealed his message to the young man, and a prophet was born.

Muhammad also had a unique experience. His father died before he was born, and his mother passed away when he was less than six years old. He was cared for first by his grandfather and then by his uncle. Being an orphan, he was not treated with any special dignity or deference and thus grew up feeling very humble. His mother had sent him to a foster mother in the countryside as a toddler, as was the custom in those days. Here he could learn rural values, which fostered thrift and good character. Because of his time there, Muhammad had better manners than most other children in Mecca. When he was a teenager, he was given the job of tending sheep in the pastures. This gave him a lot of time to think. He developed a reputation for honesty and trustworthiness and never acquired a taste for idol worship. These qualities led him to look for God.

ASK THE IMAM

The Qur'an contains a chapter that starts off by scolding Muhammad for ignoring an old blind man who interrupted him while he was trying to convince a Meccan noble about the merits of Islam. This is an example of an unintentional error in judgment committed by a sinless prophet.

So if the people selected by God to be His prophets were basically good and introspective before receiving their commission, how did they act after becoming God's elect? Did they ever sin? This is where Islam parts ways with the Jewish and Christian concept of prophethood. Whereas the Bible sometimes portrays the prophets as struggling with moral issues and even weak to temptation, Islam holds that all prophets were *sinless*. What does this mean? Were they demigods? No, they were still men open to human frailties. Sinless doesn't mean *perfect*. It doesn't mean that they didn't make mistakes or errors in judgment on temporal matters. What it signifies is that all persons chosen to be prophets had their records cleared, their hearts purified by God, and thereafter never intentionally did any immoral action again.

The Books of God

Islam accepts that written revelations given by God existed before the time of the Qur'an. As you learned in Chapter 9, there are two types of prophets: regular prophets who received prophecies, and messengers who received codified "books" that were meant to be passed down. Tradition states that there were 313 messengers. If we use that figure, it means that there were as many revealed religious texts. These would be the holy books found throughout the world from the ancient Chinese and Greeks to the Toltecs of Mexico or ancient Jews of Palestine. Not every "book," or *kitabullah*, necessarily needs to be written down, according to Islam, because oral transmission would suffice in most cases.

So where do all these revelations come from? The Qur'an says that God keeps a special book with Him called the "Mother of the Book." This is the source from which all revelations are derived. When a messenger is supposed to receive a message from God, the Angel Gabriel, who is nicknamed the *Spirit of Holiness* in the Qur'an, takes the revelation from the "Mother of the Book" and brings it to the messenger entitled to get it. Because there were so many revelations, Gabriel must have been very busy! Of these many "Books of God," the Qur'an mentions five by name:

- The Scrolls of Abraham (*Suhuf*)
- The Law of Moses (*Taurah*)
- The Psalms of David (*Zabur*)
- The Gospel of Jesus (*Injeel*)
- The Reading of Muhammad (*Qur'an*)

What happened to all the rest of the many revealed books? This problem is best left to literary historians to unravel. Religious texts abound throughout the world's ancient civilizations. Some have survived; some have been heavily edited; others were lost or destroyed in the great movement of conquerors and conquered; yet others may survive buried in the recesses of a civilization's historical literature or popular myths. The Qur'an declares: "All [Believers] believe in God, His angels, His Books and His Messengers. They say, 'We do not discriminate against any of His Messengers.'" (Qur'an 2:285)

So Islam accepts all previous scriptures and prophets that were truly sent by God. (Fakes and imposters excluded, of course.) The caveat is that all other religious books have had their integrity compromised, and therefore the job of the Qur'an is to correct the mistakes of previous scriptures. Islam does not accept the Bible that was compiled in the fourth century as being completely authentic revelation. The Qur'an accuses Christians and Jews of mixing their scriptures with other things besides the pure words of the prophets. The job of the Qur'an, then, is to refresh the message of God to the world once more. Thus, Muslims would say that their holy book is a compliment to the scriptures that went before, and that it sets aright things that may have become jumbled, covered over, or lost in previous ages.

The Least You Need to Know

- Islam accepts all the major biblical prophets (and prophets not mentioned in the Judeo-Christian tradition) but explains their life and mission in a unique way.
- Prophets are sinless but can make honest mistakes.
- All true religions originated from God, and Muslims are taught to be tolerant of others' beliefs because of it.
- Muslims do not accept the Bible as the word of God but do believe that it is based on what was once authentic revelation from God.

Jews in Islam

In This Chapter

- Learn about the special status both Jews and Christians occupy in Islamic thought
- Bring to light the influence of Judaism on pre-Islamic Arabia
- Find out how Jews and Muslims interacted in the early days of Islam
- Know what the Qur'an says about Judaism
- Discover the Golden Age of Judaism in the classical Islamic Empire

The Qur'an and the hadiths both make frequent mention of Jews. They discuss in detail the beliefs and practices, as well as the merits and drawbacks, of the Jewish religion. Whereas the earliest revelations of the Qur'an concern the evils of idolatry, later revelations spend more time on interfaith issues. This change in emphasis is the result of the conditions that Islam underwent. When Muhammad began preaching in Mecca, his audience consisted mainly of Arab idolaters. After he moved to cosmopolitan Medina, 13 years later, the audience expanded to include not only idolaters, but also three well-settled Jewish tribes (and a few scattered Christians).

Although Muslim-Jewish relations endured much strain in the waning years of Muhammad's rule in Medina, this hostility soon abated. In fact, Jews never had anything to fear from the rise of Islamic civilization. While Christians in Europe were busy persecuting Jews all throughout the last thousand years, culminating in the Holocaust, Jews who lived in the Muslim world enjoyed tolerance, peace, and prosperity. The Qur'an mentions with reverence the major Jewish prophets and even calls the founding of ancient Israel an act of righteousness.

In recent times, however, political conditions have cast a pall over Muslim-Jewish relations that never existed before. The tension of the Arab-Israeli conflict has divided Muslims and Jews irreparably, it seems. However, recent efforts have been made to heal some of the mistrust, and tentative steps toward peace may yet restore amicable relations between the followers of the world's two purest monotheistic religions. In this chapter, I explore the place of Judaism in the Qur'an, Muhammad's interactions with Jews in Arabia, and the long history of mutual tolerance that came to an end in 1948.

The People of the Book

The Middle East, the crossroads of the world, is the birthplace not only of Islam but also of Judaism and Christianity. Because the Qur'an was first revealed in the Middle East, it is only natural that the majority of its contents reference people and places found there. Islam, then, has certain similarities with Judaism and Christianity, arising from the fact that they share the same basic geographic and historical background. This makes all three religions cousins of sorts. Islam is even classified as a Western religion.

Given that Islam recognizes that Jews and Christians received authentic prophets and revelations in the past, the Qur'an uses a special title to separate them from mere idolaters. This term is *Ahl al Kitab*, or People of the Book. It is an allusion to the fact that Jews and Christians received holy books from God long before and can be counted on to have certain ideas and concepts that are similar to Islam's.

DEFINITION

Ahl al Kitab means People of the Book. It is the term used to describe Jews and Christians in the Qur'an. It refers to the fact that God revealed books to their ancestors.

The People of the Book have such an elevated status that, according to Islamic Law, a Muslim man is allowed to marry a practicing Jewish or Christian woman. (And he is not allowed to force her to convert or curtail her religious freedom.) In addition, meat prepared by Jews and Christians based on their religious dictates (the kosher standard) is permissible for Muslims to eat. (Think of the great boom kosher delis will experience as the Muslim population in the West continues to increase!) Thus, Islam considers Jews and Christians to be co-religionists after a fashion.

Judaism and Islam

Over the centuries much misinformation has surfaced concerning the concept of Judaism in Islam. Some of it can be traced to long-held prejudices and historical misunderstandings, and some of it is because the current state of relations between Israel and the Muslim world leaves a lot to be desired. Sadly, in modern times, the misinterpretation of historical events and the use of Qur'anic verses out of context have allowed some Western writers to contribute to the problem. Nevertheless, except for a rocky start and the unfortunate enmity prevalent today, the history of Jewish-Muslim coexistence has been remarkably friendly.

With that said, we can take a closer look at how Islam really perceives the Jewish people. To unravel this issue we have to look at three areas:

- The interaction between Muslims and Jews in Medina in the Prophet's time

- The perception of Judaism in the Qur'an

- The relationship between Jews and Muslims throughout the succeeding centuries

When Islam began in Mecca in the year 610 c.e., no Jews inhabited the city. Muhammad was dealing with an Arab society steeped in idolatry and tribal custom. There was no police force or central authority governing the city. At best, a council of rich tribal heads dictated local policies, and these decisions were usually guided by self-interest. Public drunkenness, prostitution, infanticide, spousal abuse, the worst form of abject slavery, and robbery and banditry were the order of the day. Consequently, we find that the Qur'anic revelations were mainly directed against these and other vices. After Muhammad and his followers migrated to Medina (which was formerly called Yathrib) to escape the persecution of the Meccans, Muslims found themselves in a city that was divided among three factions. One consisted of a group of the following three Jewish tribes who lived in and around the city:

- The Banu Nadir

- The Banu Qaynuqa

- The Banu Quraiza

The other two factions consisted of two Arab tribes who frequently fought wars with each other. They were known as the Aws and the Khazraj. The Jewish tribes often played one Arab tribe against another and thereby exercised a certain amount of dominance in city affairs, even though their numbers were small compared with the rest of the population. Jews also exerted a sort of moral authority over the Arabs by pointing out that monotheism was better than the idols they worshipped. This helps to explain why the Arabs of Medina were more amenable to Muhammad than the Arabs of Mecca. The citizens of Medina were already primed for religious discussion. (Jewish leaders often predicted to the Arabs that a new prophet would come and destroy them and their idols and ally himself to the Jews.) This was the political and religious makeup of Medina in 622 c.e.

Muhammad had been invited to live in Medina by representatives of both Arab tribes, who were tired of the constant warfare. This united decision on the part of the more numerous Arabs had the effect of limiting the influence of the Jewish tribes in the city. When Muhammad first arrived, though, the Jewish tribes acquiesced peacefully and accepted his civil leadership. Why did they do this? The answer lies in shared religious concepts.

ASK THE IMAM

During the first 15 years of Islam, Muslims were told to pray in the direction of Jerusalem. After a year and a half in Medina, a revelation instructed them to pray in the direction of the *Ka'bah* in Mecca.

The Jews had learned that Muhammad was preaching against idolatry and thus felt something of a common cause with him, for Judaism was also critical of this Arab custom. In addition, the Qur'an, as it was being revealed, spoke respectfully of Jewish prophets, and this had the effect of causing many Jews to sympathize with Islam. Moses, Job, Saul, David, and Solomon all had a revered place in Islamic theology. Many Jews thought that Muhammad would actually convert to Judaism and increase Jewish power throughout central Arabia.

Many were even further impressed when Muhammad demonstrated his considerable political acumen by drafting a constitution for Medina, spelling out the rights and responsibilities of all groups resident within the municipality. This lengthy constitution included the following terms:

- Everyone must live in peace within the city.

- No side will make any alliances with an enemy of any other party in the city.

- All citizens of Medina have the right to be secure and have their economic rights respected.

- If the city is attacked, all parties will join together in its defense.

In addition, Muhammad made a separate treaty of friendship between the rapidly growing Muslim community and the three Jewish tribes. The treaty bound each side to respect the other and also reiterated the illegality of forming alliances with outside parties against one another. Its acceptance by both sides demonstrated their willingness to accept the legitimacy of Muhammad's authority in Medina.

Tension soon arose, however, after several Jewish families converted to Islam. Among them was a prominent Jewish rabbi named 'Abdullah ibn Salam. He kept his conversion a secret at first but then declared it publicly in a meeting of Jewish clan leaders. Add to the situation the fact that Muhammad was *not* converting to Judaism and that the Qur'an was not particularly supportive of certain Jewish beliefs, and you can see the beginning of a rift. Some Jews began to charge that Muhammad could not be a true prophet because he was an Arab and not one of *God's chosen people.* They also began quizzing him at every opportunity about arcane facts concerning the prophets of old in order to trip him up. As the months went by, the situation went from bad to worse.

The Qur'anic revelations received by Muhammad painted a picture of Judaism, as it was then practiced, that was extremely unflattering. The Qur'an accused the Jews of practicing racial discrimination and hypocrisy. It said that they were not following the teachings of Moses and that their customs had no authority from God. But the worst of it, from the Jewish point of view, was still to come. When Muhammad first arrived in Medina, the Jews had been hopeful that he would denounce Jesus as an impostor. (Judaism holds that Jesus is a false rabbi.) But instead of rejecting Jesus, the Qur'an called him the Jewish Messiah and a messenger from God who was sent to call the wayward Jews back to true faith! Such a view was totally unacceptable to the Jews, and the situation deteriorated from there.

Muhammad had been engaging in dialogues with Jewish leaders over religious issues and had succeeded in making some more conversions. However, after six months in Medina, the Jewish clan leaders began a vicious propaganda campaign against Muhammad, and much slanderous talk was directed against the Muslims. Some Jews actually pretended to convert just so they could gain entry into Muslim meetings and ask confusing questions to sow doubt into the minds of recent converts. The Aws and

Khazraj tribes, who had almost all converted to Islam, were soon engaged in a war of words with their Jewish neighbors. The breaking point would soon be upon the city.

The Only Muslim-Jewish War

The Jewish tribes of Medina grew increasingly hostile to the Muslims as a result of the major doctrinal disputes and the clash of cultures. One by one each tribe engaged the Muslims in battle (even though they had signed peace treaties). The first tribe to pick a fight with the Muslims was the Banu Qaynuqa. After declaring war on the Muslims, they were surprised to find that their neighborhoods were immediately blockaded. The Banu Qaynuqa surrendered under the terms that they would have to pack up their belongings and leave Medina forever. That tribe moved into northern Arabia and eventually settled in Palestine.

The second tribe to fight the Muslims was the Banu Nadir. They were the most active in intriguing against the Prophet and even tried to assassinate him. Again, when actual fighting broke out, the Muslims surrounded the fortresses of the Banu Nadir and forced their capitulation. The Banu Nadir were then ordered to pack up and leave as well. Most went to Palestine, but a contingent went to live in a Jewish community called Khaibar in northern Arabia.

The third tribe, the Banu Quraiza, avoided all conflict with the Muslims, and its leaders were determined to abide by the terms of their treaty with the Muslims. But the leaders of the Banu Nadir wanted revenge and thus sent ambassadors to Mecca, which was the center of idol worship. They convinced the Meccan leaders to arrange a grand coalition of dozens of Arab tribes in order to destroy the Muslims in Medina. The astonished Meccans asked the Jewish ambassador whether the Banu Nadir considered idol worship superior to Islam and its emphasis on one God. The envoy said that the Arabs' idols were better.

A force of over 10,000 Arab warriors assembled and laid siege to Medina for about a month. Never had the Muslims been in such danger before. They feared that if the idolaters breached the great trench, hastily dug around the city by the Muslims, the Arabs would show no mercy. The worst danger, though, lay in the Muslims' rear line. The Banu Nadir, after much hard negotiating, brought the Banu Quraiza into the war and extracted promises from them to attack the Muslims from behind when they least expected it. Muslim women and children were sheltering in the buildings closest to the Banu Quraiza's fortress, and if they were attacked then the Muslim line would crumble from within. Muhammad got wind of the intrigue, however, and skillfully used an undercover agent to cause dissension among the besiegers. He then sent a few soldiers to cover their newly exposed rear, which was now facing another enemy.

It took a fierce sandstorm to break the ranks of the Arab forces, and after they had retreated in disarray, the Muslims attacked the traitors. After a hard-fought battle, the Banu Quraiza agreed to surrender on the condition that their fate be judged by the chief of the Aws tribe, with whom they had always had good relations. After the Banu Quraiza's warriors were taken into custody, the Aws chief asked the clan leaders what their punishment should be for betrayal according to the Torah. The answer was capital punishment, of course, and the clan leaders were then executed by the verdict of their own religion. (The remaining men, women, children, and other noncombatants remained unharmed and were forced into indentured servanthood. All their property was also seized.)

DISPELLING THE MYTH

Muhammad ordered Muslims to be kind to their Jewish neighbors and to share their food with the Jews. He also had business dealings with Jews and never failed in his end of the bargain. Jews continued to live in Medina throughout Muhammad's rule and even for many centuries after his passing.

As can be expected, the Qur'an grew increasingly stern in its tone as all the afore-mentioned events unfolded. However, the Qur'an still maintained that all people were equal in God's sight and that it was only in the strength of their faith that they could be judged. Muhammad kept his end of the treaty at all times, and many Jews converted to Islam of their own free will. He never forced any conversions nor did he act in an unjust manner. One of his wives, Safiya, was also a Jewish Muslim; although some people grumbled and accused her of being duplicitous, Muhammad publicly defended her honor and silenced the detractors.

The expulsion of the three organized Jewish tribes was due to their own duplicity and treachery. Western writers have recognized this reality and have not spent much time weaving a false web. There were still many Jews living in the city of Medina afterward, and religious toleration was the order of the day. The only burden Islamic law laid upon non-Muslims is what is known as the *Jizyah*. This is a tax that non-Muslims must pay to the government as compensation for not being drafted into the army in times of need. (All Muslim men are eligible for the draft, and non-Muslims are forbidden to join the army in an Islamic state.) Even as Muslims pay *Zakah*, non-Muslims must pay their fair share as well.

Jews in the Muslim Empire

The history of Islam from Muhammad's time until the advent of the twentieth century is one of remarkable tolerance toward Jews and Judaism. Even as Jews were persecuted in Europe during the Middle Ages, they almost always enjoyed political and religious freedom in Islamic societies. The greatest example of that is found in the period known as the Golden Age in Spain. From the eighth century until the fourteenth century, Muslims ruled nearly all of Spain and a small sliver of France. (The last tiny Muslim stronghold of Granada was overrun by Christians in 1492.) During that time, Jewish citizens of the state had rights nearly equal to their rights in America today. Jewish historians refer to the time their people lived in Muslim-ruled Spain as the Golden Age of Judaism.

Jews were also prominent in the courts of Baghdad, Cairo, Istanbul, and elsewhere, being palace physicians, finance officers, and even *viziers*, or government ministers. The Islamic *Millet*, or Sectional system, operated to the benefit of religious minorities by setting up an official board of people from every religion who ruled over their co-religionists according to their own religious laws. (Non-Muslims are exempt from following Islamic Law.) Important synagogues dot the major cities of the Middle East and, save for the modern Arab-Israeli conflict, relations between Jews and Muslims have been quite fair for more than a thousand years.

As you can see, Islam is not an anti-Jewish religion. It recognizes the legitimacy of the Jewish prophets and the right of Jews to follow their own religious beliefs. Islam merely points to what it considers the collective failure of the Jewish people to live up to the best ideals contained in their revelations from God. In this regard, Islam is no different from Christianity, which offers exactly the same explanation. Jesus is quoted in the Christian New Testament as calling Jewish religious leaders "Whited Sepulchers," "a generation of vipers," and many other strong epithets to emphasize how he felt they had warped God's true teachings away from what they were intended to be. What must be remembered is that Islamic history is filled with general tolerance for Jews while Christian history, sadly, is a tragic record of forced conversions of Jews, massacres, discriminatory laws, and humiliation. This is a reality that is often not considered but can be a basis for revived mutual respect and tolerance.

Islam teaches that the true message of the Jewish prophets found its fulfillment in the person of Muhammad and that he is the most like Abraham in his life and example. It is unfortunate that political strife has interrupted the dialogue between Islam and Judaism, but that may change in the future if the conflict in Palestine finds a successful resolution. All of the demagoguery and inflammatory rhetoric on both sides is not because of religion, but because of each side feeling that it has been wronged in some way.

DISPELLING THE MYTH

Islam does not teach its followers to discriminate against Jews. When a Jewish funeral procession was passing by him in Medina, Muhammad stood up in respect for the deceased. When asked about it, he remarked that we're all equal in death.

The Least You Need to Know

- Islam does not teach its followers to be anti-Semitic. The intractable Arab-Israeli conflict, which has festered since 1948, is a political condition that is often unfairly cloaked in religious rhetoric.
- Islam accepts all the major Jewish prophets, including Moses, Job, Saul, David, and Solomon.
- Many Jewish teachings are compatible with Islam, such as monotheism, kosher standards, angels, and prophets.
- The Qur'an contains more than a hundred verses that discuss Judaism, Jews, and issues related to the ancient Israelites.
- Jews lived generally at peace in the Muslim world for more than a thousand years and did not suffer persecution in any comparable way to that of their co-religionists who dwelled in Christian Europe.

Christianity and Islam

In This Chapter

- Learn about the historical ups and downs of Muslim-Christian relations
- Discover Jesus and Mary through the lens of Islam
- Take a look at Muhammad's experiences with Christians
- Know what the Islamic position is on all the major Christian doctrines

The two largest religions in the world today are Islam and Christianity. They also happen to be historically separated by only 600 years. Given that both religions began with charismatic leaders, it's not surprising that their relations would be equally charged with emotion, fervor, and sometimes conflict. Islam accepts the founder of Christianity, Jesus Christ, as a true prophet from God, while denying that he is a god or God Himself. The Qur'an even devotes whole passages in commenting on the Christian religion. Christianity, which came before Islam, has not yet accepted the validity of Muhammad's message and consequently most Christians know little of this rival faith.

The situation is changing, however, with the growth of more diverse multicultural societies in the West. With more Muslims than ever either moving to the West or converting from among the Western population, people here have had to take a closer look into their neighbors' beliefs. The growth of interfaith dialogue, long the province of Jews and Christians, has recently expanded to include Muslims as regular participants. In this chapter, I explain the long and fractious history of relations between these two world giants and show the efforts that both traditions are making toward living together in harmony and mutual tolerance.

Setting the Stage

The history of Muslim-Christian relations has followed a thorny pattern of shifting political realities. Both religions, being missionary oriented, have been the big boys on the block, fighting in every arena for land, dominance, converts, and influence. Whereas Muslims and Jews got off to a rocky start but then settled into a tolerant relationship (until very recently), Muslims actually had good relations with Christians in the early days of Islam. The Qur'an even looks fondly upon them and predicts a certain amount of mutual goodwill:

> You will find that the closest to you in love are those who call themselves Christians because there are priests and monks among them who do not behave arrogantly. (Qur'an 5:82)

It was only after the initial spirit of tolerance abated on both sides that centuries of conflict ensued (culminating with the era of Colonialism when Christian European powers completely dismantled Islamic civilization). The so-called Islamic Resurgence that is much maligned in the West today is really nothing more than the Islamic world trying to right itself after the last knockout punch it received. Islam can recover because it has a definite explanation of what happened and a sense of certainty to propel it forward again. Muslims, when their nations were being dominated by direct European rule, never felt that their religion was to blame or that Christianity was superior. Instead of blaming God for their malaise, they turned inward and began blaming themselves and their own shortcomings.

Muslims consider Islam to be a complete way of life, no matter what political situation they are in, so the urge to tell others about their beliefs is alive and well. Indeed, to this day, the war for converts between Christianity and Islam is a daily struggle, with more people converting to Islam from Christianity than the other way around. What gives Islam a certain measure of insulation that protects its followers from accepting Christian dogma? The answer lies in the explanation of Christianity given in the Qur'an itself. Just as the Qur'an contains a full discussion of Judaism and its merits and drawbacks, it also has a complete analysis of Christianity. So while the average Christian might be completely in the dark about Islam, the Muslim is already well versed in both faiths. Talk about a home-court advantage!

Muhammad and the Monk

Muhammad grew up in the city of Mecca in Arabia. Only a handful of people who claimed to be Christians lived there among the thousands of Arab idolaters, and there was no organized church or place of worship. Indeed, a generation before Muhammad was born Christianity was all but made illegal by the reigning idolaters, who feared the loss of their religion. And what of the closet Christians of Mecca, or the few Christianized tribes in northern and southern Arabia? As many writers have lamented, the Christians of Arabia were not known as paragons of virtue, being a part of the lifestyle and grit of a rough-and-tumble environment. Furthermore, there weren't any centers of Christian learning or repositories of centuries-old knowledge. The main centers of Christianity were far to the north in the Byzantine Roman Empire or across the Red Sea in Egypt and Abyssinia. Arabia was a land virtually untouched by the Gospel.

What were Muhammad's first contacts with Christians? As I discussed before, he rejected idol worship from an early age and grew up as a poor orphan in the care of relatives. When Muhammad was about 12 years old, however, he had his first foreign adventure. He accompanied his uncle on a business trip to Syria, an event that in those days was like a rite of passage for young men. Caravans made up of dozens of horses and camels snaked their way through northern Arabia and into Syria, heading for the great trading bazaars where everything from Chinese silk to Germanic metal-work could be had.

 FROM THE SOURCE

According to Muhammad, "Every Prophet sent by God has been a shepherd. Moses was a shepherd, David tended animals, and before I became a Prophet, I also was a shepherd."

Just inside the southeastern region of Syria lived a Christian monk named Bahira. His usual habit was to watch the roads during the day, and when he saw this particular caravan coming in from the Arabian road, he noticed some strange portents. Clouds seemed to be following overhead, shading the travelers. He sent a boy to invite the weary merchants to his monastery. The young Muhammad was also brought to the dinner prepared for the men, though at first he had been left to tend the camels.

Bahira was fascinated by the boy and, after interviewing him, predicted privately to the boy's uncle, Abu Talib, that his nephew would be a prophet one day. The practical uncle dismissed the idea, and the next day the caravan went on its way. After a few weeks spent in the bazaars of Syria, the group returned uneventfully to Mecca, where Muhammad continued his normal routine of tending his uncle's flocks of sheep in the scruffy hills around the city.

An Interesting Proposal

When Muhammad turned 25 years old, he received an offer of employment from a 40-year-old Meccan widow named Khadijah. She wanted the young man to lead her next caravan to Syria. (His uncle, Abu Talib, had put in a good word for him.) He agreed, and the trip was very successful financially. This was Muhammad's second and final business trip to Syria. Khadijah was impressed by Muhammad and soon offered her hand in marriage to him. He accepted and for the next 15 years lived the life of a quiet family man.

But years later, as he neared his fortieth birthday, Muhammad grew restless and wanted to connect with his spiritual side. He would often retreat to a mountain cave to meditate. One night, while meditating in his usual spot, he was visited by the angel Gabriel, who announced to him that he was chosen to be the last prophet of God. Understandably, Muhammad was shaken, and he ran home and hid under his bedsheets. The next day his concerned wife took him to meet her old, blind cousin, Waraqah. He was a Christian and knew how to read and write, though he was forbidden by Meccan law from spreading knowledge of his faith. (Christianity was outlawed in Mecca before Muhammad was born because it was perceived as a threat to idolatry.) Waraqah listened to Muhammad's account and then told Muhammad that the angel who had come to him was the same one who had gone to Moses. He then said that Muhammad was going to be a prophet and would be opposed by his people. A few months later Waraqah passed away.

These two people, Bahira (whom he met one time at a banquet as a boy) and Waraqah (an old reclusive cousin of his wife with whom he was never known to associate), represent all of the contacts Muhammad had with Christians for the first 40 years of his life. Christian evangelists have often charged that Muhammad was instructed by closet Christian scholars in the ways of religion and that he simply took it from there and made up his own faith. This simplistic view, however, is unsustainable when one considers the depth of Islam and the fact that Muhammad had only the most limited contacts with Christians. There were no wandering evangelists or seminaries in Mecca, and Muhammad's enemies never seriously pursued such a charge against him because they knew him from childhood and they knew his circle of friends and acquaintances.

In fact, Muhammad had no significant interaction with Christians until he and his followers moved to Medina after 13 years in Mecca. A few Christians lived in Medina, and farther to the north were Christian Arab tribes. Muhammad spent a great deal of time setting up dialogues with these people and succeeded in converting several visiting delegations of Christians to Islam. Not all Christians who came converted, but Muhammad still showed them great respect. He even allowed a group of Christians to use the main mosque of Medina for their Sunday worship services.

As he did with the Jews, Muhammad made a treaty of peace with the closest Christian community. These were the Christians of Najran, a small area hundreds of miles away in central Arabia. In that treaty, both sides agreed to respect the rights and beliefs of the other. During the time that Muhammad lived in Medina, there were no conflicts between the Muslims and Christians. There would eventually be a war with the Byzantine Romans to the north, but it would be a war for defensible borders and not a fight over religion.

Christianity and Jesus in the Qur'an

The Qur'an describes the state of Christianity and its doctrines as they were in the seventh century, long before the Protestant Reformation. Beyond disagreement with a few particular Christian concepts, the Qur'an accepts and promulgates many teachings that are accepted in Christianity. What must be remembered here, as we take a survey of what Islam says about Christianity, is that Muhammad never went to a School of Divinity, he never read the Bible, and he never had access to any books or traveling evangelists. In fact, he couldn't even read!

Just how does Islam explain Christianity and what it stands for? You will find that Christianity is given as much coverage in the Qur'an as Judaism. In fact, the first nine chapters of the Qur'an contain hundreds of verses related to these two topics. Perhaps the best place to start is with Islam's concept of Jesus and where he came from. Jesus holds a particularly high place in Islam, and he is honored in many verses in the Qur'an. For example, we read, "And We made Jesus, the son of Mary, and his mother a sign for mankind." (Qur'an 23:50) Let's see how the Qur'an narrates his life.

The Islamic view of Christianity begins before the birth of Jesus. According to the Qur'an, the Jews of Roman-ruled Palestine were somewhat removed from the pure traditions of the prophets of old. In those difficult times under occupation, a young woman named Mary was chosen to be the mother of a special, anointed child—Jesus, the Messiah. He was born to her without a human father through the agency of divine action. The basic details in the Qur'an differ little from the familiar biblical tale. Jesus is further mentioned in the Qur'an as a dutiful boy who always obeyed his mother.

When he attained to his full age of manhood, his mission of prophethood began. The Qur'an recounts that he attempted to teach his people about true faith in God. He taught that the corpus of Jewish law was filled with unnecessary rules, though some of it was valid. He wasn't teaching a new religion; he was mostly trying to reform the old one. But no matter where he went, he had a hard time getting people to listen. This is when he called for disciples to follow him. He recruited a dedicated cadre of people who assisted him in his mission. The Qur'an mentions neither how many he found nor their names. The immediate effect, however, was that many new converts to Jesus' way were gained.

 ASK THE IMAM

Muslims accept the virgin birth but do not say it is a sign of divinity. Rather, Islam teaches that God created Jesus with a mere command as a miracle for people to ponder.

The Qur'an records that fierce opposition to Jesus came from the leaders of the Jewish community. They called him an impostor and contrived a plot against him. After they succeeded in having him arrested, they tried to get him executed. Here is where the story gets interesting: The Qur'an claims that Jesus was not killed or crucified, but that it was *made to appear so to them.* Islam is uncompromising on this issue. God saved Jesus and took him to Paradise until the hour would come to complete his mission in the end of time.

So from the point of view of Islam, the Christian doctrine that Jesus is God is moot, because Jesus didn't die anyway, and certainly not for the sins of humanity. So who was crucified on that fateful day? If anyone was executed, it may have been the man who betrayed Jesus. If he looked sort of like Jesus, in the confusion the Romans may have grabbed him and killed him, thinking all Semites looked alike. In any case, Islam says the method of deception is unimportant. What matters is that people thought that Jesus died, when he didn't.

Original Sin and All That

The Qur'an gives a rebuttal to every major Christian doctrine. It also recognizes that Christianity has many different sects, each with slightly different teachings, and thus addresses many issues without regard to the uniqueness of each Christian group. Here is a summarized version of what Islam says about some of the more well-known teachings of Christianity:

Original sin   Islam says Adam and Eve were forgiven by God after eating from the tree and passed on no taint of sin to their descendants.

Atonement   God doesn't need to sacrifice Himself to atone for the sins of mankind because He can forgive anything He wants, anytime He wants.

Trinity   Islam says that God is not divided into parts or separate persons.

Marriage prohibition   The Catholic Church forbids priests to marry, but the Qur'an calls this an invented practice.

Monasteries and convents   The Qur'an says God never authorized this lifestyle.

Confession   Islam requires people to ask God for forgiveness directly. No man can act as an intermediary or facilitator.

The Holy Spirit   Islam says that there is no Holy Spirit other than the angel Gabriel who has that nickname. Speaking in tongues or laying on of hands to heal sickness is not known or accepted in Islam.

Salvation and redemption   Islam says our sincere faith and virtuous actions get us into heaven, not just a one-time conversion moment.

Will there be Christians and Jews in Paradise? According to Islam the answer is yes. The Qur'an states that any follower of those religions who "believes in God and the Last Day and does what is right will have nothing to fear or regret." Does this mean that Islam accepts Christianity and Judaism as valid paths to salvation? Yes and no.

The Islamic principle is that you will be judged by what you knew. If a person only knew about Christianity or Judaism or whatever and never heard of Islam, then God will take that into account on Judgment Day and judge the person fairly by it. If a person finds out about Islam, then it becomes incumbent upon him or her to accept it and leave behind the former religion. This is because Islam is considered to be God's last and, therefore, most complete message to the world.

Interfaith Dialogue

The Qur'an is very enthusiastic about interfaith dialogue. Muhammad himself often engaged in this practice with Jews, Christians, and idolaters. The Qur'an even encourages Muslims to invite people to such meetings by saying, "Come! Let us gather together our sons and your sons, our women and your women, ourselves and yourselves: then let us earnestly pray and invoke the displeasure of God on those who are deceitful!" (Qur'an 3:61)

The history of interfaith contacts has often been intimately tied to the political circumstances of the day. For most of Muslim history the dialogue was between parties of equal strength, that is until 1918 (the end of the First World War). Prior to that year there still remained a unified Muslim Empire consisting of an appreciable amount of territory. With the dismantling of the Ottoman Empire, however, interfaith dialogue has taken on the tone of conquered and conquerors. The five nations that have done the most harm to the Muslim world—Britain, France, Italy, the Netherlands, and Russia—suppressed the teaching and practice of Islam and went to great lengths to set up missionary schools and other forms of institutional Christianity in the lands they controlled.

Muslim civilization, on the contrary, from its earliest years until the thirteenth century has almost always encouraged the equal participation of non-Muslims in religious debate and inquiry and rarely attempted to suppress the religious rights of others. Although one can always find aberrations, Muslims have respected freedom of conscience in others. Succeeding Islamic Empires (like the Ottomans) have even paid for the construction and upkeep of churches and synagogues, considering the maintenance of religion for all citizens in an Islamic state to be a duty of the government!

With this diversity of religion in the classical Muslim world, one finds that a great amount of dialoguing went on. On closer scrutiny we find that the great Muslim caliph, Harun ar-Rashid, for example, who ruled in Baghdad in the late eighth century, kept a staff of scholars representing Muslims, Jews, Christians, Hindus, and Buddhists who routinely held regular debate sessions on each other's religions. He even sent a delegation to Charlemagne (along with an elephant as a gift) and opened the lines of communication between Europe and the Middle East.

The Crusades also presented ample opportunities for dialogue. Although the initial onslaught of the European invasion of Palestine was violent and merciless, as the Crusaders settled on their conquered fiefs all along the Mediterranean, daily life and trade brought them into contact with Muslim ideas and values. The whole concept of chivalry, for example, was adopted by European knights from Muslim warriors who practiced *futuwwat*. King Richard the Lionheart once met in a truce with Saladin, the great Muslim hero, and, over a game of chess, they talked about issues between their religions.

> **DEFINITION**
>
> *Futuwwat* was the Muslim chivalric code by which a Muslim soldier would give quarter to an injured opponent, protect women and children, and fight with honor at all times. The Crusaders brought these ideas back to Europe and thus European chivalry was born. Hail King Arthur!

The Activist Popes

Perhaps no one has been more instrumental in reviving interfaith dialogue in modern times than Popes Paul VI and John Paul II. It was the defining statements enshrined in the Second Vatican Council of 1962 to 1965 that opened the door for Christians to have open fellowship with Muslims. This council declared that Christians should accept and respect Muslims as followers of God and of the example of Abraham. The major document of Church policy, the *Lumen Gentium*, had this to say:

> The Plan of salvation also includes those who acknowledge the Creator, among whom are, in the first place, the Muslims. These profess to hold the faith of Abraham, and together with us they adore the one, merciful God, judge of humankind on the Last Day. (*Lumen Gentium*, 16)

Following these and other extremely conciliatory statements, Pope Paul VI embarked on a short tour of the Muslim world and engaged Islamic scholars in ecumenical dialogue in places as diverse as Jordan and Uganda. But it was the efforts of Pope John Paul II that opened the doors to full-blown regular dialogue. Not only was he an extremely prolific traveler among Muslims, but he also apologized to Muslims for the conduct of Christians during the Crusades. He made history as the first pontiff to visit a mosque in Syria and allowed the construction of a small mosque in Vatican City. His vision gave rise to a spirit of Muslim-Christian toleration that has not been seen for over a thousand years.

The varied history of Muslim-Christian-Jewish dialogue that has continued since then in an on-again, off-again fashion is a rich tapestry with many colorful threads of thought. In recent years such activities have become more public, and greater tolerance among the people of all three religions in the West has brought many benefits to our societies. As the Second Vatican Council wrote:

> Over the centuries, many quarrels and dissensions have arisen between Christians and Muslims. The Sacred Council now pleads with all to forget the past, and urges that a sincere effort be made to achieve mutual understanding: for the benefit of all, let them together preserve and promote peace, liberty, social justice and moral values. (*Nostra Aetate*, 3)

DISPELLING THE MYTH

The first public dialogue between Muslims and Christians happened after Muhammad sent a refugee column to Abyssinia in Africa to escape Meccan persecution. The Meccans sent ambassadors to the king there to ask for their arrest, but in a public interview the Christian king, Najashi, ruled that the teachings of Islam were closer to Christianity than to idolatry. He allowed the Muslims to stay.

The Least You Need to Know

- Islam accepts the virgin birth of Jesus and his role as Messiah to the Jews. The Qur'an, however, denies that he is God or the Son of God, rather considering him to be a prophet.

- Muslims do not believe that Jesus was crucified nor that the Romans killed him in Jerusalem. Muslims hold that God answered Jesus' prayer and removed him from the physical world to await the end-of-time and a triumphant return to Earth.

- Christianity and Islam have had many centuries of interfaith dialogue interspersed with wars and periods of mutual fear and distrust.

- European Christians completely occupied the Muslim world during the era of Colonialism and targeted Islam for elimination. The Islamic resurgence today is merely an attempt by Muslims all over the world to regain their values.

Regulating Life Within the Laws of Islam

Muslims consider Islam to be a complete way of life. It touches upon every aspect of our personal, familial, and social lives. The foundation of Islamic guidance comes from two main sources: the Qur'an and the sayings of Muhammad. How did both of these come into existence, and how do Muslims use them to guide their lives? In this part, I explore both sources in detail so you can understand why Muslims do what they do.

Exploring the Sources of Islam

In This Chapter

- Learn about the Islamic scripture, the Holy Qur'an
- Discover the place of the hadiths, or prophetic sayings, in formulating Islamic teachings
- Find out who the companions of Muhammad were
- Meet the traditional scholars of Islam
- Discover the world of Islamic Law and how it is created

Every religious tradition has, as its foundation, a body of knowledge from which each successive generation can draw the fundamentals of their faith. Christians have their Bible and the works of countless theologians stretching over a thousand years. Judaism, Hinduism, and Buddhism have similarly ancient sources combining both scripture and a process of doctrinal development by their luminaries. Islam, on the other hand, is derived from only two main sources, both of which passed through one man and were completed in less than 25 years. In this chapter, I delve into these two sources and see what they say about Islam.

The Qur'an, which is considered to be the literal Word of God, forms the basis of Islamic teachings. The hadiths, or sayings of the Prophet, are considered a commentary on how to apply the Qur'an to daily life. The *companions* of the Prophet, those people who knew him and learned directly from him, are taken as a further source for elucidation and interpretation. Finally, throughout the centuries many great scholars have applied themselves to codifying, investigating, simplifying, and explaining the details of Islam for the common person. They did not introduce any new precepts or practices per se, however, because Islam has a strong tradition against making new additions. Thus, Islam holds a unique place among the religions of the world in that it is the only faith whose doctrines were not created centuries after the death of its founder.

A Closer Look at the Qur'an

Iqra. This command, meaning "Read," was the first word revealed of the Qur'an to Muhammad in the year 610 c.e. He was sitting in a mountain cave, just outside the city of Mecca, thinking about the meaning of things, when a brilliant flash of light overcame him. A hidden voice commanded him to *read.* Its tone was both frightening and compelling. But Muhammad was an illiterate. He never learned how to read, so he meekly answered, "I can't read."

Suddenly, he felt himself being squeezed so that the very breath seemed to rush out of him. When he could bear it no longer, the commanding voice repeated, *"Read."* Confused about what to do, Muhammad protested, "But I can't read!" The same crushing feeling overwhelmed him, and he could hardly stand it when the pressure was released and the voice ordered a third time, *"Read."* Muhammad, not wanting another bout with the pain, answered, "What should I read?"

The voice began to recite melodious-sounding words: "Read in the Name of your Lord Who created humans from a clinging [zygote]. Read for your Lord is the Most Generous. He taught people by the pen what they didn't know before." (Qur'an 96:1–5) Muhammad ran home scared and begged his wife, Khadijah, to comfort him. But the revelation was no apparition or evil omen, as he had thought. Khadijah told him that God would never let harm come to him on account of his honesty and generosity. She didn't know how right she was.

For the next 23 years he would receive revelations from God, carried by the archangel Gabriel. These revelations constitute the Qur'an, a name that literally means the *Reading* or the *Recital.* The Qur'an was given orally to Muhammad, and he would ask people to write down the verses as he dictated them. The Qur'an was therefore not revealed all at once. In fact, it grew larger over time until the last month of Muhammad's life when it took its final form of 114 chapters called *surahs,* each *surah* of varying length. The *surahs* comprise over 6,600 verses called *ayahs* that cover a wide variety of subjects. Sometimes whole *surahs* were revealed together; other times groups of *ayahs* would come, and Muhammad would tell people in which *surah* to include them. (Muslims believe that he made the arrangement of all chapters and verses under the direction of the archangel Gabriel.)

The revelations usually concerned issues at hand. When Muhammad was in Mecca, where his new followers were struggling to develop a strong foundation for their faith, the content revolved around monotheism, virtuous living, and the eventual triumph of Islam, even though it was a persecuted religion. Later in Medina, when Islam had become settled into the life of the city, laws and social dictates were the core of the message. Sometimes non-Muslims would challenge Muhammad to talk about arcane subjects that they knew he wouldn't know anything about, and suddenly a revelation would come explaining the matter. For example, a group of people in Medina asked him about Joseph and his adventures in Egypt, trying to stump him. An entire chapter of over a hundred verses (called *Surah Yusuf*) was revealed right there in answer.

Muhammad described four ways in which he received revelations from God. The first was through dreams at night, when the verses of the Qur'an were implanted in his mind. The second was through instantaneous revelations in his heart during the day. The third way, which he said was the hardest to bear, was foreshadowed by a loud ringing sound in his ears and then the verses would flow. The last way involved the archangel Gabriel appearing as a man, sometimes visible to other people and sometimes not, who would then instruct Muhammad in what to say. God never appeared to Muhammad, for Islam says that God is too exalted to show Himself to us as if for our inspection.

Style and Content

One of the many features of the Qur'an that Muslims consider miraculous is its style. Muhammad was not known to be a man of poetry before the Qur'an began to flow from his lips. He also never participated in the oral poetry contests that were a mainstay of life throughout Arabia. Yet this same man suddenly began to recite what is still considered today to be the greatest book in the Arabic language. The use of lucidly phrased metaphors, the flow of the text, and the engaging syntax are held up as the highest standard for Arabic lexicographers, and no other book is so highly esteemed from a grammarian's standpoint.

How is the Qur'an's unique style expressed? To answer this question, we need to look at two areas: presentation and content. The Qur'an employs a variety of literary mechanisms, from straight line-by-line or metered rhyming to flowing prose and passionate essays. Through a skilled mixture of the different techniques, the listener is taken on a rapturous ride through feelings, thoughts, emotions, and dreams. The opening verses of Chapter 36 of the Qur'an provide an example. In this *surah*, entitled

Ya Seen, we read the opening verses in transliteration. The underlined words show the repetition of sounds:

> Ya Seen. Wal Qur'anil <u>Hakeem</u>. Innaka lamin al <u>Mursaleen</u>. 'Alaa siratim <u>Mustaqeem</u>. Tanzilul 'azeezil <u>Raheem</u>. Le tunzera qawman ma unthera aba-uhum fa hum <u>ghawfiloon</u>. La qad haqqal qawlu 'alaa ak tharihim fahum la <u>yu-minoon</u>.

If you noticed the transition from one rhyme to another, you can see how the Qur'an can continually engage the ear of its listeners with something fresh and new. For this reason, Muslims never consider a translation of the Qur'an as equal to the Arabic text. The Qur'an itself makes a note of this unique style and its purpose when it declares that it is a book that is easy to remember. In longer passages you will find quite a lot of transition in style over the course of many different topics. (Although some Western scholars have criticized this literary technique, it is in fact one of the strengths of the Qur'an, distinguishing it from all other Holy Books.) When the Qur'an is recited out loud by a skilled reader, its beauty can move listeners to tears. (Qur'an reciting contests are held every year all over the Muslim world with the most important ones being in Malaysia and Saudi Arabia.)

DISPELLING THE MYTH

One of the most adept poets of the Arabs, Tufayl ibn Amr Ad-Dawsi, wanted to investigate what he had heard about Muhammad and the Qur'an, so he went to Mecca and asked Muhammad to recite some of it to him. After listening to it he exclaimed, "I swear by God, I have never heard such beautiful words before."

The second miraculous aspect of the Qur'an concerns its content. The Qur'an covers a variety of subjects, including religious doctrine, law, social values, morality, history, prophets and their struggles, philosophy, and science. Without containing a single unified narrative on any of those subjects, the Qur'an skillfully weaves components of each into self-contained chapters that reference one and then the other to provide coherent essays appealing to a variety of listeners.

Muhammad never went to school. During his life he never read a book, nor was he ever tutored or engaged in learning of any kind. Then suddenly, when he turned 40 years old, the epitome of eloquence flows from his tongue? This is quite inexplicable. Only a century ago, Western scholars of Islam were claiming that Muhammad had epilepsy (which is not true) and that the Qur'an came during seizures. Do epileptics conjure rapturous poems and essays in such states? Other Westerners have charged that Muhammad made up the Qur'an, though they can't explain how. But as Dr. Maurice Bucaille observed, in refuting those who have suggested that Muhammad wrote the Qur'an himself, "How could a man, from being illiterate, become the most important author, in terms of literary merits, in the whole of Arabic literature?" Muslims would say that it is no less than direct revelation from God.

Meccan and Medinan Revelations

The verses of the Qur'an are divided into two main categories based on the period of the Prophet's mission in which they were revealed. The first 13 years of prophethood were spent in Mecca, a hostile environment for the Muslims in which the reigning idolaters made life miserable for the new religion and its followers. The second period began with the *Hijrah*, or migration to Medina, when Islam became the dominant force in city politics and thus was no longer directly under fire.

Meccan revelations, as they are called, center on two main themes: confronting backward Arab tribal customs and pointing out the foolishness of idolatry. Some of the customs that the Qur'an spoke out against are as follows:

- Burying unwanted baby girls alive (infanticide)
- Believing in superstition and practicing witchcraft
- Men inheriting their widowed mothers as wives of their own
- Blindly following tradition for its own sake

The campaign against idolatry was especially urgent because the Qur'anic revelations were making it increasingly clear that the shrine of Abraham, the *Ka'bah*, was no place to store 360 tribal idols. Mecca was so decadent that idolaters often circled the *Ka'bah* naked, paying homage to their idols. The Qur'an mentioned specifically three gods that the Arabs worshipped and called such practices idiocy. Instead of praying to lesser gods for daily benefits and luck, Islam asserted, why not pray to the only true God, Allah?

Understandably, the Meccans didn't take kindly to Muhammad's preaching and teaching, and they began to harass the Muslims daily. Muhammad was often punched and shoved in the streets. Once he was almost strangled to death by an irate Meccan near the *Ka'bah*. Other Muslims were brutally tortured, and a few were murdered. (The first martyr of Islam was a woman who refused to go back to idol worship.)

Consequently, Meccan revelations also contain the stories of past prophets who suffered hardships; this was a way to show Muhammad and his followers that others also endured rough times, but God's help eventually saved them.

Medinan revelations, or those delivered to Muhammad after he and his followers escaped Mecca, were concerned with how to build an Islamic society. The values and manners of Islam and the particulars of Islamic Law grew in importance and application. Verses regulating inheritance, marriage and divorce, the conduct of statecraft, civil laws, and criminal punishments made an appearance. An extensive collection of verses on relations with Jews and Christians was given as well. It was also during this period that alcoholic beverages were made illegal. But by this time Muslims were so staunch in their faith that they had no problem in smashing their wine vessels in the streets. This is one Prohibition that didn't fail.

The Compilation

The Qur'an was an oral message given to Muhammad through the archangel Gabriel. Muhammad himself couldn't write, so he asked his literate followers to be his secretaries. Even in the earliest days of Mecca, the Qur'an was being recorded. Paper was unknown in Arabia at that time, so the materials used consisted of Egyptian parchment, leather scrolls, and the shoulder blades of camels (which were sort of like large slates). During the Medinan period, the entire collection of written *surahs* was kept in a large leather bag in the possession of the Prophet. At one time the Prophet had over 20 secretaries writing down his words.

There was no need to put everything together in book form because the tradition established by the Prophet was for people to memorize as much of the Qur'an by heart as possible. By the time of the Prophet's death, hundreds of people had memorized the entire book in its properly arranged order. Nearly everyone else knew at least significant portions by heart. And with the Prophet's emphasis on literacy, more people than ever before were learning how to read and write, so written pages of Qur'anic verse began to circulate far and wide.

During the rule of the first Muslim caliph, Abu Bakr, a rebellion arose in southern Arabia, and during one battle more than 70 of the most prominent memorizers were killed. Umar ibn al Khattab, one of the top companions of Muhammad, prevailed upon Abu Bakr to prepare the Qur'an in a single book form so that its proper order and reading would never be lost. This was done under the meticulous supervision of the Prophet's chief secretary, Zayd bin Thabit, who was able to utilize newly introduced paper products from China. The book was kept in the care of one of the Prophet's widows and no more thought was given to the issue.

Later on, during the rule of the third Muslim caliph, Usman ibn Affan, non-Arab converts began arguing about the proper way to pronounce the verses of the Qur'an as well as the meanings of the words contained within. They even began writing personal copies, incorporating their own variant spellings, arrangements, and pronunciations of words. The problem became so serious that some of the old-time companions of the Prophet thought the Qur'an might be lost in a sea of competing versions. Usman acted decisively and ordered that the official edition, prepared in the time of his predecessor, Abu Bakr, be verified and duplicated, and one copy of it sent to every major Muslim city. Again, Zayd bin Thabit was given the responsibility for this task, and he headed a team of four who had committed the Qur'an to memory to ensure the utmost veracity. From the five or seven copies that they prepared, scribes in the far-flung regions of the Empire could make further copies, so all controversies and disagreements would be laid to rest. All the faulty copies people had made themselves were to be burned so that only the authenticated edition would circulate.

DEFINITION

A **Hafiz** is a person who has committed the entire Qur'an to memory. The name literally means a *Guardian*. The Holy Qur'an is the most memorized book in the world.

Two copies of those *Usmani Qur'ans*, as they are called, exist to this day in museums in Turkey and Tashkent. They have exactly the same text as any Arabic Qur'an today. To those who have suggested that the Qur'an we have today is not completely in line with the one Muhammad recited, the reply is simple: All of the people who were involved in recording the Qur'an both during and after Muhammad's time were memorizers of the book. In addition, there were hundreds of other such people who would have noticed any alterations in the text.

The Teachings of the Prophet

"O You who believe," the Qur'an exhorts, "obey Allah and obey the Messenger." In another verse we read, "You have a beautiful pattern to follow in the Messenger of Allah." These are just two of the many *ayahs*, or verses, that tell Muslims to follow the teachings of the Prophet Muhammad. But isn't the Qur'an one such teaching? The Islamic answer is no. The Qur'an is God's literal Word merely transmitted through the mouthpiece of Muhammad. The Prophet's teachings are something else entirely. This is why the *Shahadah*, or Islamic Declaration of Faith, has two parts—in order to remind people of this.

Muhammad's life example, called his *Sunnah*, or Way, represents his own interpretation of how to live by the dictates of the Qur'an. One often-used example concerns the five daily prayers of Islam. The Qur'an tells Muslims simply to pray at fixed times, but it doesn't tell them how to pray. It mentions nothing about reciting *surahs*, bowing at the waist, saying certain phrases, and so on. These the Prophet taught in his own words. The archangel Gabriel, Muslims believe, was providing Muhammad with guidance on this and all other issues, but the knowledge was filtered through Muhammad's speech, experiences, and actions. Thus the *Sunnah* of Muhammad is considered to be the second most important source of Islam.

FROM THE SOURCE

Muhammad, during his last major public address, said, "I'm leaving you with two things. If you hold fast to them you will never go astray. They are the Book of Allah and my Sunnah."

How Are Hadiths Different from the Qur'an?

The Qur'an contains verses that have their own style. From rhymes to prose, there is a certain way that the information is presented and certain types of grammar constructions. Muhammad's own sayings, or hadiths, which form the basis of the *Sunnah*, are what he said on a daily basis in the course of normal life. When he spoke to people of his own volition, he neither rhymed nor recited in a melodious voice. Here is an example of the difference in style. The first selection is a verse from the Qur'an. The second two selections are well-known hadiths of the Prophet, taken from the collection of the ninth-century scholar Imam Bukhari.

Qur'an:

O You who believe, shall I lead you to a bargain that will save you from a painful doom? It is that you believe in Allah and His Messenger and then strive in His cause with your wealth and your persons. That is best for you if you only knew. (61:10–11)

Hadiths:

The older a person gets the more his desire for two things increases: wealth and longevity. (Bukhari)

Learning is a duty on every Muslim, male and female. (Bukhari)

As you can see, the Qur'an contains a distinctly religious tone while the hadiths are more like statements or pronouncements such as an orator might make or a teacher might say to his or her students.

DEFINITION

A **hadith** is classified as anything the Prophet Muhammad said, did, or gave silent approval to.

Who Recorded the Hadiths?

During the Meccan period and early Medinan period, Muhammad used to forbid his followers to write down his personal sayings for fear that people would mix them up with the Qur'an. Near the end of his life, however, when the sanctity of the Qur'an was secure and lots of people knew the entire Qur'an by heart, he relaxed this prohibition. Many of his followers began to write down what they had learned from him on a variety of topics.

One of the earliest collections of Muhammad's sayings to have survived to this day is called the *Muwatta of Imam Malik*, which was written in Medina within 80 years of Muhammad's death and draws on many firsthand witnesses and the children of those who lived and worshipped in the Prophet's time. Given that most early Muslims could still not read or write, though, a large majority of the Prophet's sayings were passed on orally from parent to child for several generations. As the population increased and the movement of people became more pronounced, many of those who knew or who had learned the oral hadith traditions became scattered.

Starting in the late seventh century, but gaining real momentum by the eighth, scholars who wanted to collect these elusive sayings and preserve them for later generations began traveling all over the Muslim Empire looking for people who had these hadiths or who had learned them from others. One of the early Caliphs, Umar ibn Abdul Aziz (who ruled from 717–720), actually commissioned a historian to compile the Prophet's sayings in an official public record. He was just one of many Muslims who began to look seriously into this task.

Because there are always dishonest people and forgetful ones, these early scholars developed a system for sifting through the collected data to determine whether a hadith was authentic or fabricated. This process involved a grueling investigation into the genealogy of the person giving the hadith, focusing on the moral character of the narrator and whom he or she had heard it from, and so on. If any discrepancy was found, the hadith would be labeled as not fully reliable or even false. All of this information is recorded as a chain (called an *isnad*) going back to the original person who heard the hadith from the Prophet.

DISPELLING THE MYTH

Imam Bukhari (d. 870), the most famous collector of hadiths, gathered more than 600,000 hadiths but included only 2,602 in his official book because the rest he could not prove with sufficient certainty that the Prophet said them.

Imam Bukhari, considered by Sunni Muslims to be the foremost authority of hadith who ever lived, heard that there was a man in a far-off land who had a unique hadith. The Imam traveled for weeks to reach the man's city and asked where this person could be found. When the Imam approached the man's house, he saw him trying to coax his donkey to move by pretending he had food in his hand. The Imam concluded that the man was a liar and left without ever speaking to him.

The 'Ulema: Scholars of the Faith

The body of Islamic knowledge is quite extensive. Areas of study can include Arabic grammar, the Qur'an, the hadiths, Islamic Law, biographies of the *sahaba*, philosophy, interfaith dialogue, the life history of Muhammad, and political and economic theory. Most people don't have the time to delve very deeply into these subjects, so religious scholars fill the gaps in knowledge. The difference between Islam and other religious traditions, however, is that Muslim scholars (the *'Ulema*) are not charged with formulating new doctrines. Rather, they organize and interpret the data given in the Qur'an and the hadiths.

The only areas in which new additions to Islamic Law can be made are those involving an unexpected issue that confronts the Muslim community. For example, how does Islam view test tube babies or cryogenic freezing or even organ transplantation? Islamic scholars, who often work independently of each other under little to no regulation, consult a descending order of sources to arrive at an answer that is within the general spirit of Islam. This is called the science of *Fiqh*, or deducing legal positions. The four sources consulted are …

- The Qur'an (the word of God).
- The hadiths (the basis of the Prophet's *Sunnah*).
- The consensus of the *sahaba* on an issue (*'Ijma*).
- Independent reasoning or analogy (*Qiyas*).

In the last source, the scholar himself or herself tries to come up with an answer from his or her own logic and ability to reason. Sometimes scholars have to get very creative to provide answers for the community. The word *Ijtehad* is the name for this process of coming up with definitive rulings that rely on a lot of independent thought. It is through this process that the corpus of Islamic Law is a living, breathing institution that can adapt to any age or circumstance. Recent legal rulings, called *fatwas*, have declared that it is allowed to say the call to prayer over a loudspeaker, to perform prayers in a spacecraft, to donate organs, and to trade stocks that are not connected with vice.

DISPELLING THE MYTH

There is no prohibition against women being scholars in Islam. Throughout Islamic history until this day, many famous *'Ulema* have been females revered for their learning and sagacity. Because there is no clergy in Islam, only a society of scholars, the certifying authority is widespread from recognized Islamic colleges.

Early Theologians

Not everyone is qualified to issue *fatwas* or engage in *Ijtehad*. Although no central hierarchy exists among Muslim scholars, such as in the Roman Catholic Church with its ecclesiastical structure, there are certain recognized qualifications for being accepted as a religious authority in Islam. A person has to study in an accepted Islamic university or with a graduate who has been given permission to teach higher studies. Such independent teachers are often called *shaykhs*, an old Arabic term that means chief or leader. People who complete programs of study, which usually last about five years, are given a certificate called an *'Ijazah*, the equivalent of what we would call a Master's degree in Islamic studies.

Some of the most famous *sahaba* of the past and their students are still remembered by Muslims. Names like *Hassan al Basri* and *A'ishah bint Abi Bakr* are spoken of with reverence. It was during this early generation that the teachings of Islam were systematized and made more comprehensible to the masses. All of the major Islamic sciences from *Fiqh* to Arabic lexicography were initiated within the first two centuries of the Islamic expansion. The foundation of this knowledge still defines traditional Islamic education today.

The Five Imams

The science of *Fiqh* was initiated by a variety of concerned scholars in the first centuries of Islam. They often worked together at first but then formulated their legal processes of *Ijtehad* independently. Each scholar attracted numbers of students who carried on the work after their founder's passing. These growing legal traditions attempted to explain the teachings and application of Islam to the masses.

This service was necessary because many verses of the Qur'an can be interpreted in different ways. In addition, some of the hadiths are vague or even confusing for the average person to understand. Because people see things differently, each of these schools of thought, or *madh-habs*, varied slightly in its findings. When talking about issues of *Ijtehad* where no clear-cut Islamic answer is available, the amount of disagreement can increase. For example, the Qur'an declares that Muslims are allowed to eat "flesh from the sea." Some scholars thought this meant only fish, while others included clams, crustaceans, and anything else that lives under the water. Although the *madh-habs* agree on more than 80 percent of the issues related to Islamic beliefs and practices, it's over the peripheral issues that disagreement and controversy sometimes ensue.

Each of these schools of thought began to be known by the name of its founder. The four *Sunni* and one *Shi'a* (for an explanation of the differences between these two major sects of Islam see Chapter 26) *madh-hab* that have survived to this day are as follows:

The Hanafi   Founded by Abu Hanifa (700–767). He emphasized reason and analogy in the development of Islamic Law.

The Shafi   Founded by Muhammad Al Shafi'I (767–820). He was the first to classify the four main sources of Islamic Law ranging from the Qur'an and *hadith* to *Ijma* and *Qiyas*.

The Maliki   Founded by Malik ibn Anas, the author of Al Muwatta (716–795). Imam Malik emphasized the importance of following the legal traditions of Medina.

The Hanbali   Founded by Ahmed ibn Hanbal (780–855). This is the most conservative of the surviving four schools of Sunni Islamic Law. Ibn Hanbal crafted his understanding of Islam in response to a new Muslim ideology based on rationalism. The Wahhabi movement, which has governed Saudi Arabia for almost two centuries, favors this stricter school of *Fiqh*.

The Ja'fari   Founded by Imam Ja'far as Sadiq (699–765). This is the principle Shi'a school of Islamic Law and is not recognized as valid by more conservative scholars of the Sunni tradition. A majority of its principles conform to those of the other schools of thought, though there are significant differences.

Muslims everywhere generally adhere to one of these five schools of thought, taking all of their questions about how to follow Islam to the scholars and manuals produced by each. Most Muslim countries have areas of concentration in which the majority of the people follow one or the other. The modus operandi that has prevailed for centuries between the adherents of each legal tradition has been that all are valid legal paths to being a good Muslim, so no one should criticize another's *madh-hab*. Muslims commonly identify themselves by the legal tradition they follow.

The Least You Need to Know

- Muslims consider the Qur'an to be the literal Word of God dictated to Muhammad by the archangel Gabriel.

- The sayings of the Prophet are considered secondary in status to the Qur'an. The details of how to practice Islam are given in the hadiths.

- The companions of the Prophet are those who carried the message of Islam forward both before and after Muhammad's death. Muslims revere them as examples of strong faith.

- Islam is interpreted for everyday Muslims by scholars. A scholar in Islam is similar in status to a theologian in Christianity and Judaism, with the exception that a scholar does not create doctrines.

- Muslim scholars are considered to be the authorities on Islam but are not considered holy in the same way a priest or rabbi is. Women can become scholars in Islam as well.

Living Islam

In This Chapter

- Learn about the Islamic view of family and marriage
- Step into a mosque and look around at what's inside
- Discover the ceremonies that mark the passage of life for Muslims
- Mark the holidays of Islam and discover their significance
- Find out what Muslims can and cannot do
- Learn about the dietary restrictions that affect every aspect of Muslim life

Islam is not just a religious or spiritual discipline. It also provides guidance for every aspect of a person's life both at home and out in society. The very basis of a healthy community, after reforming one's own self, is the family. "Save yourselves and your families," declares the Qur'an, and this theme encompasses a large part of a Muslim's life. Islam holds that the best places to be are in the home or in the mosque; when out in the world at large, one had better avoid the many snares and traps of *Shaytan*.

But Islam is not a dowdy religion, consigning its followers to just praying, fasting, and staying out of trouble. It is also a community experience, and wholesome activities to celebrate life are not only encouraged but religiously mandated. People should come out to mingle and build stronger bonds among themselves. For this reason Islam promotes public ceremonies to mark the passage of life-changing events. There are also two annual holidays for people to come together in joy and merriment. In this chapter, I show you the familial and social aspects of Islam.

Islam and the Family

Islam has a definite conception of the ideal family life. The Qur'an describes the relationship between a husband and a wife as "two garments that protect each other." Both have equal status as adults, and neither is encouraged to lord it over the other. With that said, Islam also assigns the husband the role of the head of the family. It doesn't mean that the husband is to be the dictator of the family, though, but rather the caretaker of everyone's safety and well-being. Consequently, on Judgment Day a man will have to answer for how he shepherded, cared for, guided, and provided for his family.

DISPELLING THE MYTH

Although there are patterns of discrimination against women evident in some conservative Muslim societies, according to longstanding Islamic legal theory, women are allowed to work outside the home, are entitled to an education, and can hold positions of authority over men in the workplace. The only caveat is that a mother is encouraged to put her family first before a career, but this is not a legal requirement in Islamic Law.

As the Qur'an itself explains: "Men are the appointed protectors and maintainers of women because Allah has given them more responsibility than them." (Qur'an 4:34) Never are men called smarter, more deserving, or more capable than women. They are simply given the responsibility to work (and the added physical strength to go along with it) so that women have a greater freedom to make choices that will ensure they don't need to sacrifice their family life for the sake of supporting themselves. Looked at from a certain angle, God has eternally doomed men to work for women!

Muslims take Muhammad's experiences with his extended household as examples of how interfamilial relationships can be conducted. Muhammad's marriage to Khadijah lasted for over 20 years, and he had no other wife during this time. Khadijah is held up as the ideal wife—caring, supportive, and compassionate. With her prowess in economic affairs, she helped to fund the Prophet's activities. A year after her death, Muhammad's companions encouraged him to marry again, so he married an older widow who had no support. He would later take more wives, widows mostly, for the same charitable and kindly reasons. During those years people frequently asked his wives about how he treated them and what he did around the house. Besides praying quite often, they reported, he was always friendly, kind, helpful, and never overbearing or demanding. Thus, ample opportunity existed for people to see how a prophet coexisted with his family.

The Ties That Bind

Islam envisions a society in which people are connected on many levels. Families are united, and divorce is rare. Communities are made up of settled people who look out for each other, and everyone attends the mosque regularly. As such, the ties of neighbors are continually strengthened. If one household is in need, others step forward to assist. Crime is rare, and the citizens are literate and thoughtful. Has such a utopian vision ever existed? Actually, for a large chunk of Islamic history, many communities functioning around the world have come close to this ideal.

When Muslims look at modern society with all of its problems, they sometimes get the urge to become insular. Issues such as abortion, teen pregnancy, rampant promiscuity, dating, drug addiction, violent youth culture, and alcoholism were virtually unknown in the traditional Muslim world until recently. One of the reasons for the growth of Islamic parochial schools in North America is the alarming trends that seem to be tearing apart American society. Do Muslims claim that Islam has the answers to these problems? Yes; but in the meantime, few Muslims are willing to allow their families to assimilate into the more negative aspects of modern culture.

The Ideal Muslim Home

In an Islamic home the father is a responsible man who works hard for his family. He is neither arrogant nor cruel and shows tender kindness to his family. Toward his wife, he is loving, and he caters to her sexual needs through caressing and tenderness. These symbols of intimate affection were described by the Prophet as the *ambassadors*, which must come before intimate relations. He is never alone with another woman, even at work, and he consults his family on all major decisions. He does not physically or emotionally abuse his wife because he knows the Prophet Muhammad never hit or disrespected a woman in his whole life. The children are obedient and respect their father completely. Their greatest shame is to cause their father to become angry.

The wife is cooperative with her husband in all things that require a team effort. She is not a slave, a servant, nor a second-class citizen. She is her own person with her own financial assets, hobbies, and interests. The Qur'an describes the relationship between a man and wife as that of helpers to each other. The Prophet Muhammad said that mothers deserve three times the respect as that given to fathers, and this is on account of the sacrifices women make for their families. With that said, the wife understands the grave responsibility upon her husband's shoulders, for on Judgment Day the father will bear the blame for any failures to protect his family.

She doesn't refuse his sexual advances so as not to alienate him, and she doesn't have any friends that he dislikes. She upholds his reputation and doesn't spill his secrets in public. Though she may work if she wishes, her money is her own. She would never sacrifice her children's moral, physical, and emotional needs, however, solely for the sake of personal goals. She doesn't wear much makeup in public or dress specifically to attract other men's eyes, and she looks forward to Paradise, which is promised to those women who are sincere helpmates to their husbands.

Spare the Rod

How should a child be raised according to Islam? The answer is best expressed in the words of the Prophet Muhammad, who said that when children are under the age of 7, we should be easy with them. From the ages of 7 to 14, we should be strict with them, and after 14 we should be their friend. This three-stage developmental process takes into account every level of intellectual and emotional capacity. Small children don't always understand what they're doing, so punishment must be withheld as much as possible. Teenagers are prone to trouble, so a firm hand is in order; after puberty, Islam considers a person an adult.

It is the responsibility of the parents to rear their children properly and to teach them manners, religious obligations, and worldly knowledge. Abu Bakr, a famous companion of the Prophet, once noted that the child who is taught to be good at an early age has an easier time being virtuous later on in life. Another famous companion, 'Ali ibn Abi Talib, once counseled, "Raise your children differently from how you were raised because they are meant for a different time than you."

The Prophet Muhammad, whose *Sunnah* is considered the ideal model for all Muslims, used to hug and kiss his children and grandchildren and always made time to play with them. He also did not complain about what they did. Anas bin Malik, who as a boy came to serve the aged Prophet, later remarked, "I served the Prophet for 10 years and never once did he say, 'Why did you do this?' or 'Why did you do that?'"

FROM THE SOURCE

According to Muhammad, "Paradise lies under the feet of mothers."

Welcome to My Mosque

The mosque, or *masjid*, is the focal point of the Islamic community. It is open for the five daily prayers, and Muslims routinely congregate there for prayer, meditation, and reflection. In the Prophet's day, the main mosque of Medina was used for community meetings, planning sessions, and even as a homeless shelter for the poor people who embraced Islam and needed a place to stay for the night.

In North America today, the mosque still retains many of its traditional functions. Community dinners are usually a monthly occurrence. Weddings and funeral prayers are often performed there as well. A new innovation that is common mostly to mosques in the Western world is the addition of a weekend school for the children of the congregation's members. On Saturdays or Sundays, children attend the school to learn about the fundamentals of their religion and to socialize with other children of similar backgrounds.

There are currently over 2,000 mosques spread all across Canada, the United States, and Mexico. Most have congregations numbering less than a thousand, but a few serve several thousand people annually. Most mosques are operated by an elected body whose terms are limited. Unlike most Christian churches or Jewish synagogues, however, the public leadership of a mosque usually lies with a president, director, or chairman of the board while the post of Imam (a traditional title for a prayer leader) is limited to leading prayers, performing weddings and funerals, and teaching religious classes. In the past most Imams were imported from overseas but with the rise of an indigenous number of Islamic scholars and activists one can find increasing numbers of American-born Imams in our nation's mosques.

What Happens in a Mosque?

The main activities one finds in a mosque are prayer and teaching. The most attended prayer, of course, is the Friday service called *Salat ul-Jumu'ah*, or the prayer of gathering. It is an obligation on all Muslim men over the age of puberty to attend. Women are allowed and encouraged to attend as well, though there is no sin recorded for them if they pray at home. This is a mercy owing to the fact that many women have child-rearing responsibilities, such as breastfeeding and the like.

Hyper-spiritual Muslims, who are known as *Sufis*, sometimes sit in large circles in mosques and chant Islamic phrases and the names of God in unison. Other Muslims simply go to the mosque to read and study the Qur'an in a quiet atmosphere. Loud shouting and calling out are frowned upon, and men are encouraged to apply scented cologne when they arrive. (Women are asked to wear more-muted perfumes that do not surround them in an envelope of scents so as not to attract undue male interest.)

When the time for any particular prayer arrives, the *muazzin* gives a shortened version of the prayer call and people arrange themselves in straight rows behind the Imam. Men line up in the front rows, followed by rows of children, and finally the women line up behind. There is no gender discrimination here, as was explained in Chapter 11. With all the bowing and prostrating that goes on, it is best that the sexes are not mixed together.

DISPELLING THE MYTH

Although non-Islamic backward cultural practices in some Muslim countries result in women being discouraged from attending public religious services, Muhammad said, "Do not prevent the female servants of Allah from going to the mosque."

Friday, the Day of Gathering

On Fridays, Muslims all over the world attend a half-hour service in which they listen to a two-part speech, which is then followed up by a group prayer. The service is held in the early afternoon, and many Muslims in North America are forced to ask their employers for an extra-long lunch break on Fridays. This is because *Salat ul-Jumu'ah*, as it is called, is classified as a religious duty upon men. The Qur'an states:

> O you who believe! When the call for prayer is made on Friday, hasten to the remembrance of Allah and cease your business. That is better for you if you but knew. (Qur'an 62:9)

Friday is not considered like a Sabbath day or a day of rest. Muslims are asked to stop working and come together as a community for less than an hour and then they can go back about their business. It's really quite interesting that in some Muslim countries where there are large Christian populations, the governments usually designate Friday and Sunday as weekend days, with Saturday being a workday. Other nations keep the traditional Western days of Saturday and Sunday for rest and merely mandate that for the time of Friday prayers workers can get a break in the workday.

What Is an Imam?

An *Imam* is a person who leads the prayer in the mosque. It is a term sometimes applied to the leader of the community, as well. Basically, an Imam serves a function similar to that of a priest or rabbi. He conducts religious services, performs marriages and funerals, gives counseling, and teaches adult and children's classes. An Imam gains his position by first completing a course of study in a recognized Islamic college. Then he is hired by the mosque's board of directors and retained on salary. Imams are not considered holy men, nor are they ordained in official ceremonies like functionaries in other religions. Their status is based on their learning and piety and nothing more.

Ceremonies for Life

Islam provides a way for people to mark the passage of time with rites and ceremonies. No one would deny that significant events require special recognition, and neither does Islam. The traditions for marriages, births, and funerals were all taught by Prophet Muhammad and personally conducted by him for the community on numerous occasions. This section introduces the three ceremonies that Islam recognizes.

Nikah: Marriage in Islam

Nikah is the word for marriage in Islam. It is considered a civil contract between a man and a woman for the purpose of forming a family and engaging in marital relations that are allowed and wholesome. It is not considered a religious sacrament. The Prophet encouraged people to get married as soon as they were financially able so that the "raging hormone syndrome" can be satisfied within the bounds of marriage. Ideally, young men and women should get married any time between the completion of puberty and their late twenties.

No dating in the traditional sense is allowed in Islam, so how do prospective partners meet? This question often comes up in public presentations of Islam. It may surprise you to learn that dating was unknown in America just a hundred years ago. Prior to the modern anything-goes era, people used to be paired up by relatives and matchmakers and through contact at social functions or in school. Islam employs a similar mechanism for getting people together. When a match is found, marriages usually take place in either mosques or in community halls.

Aqiqah: Welcoming Baby

The arrival of a new baby brings joy to any family. Islam has a way to cement that joy in a ritual called the *Aqiqah*, or Welcoming Consecration, which is held seven days after birth. When a baby is first delivered, the father or mother whispers the Islamic call to prayer in the newborn's ear, welcoming the baby into the life of the world where the responsibility to respond to Allah's call is greatest. A bit of mashed date is then lovingly fed to the baby by custom, and a supplication for its good fortune in life is made.

On the seventh day after birth the actual *Aqiqah* ceremony takes place. Families gather for a special dinner. A sheep or goat is ritually sacrificed (usually at a butcher shop), and the meat is cooked and served to the guests. A portion is also donated to the poor. The baby's hair is shaved off, and its weight in silver is given in charity. People congratulate the parents on their newborn and give gifts for the baby of money, toys, or clothes.

Janazah: Muslim Funerary Rites

The Muslim funeral procedure is conducted with a unique frame of mind. Islam teaches that death is merely a doorway into the third stage of life, our time in the grave until Judgment Day. Consequently, the traditional condolence to the bereaved is, "To God we belong and to Him we return." While sincere crying and sorrow are allowed for the mourners, loud wailing and the tearing of clothes is forbidden.

The body is usually brought to a mosque for the special funeral prayer, known as the *Janazah*, but it can be performed anywhere. It takes about five minutes to perform, and the words that the mourners recite silently to themselves center on asking God to forgive the deceased and all those who have passed away before him or her.

Completing the Qur'an

There is a very common unofficial ceremony practiced throughout most of the Muslim world called Khatmi-Qur'an, or Sealing the Qur'an. This is a celebration to mark a child's completion of their first full reading of the Qur'anic text in Arabic. It usually takes up to two years under the guidance of a teacher for children to master the proper pronunciation and to read the text clearly from the first verse to the last. Most children complete the Qur'an between the ages of four and seven. This celebration is called an Ameen Ceremony in Southeast Asia. The ceremony usually involves a dinner and presentation by the child who is being honored.

Islamic Holidays

There are two main holidays in Islam. Each comes after an important Islamic ritual and is supposed to remind the celebrant of the meaning and joy of what was just accomplished. The first holiday comes after the end of Ramadan, and the second after the *Hajj* is completed.

Ramadan and *'Eid ul Fitr*

The after-Ramadan celebration known as the *'Eid ul Fitr* (Festival of the Fast Breaking) is the most popular holiday in Islam. For obvious reasons, being released from a month-long, dawn-to-dusk fast can make people quite happy. The first day of the *'Eid* begins in the mosque with a special morning prayer service, which consists of a short congregational prayer followed by a two-part sermon reminding people of the lessons they should remember from Ramadan for the rest of the year. The *'Eid* festivities officially last for three days, and Muslims hold parties on each of the days. In some places carnivals are held. Special *'Eid* sweets are prepared, and children are given gifts.

After the *Hajj:* *'Eid ul Adha*

The second official holiday in Islam is known as *'Eid ul Adha*, or Festival of the Sacrifice. It comes at the end of the *Hajj* ritual in Mecca (see Chapter 13). No special religious rites connected to the *Hajj*'s events are held in the rest of the Muslim world, as the rituals are confined to Mecca, so this holiday is usually more muted in tone. The lesson of the *Hajj* is about sacrificing what we love for God's sake, and sermons in the mosques usually relate to this theme. The special prayer service and three-day celebration are carried out in the same fashion as for the other *'Eid*.

Halal and *Haram:* What Can a Muslim Do?

Islam classifies all actions by their merit or sinfulness. The rule in the *Shari'ah*, or Islamic Law, is that everything is allowed except what is expressly forbidden. Allowed activities for a Muslim are called *halal*, while prohibited ones are labeled *haram*. In keeping with the Islamic spirit of planning for all eventualities, there are two other main categories by which actions can be judged. These are things permissible, though not encouraged; and things disliked, though not sinful. In this section, I will explain many of these types of deeds and what Islam says about the performance of each.

The Muslim Kosher Standard

Food is one of the most important elements of our daily lives. Islam is concerned with both what we eat and how much we consume. Some types of food are *haram*, and thus Muslims, like observant Jews, must watch what they eat. Although the Muslim *halal* food standard is not nearly as strict as the Jewish kosher requirement, it is nonetheless quite rigorous. The main features of Muslim dietary restrictions are as follows:

- A Muslim can eat anything that is not forbidden or harmful.
- Animals must be ritually slaughtered by either the Muslim *zabiha* or the Jewish kosher standard.
- Pork products are forbidden, because pigs are considered unclean, as in Judaism.
- Seafood is generally allowed.
- Ingredients derived from animals such as gelatin and enzymes must be *zabiha* or kosher.

Islam Forbids Intoxicants

Islam is famous for forbidding its followers all alcoholic beverages. Wine, beer, whisky, and the like are off-limits. There is a reason for this, and the evidence is all around us in our families, communities, and nation. Drunkenness leads to violence, ill health, recklessness, family breakup, and despair. Drunk driving is one of the leading causes of death today, and a large portion of domestic violence, rape, and crime is due to the scourge of alcohol. But it doesn't stop there. Islam takes a stand on drug abuse as well.

Once a companion asked the Prophet if people were allowed to chew a certain narcotic leaf found in southern Arabia. Muhammad asked about its effects on people, and when he was told them he declared that anything that intoxicates the mind is *haram* for a Muslim. Consequently, Islamic scholars are unanimous in declaring mind-altering drugs prohibited.

FROM THE SOURCE

They ask you about drinking and gambling. Tell them: "There is both harm and benefit in them, but the harm is greater than the benefit." (Qur'an 2:219)

To go even further, Muhammad explained that anyone who buys, transports, sells, carries, serves, or stores intoxicants is equally as guilty as the consumer and is cursed by God. Even glasses specifically made for alcohol such as wine glasses and brandy bottles are illegal. Muslims are the only people in the world who can proudly state that prohibition does work if you change the hearts of the people first.

Gambling

Islam forbids all forms of gambling and games of chance in which monetary rewards are at stake, equating them with being a trick from *Shaytan* to keep people's minds off God. Any winnings are considered funds gotten unfairly, while any losses are held to be foolish setbacks that should have been avoided. Lotto, betting, poker, and all other forms of gambling are labeled as sins. Other types of activities, such as games of skill, are allowed. So go for that ring toss at the carnival in confidence, but avoid the slot machine at all costs!

Music and Islam

There is quite a lot of debate in the Muslim world today about the permissibility of music and singing in Islam. Given the rise of pop music in the last several decades, almost to the status of a religion among teenagers, you can well imagine the conversation in most Muslim homes at night. ("Why can't I go to that concert, Mom?") The reason that music is a concern at all in Islam has to do with its effects on people. When a person is caught up in a song, he or she is oblivious to most everything else. Songs also teach, and the lessons may not be the most proper ones to learn. What is generally agreed upon by Muslims is that drums and other percussion instruments are allowed, and choruses of children singing songs of joy are just fine. Traveling songs, poetry, celebration music, and the like are all allowed. The basic rule is that music should not be suggestive, immoral, or lewd. If it meets a wholesome standard, as defined in Islamic morality, then sing as much as you like!

ASK THE IMAM

Cat Stevens, the popular British singer of decades past, embraced Islam after reading the Qur'an. Today, as *Yusuf Islam,* he writes religious songs for children as well as secular music.

Animal Rights and Islam

God created animals and other living things for the benefit of humanity. But this does not mean that we have been granted license to do as we please. The Holy Qur'an teaches that every animal has its own communal life and its own way to worship God, and thus our dealings with them must be on that footing. We have been created with a greater intellect than animals and so have a special responsibility to be fair, just, and kind to all other living things. The Blessed Prophet Muhammad once said that every injustice will be paid back on the Day of Judgment; even if one goat hits another with its horns, it will be taken account of. Therefore, in our use of animals for our own survival we must do justice.

God gave us the free use of the plants and animals of this earth. He said, "Eat and drink of the good things of the earth." He also said, "It is God Who has provided you with livestock of every kind. You can ride some and others you eat ...." (Qur'an 40:79) But we must balance our use of animals and plants with our primary role as caretakers on the earth. For example, we are not allowed to harm animals or plants for no reason. The Blessed Prophet forbade people from capturing baby birds, burning anthills, and whipping animals cruelly. All the people he stopped from doing these things were just having "fun." Well, as the Prophet pointed out, it wasn't fun for the animals. Muhammad said, "If someone kills a sparrow for sport, the sparrow will cry out on the Day of Judgment, 'O Lord! That person killed me in vain! He did not kill me for any useful purpose.'" So hunting for sport is forbidden in Islam. You must eat what you hunt.

If we use animals for our work, we must feed them and not overwork them. If we eat animals, we are supposed to slaughter them according to humane rules that prevent all cruelty and suffering; and if we have them as pets, we are to feed them and care for them properly. The Prophet once told a story in which he noted that a woman who starved her pet cat to death would be tormented by that cat on Judgment Day by way of revenge. We thus have a responsibility to all living creatures around us, and even though many non-Muslims assert that animals have no rights or feelings, Islam says otherwise.

Monetary Restrictions

Islam regulates economic affairs with the same thoroughness as other areas of life. Free trade, fair competition, contractual rights, and compassionate capitalism are the hallmarks of Islamically based finance. The main features that guide Muslim financial life are listed as follows:

- Muslims are forbidden to engage in interest-based borrowing or lending. This is because interest brings a hardship on the borrower and gives the lender easy gains that were not earned.

- Muslims are exhorted to be honest in all financial exchanges. God will punish dishonest business people and reward the upright with paradise.

- Stock trading is allowed in companies that do not deal in forbidden substances or interest. Futures contracts are forbidden because no one can foresee what conditions will be like tomorrow, and to lock someone into such a contract is unfair. Mutual funds are allowed with the same attention paid to the items individual companies deal in.

- Muslims are allowed to be business partners with non-Muslims.

The Least You Need to Know

- Men are the head of the family in the Islamic family structure, but the wife has the status of an equal adult who must be consulted in family affairs.
- The mosque is considered a sort of all-purpose community center where people can worship, hold meetings, and discuss community affairs.
- Islam has two major holidays: one after the Hajj, and the other after the fasting month of Ramadan.
- The birth of a baby is celebrated in a special ceremony called an *Aqiqah*. It is customary to give gifts for the baby on that day.
- Muslims have a kosher-like standard that restricts what they can eat and consume.
- Islam forbids gambling, alcohol, drugs, and suggestive music.

Looking at the Status of Women in Islam

In This Chapter

- Learn about the role and concept of women in Islam
- Discover what it means to be Muslim and female in Muslim society today
- Find out what rights and duties Islam confers upon women
- Read up on divorce, polygamy, and Islamic Law
- Find out why Muslim women cover their hair in public

Women have always had to struggle for equality and acceptance in male-dominated societies. Sometimes local or national customs are to blame for women's woes, while other times religion (or its misapplication) is responsible. Every nation has had to deal with this issue, and some have been more successful at finding equitable solutions than others. Over the last 100 years, women in Europe and America have been able to garner such rights as inheritance, equal education, and even voting privileges, but women in much of the rest of the world seem to have lagged behind.

The perception in the world today is that Muslim women have the fewest rights and liberties of all. This view is strengthened by decrees from many conservative Muslim groups and governments that range from mundane things such as requiring segregated classrooms to more serious indignities such as forbidding women to work, go to school, or even drive a car. But are these restrictions rooted in religion or in long-held local customs and prejudices that have nothing to do with Islam? In this chapter, I discuss the real story of women in Islam, and how it is one of progressive liberation and elevation of status. It was for this reason that women in the early days of Islam were the staunchest supporters of Muhammad's mission. If women in some countries today are not enjoying the full rights theoretically bestowed upon them by Islam, it is not the fault of the religion, but of chauvinistic men who use religion selectively to maintain their dominance.

Does Islam Teach Inequality?

Many Westerners believe that Islam teaches that women are second-class citizens. Commentators often point to the many backward customs prevalent in the Muslim world as proof that religion is to blame for this sorry situation. Women who have escaped the stifling lifestyle of their home countries are held up by women's rights groups as paragons of bravery who stood up to their culture and were liberated. An episode of the *Oprah Winfrey Show* centered on one such woman, a princess from Bahrain who wanted to marry an American Marine. She had to leave her country to do it because her family forbade her marrying a non-Muslim. Unfortunately, the show's unintended side effect was to make it look like the Muslim world was the new Iron Curtain that women had to escape from! However, the Holy Qur'an lays out the case for women's equality in several ways:

> O people! Reverence your Lord Who created you from a single soul and created of like nature its mate and from those two He scattered countless men and women. Reverence Allah through Whom you demand your mutual [rights] and [reverence] the wombs [of mothers that bore you] for Allah ever watches over you. (Qur'an 4:1)

DISPELLING THE MYTH

Islamic Law considers women to be equal with men in all respects. Men and women have the same religious and moral duties, and the economic rights of women are identical to men. Husbands do not acquire the property of their wives upon marriage. Women have full right to vote in Islam and can hold positions of authority over men. All of these principles have had their examples in Islamic history and are proven from the time of the Prophet.

Muhammad himself established the equal suffrage rights of women by including them in the oath-taking practice, which was the equivalent of voting in Arab society. Islam has never taught that women should be denied a political voice, and in those Muslim countries that are not ruled by kings (which is forbidden in the Qur'an, by the way) one finds that women vote freely. Iran, which is often held up as the epitome of chauvinism, actually has more elected women in government than the United States!

Islam does not teach that women are inferior in religion or in political rights. The only caveat, as was noted in Chapter 19, is that men are called upon to be the protectors and primary providers of the family. This doesn't mean that women are weak or incapable of defending or supporting themselves, for Islamic history is full of wealthy, strong, and martial women. Rather, it elevates women by freeing them from a lot of drudgery that God has said men are primarily responsible for. According to some Islamic scholars, women are not even obligated to do the housework! (Any work they do is considered a charity on their part.) The Prophet Muhammad worked around the house as much as any other member of his family. Men are the undeclared servants of women, in an ideal Islamic sense.

The Struggle for Equal Rights

In most Muslim countries, few people have any rights, men or women. Remember that the Islamic civilization was virtually wiped out during the era of Colonialism, and thus what is left is a confused jumble of customs, misconstrued religious ideas, imported ideologies, political turmoil, and poverty. The very fact that most Muslim countries are under the sway of dictators, presidents-for-life, kings, and other tin-pot leaders is an indication of just how serious the problem is.

In most places, the struggle for women's equality is carried out under a backdrop of governmental oppression of the men. Whether it's Syria, Algeria, Uzbekistan, or other similar places, the average citizen must be mindful of secret police, arbitrary arrest, torture and imprisonment, cronyism, and bribery as a fact of life. In such conditions, it may be easier to understand a backlash against the advancement of women in society. The men may feel they are losing control of another sphere of life. This is, of course, no excuse to justify unrestricted male dominance; it is merely a way to try to make sense of the struggle women must go through.

Remember that the women's rights movement in the United States encountered such stiff opposition that it took over 100 years for meaningful equal-protection laws to be enacted in the late twentieth century. Early pioneers like Susan B. Anthony and Elizabeth Cady Stanton were ridiculed by American men as rebellious, scandalous, and downright un-Christian. Although several important rights were eventually achieved, many American women would argue that the status of their gender still needs much improvement. Indeed, this brings up the point that Muslims are consistently trying to make: even as it is unfair to look at crime statistics against women in America and conclude that Christianity is oppressive to women, so, too, Muslims would say, it is equally unfair to blame Islam for what are essentially abuses against women by men who either falsely use their religion to justify their actions or are ignorant of religion and are just criminally minded or abusive.

Still Room for Improvement

How can the lot of women in the Muslim world be improved? Education coupled with political reform is the key. Contrary to what may be immediately assumed, a more thorough religious education for men and women in which the rights of women in Islam are given prominent coverage is the best course of action. To be very frank, there is quite a lot of misinformation and faulty ideas about Islam in the Muslim world. The status of women is just one of those areas where great improvement is necessary. On the second issue, political reform, based on an Islamic model, would guarantee the safety and security of the population at large in a similar way that the American Constitution protects the rights of the average American. Despite the occurrence of the high-profile Iranian Revolution of 1979, the proper implementation of Islam in a nation is not rooted in chaos or barbarism.

Islam does not encourage the oppression of women. In fact, the teachings of Muhammad call upon men to respect the rights of women. Islamic Law contains dozens of laws for the protection of women's rights. Among these are the following:

- A woman's property cannot be seized by her husband.
- Women cannot be denied the right to an education.
- Ruining a woman's reputation is a criminal act.
- Forced marriage is prohibited.
- Women can file legal suits in court and provide sole testimony.
- Women can initiate divorce.
- Women get automatic custody of young children after divorce.
- Alimony and palimony are mandatory.
- Women can enter into contracts without interference or permission from a man.
- Spousal abuse is a punishable offense.
- Women receive equal pay for equal work.
- Women can vote and stand for civil office.

The list goes on further and covers so many areas that it rivals current Western laws regarding women's status and rights. So from the Islamic standpoint, the liberation of women is not accomplished by rejecting their religion but by actually implementing it. Replacing the current regimes in Muslim countries with Islamic governments that will rule according to the traditional understanding of Islam as it was practiced during its Golden Age (from about the ninth to the thirteenth centuries) is also essential. This is how Muslims look at the issue among themselves.

Myths About Muslim Women

Perhaps no other issue has influenced people's imagination more than the status of women in Islam. In the Middle Ages, when Europeans were engaged in warfare with Muslims in Palestine, the focus was on painting a picture of Muslims as minions of the Devil. But with the powerful Ottoman Empire holding sway over much of southeastern Europe from the fifteenth century until 1918, many Westerners began changing their views of Muslims as invincible conquerors and instead focused on the exotic excesses of Ottoman court life.

Europeans began to view the typical Muslim family as a licentious man lording over a harem of beautiful, nubile women. Many French, Italian, and British painters created fanciful images that fueled this notion and gave rise to the myth of the harem. The word *harem* itself does not mean in any way a pleasure room full of compliant women. It literally means "forbidden space" and is the term Muslims used for that area of the house where male visitors were not allowed to go. In the same way that it is considered bad etiquette to walk into the bedroom of another person's house while you are a guest for dinner, Islam also has an etiquette regarding private areas of the home.

The harem of any house was the area where women could be assured of privacy, where they could lay aside their head scarves and relax without feeling the pressure of men around. The bawdy imagery, unfortunately, comes from the un-Islamic practices of some Ottoman rulers who would literally collect women as concubines and cordon off whole areas of their palaces as pleasure gardens. These are the harems that Europeans have taken as representative of the normal state of Muslim women. (The later Ottoman sultans were the guiltiest purveyors of this practice.) Islam, as it was understood in its first centuries, did not foster or condone this type of extreme sensualism, and except for a few high-profile cases, this practice has been virtually unknown in the Muslim world.

How are Muslim women viewed today? Surprisingly, the myth of the harem is no longer as much in vogue among Westerners. Instead, it has been replaced by an equally damaging myth, that of the Muslim woman as a victim of fanatic religious zealots. This stereotype has taken off in recent years due to two main factors:

- The issue of arranged marriage.
- Cultural oddities in some Muslim lands.

We'll examine each in turn.

Arranged Marriages

Many women are wary of marriage because of the danger of being stuck with a bad man. The prevailing wisdom in our time is that dating helps people to make more informed choices by letting them see another person intimately before taking the vow of marriage. The concept of an arranged marriage, then, would seem like the antithesis of this approach. "How can you love somebody you don't even know?" is the big question.

It may surprise many to learn that arranged marriages are not an Islamic requirement. There is no teaching in the Qur'an or in the hadiths that calls for this practice. It is, rather, a cultural phenomenon that exists in many Muslim countries even as it exists in much of the non-Muslim world from Zimbabwe to China. In fact, it is really the institution of unchaperoned dating that is the new practice which much of the world is struggling to accept. Islam merely regulates the conduct of people who want to form a marriage, whether arranged by their families or by themselves. Are women sometimes forced into arranged marriages? Yes, but this abuse goes against the teachings of Islam and is not limited to Muslim populations.

Anomalies in the Muslim World

Practicing Muslims often discuss the primitive (un-Islamic) cultural values prevalent in certain parts of the world. To be fair, most Muslim women in the world are not oppressed or held back any more than women may be anywhere else in the world. In fact, Muslim women in such places as Malaysia, India, the United States, Turkey, and England are often highly educated and mobile. It is the utter inexplicability of several lingering (and often un-Islamic) cultural values, however, that people tend to take the most interest in.

The first anomaly I will examine is the so-called honor killings that sometimes occur in Palestine, Jordan, Turkey, and other similar places. The idea is that if a girl brings dishonor on the family by either dating, refusing a marriage arrangement, or being promiscuous, then a family member must kill her to protect the family's reputation. There is no sanction in Islam for such a horrible practice, and Muslim scholars in those countries have issued *fatwas* against it repeatedly. But people don't change their values easily and they frequently cling to odd notions of macho culture more strongly than to authentic religious dictates. This is a worldwide phenomenon, as other ethnic and religious groups also engage in such negative cultural practices. (Have you ever heard of the concept of *machismo* in South America, which also causes untold suffering to many women? What about sexism in French culture?) To make it perfectly clear, there is no verse in the Qur'an or saying of the Prophet or even principle enshrined in Islamic Law that permits this practice. It is backward, evil, and thankfully dying out—though not fast enough!

The second anomaly is that of female circumcision. This practice is mainly found in a few isolated regions of Africa and is not sanctioned or required by Islam. It is a pre-Islamic cultural relic that Christians, Muslims, and animists engage in equally. When the issue first came up among women's rights groups in the West, their initial response was to blame Islam. However, after news reports found that African Christians were as likely to engage in the practice, Islam was no longer mentioned as the cause. When the Prophet Muhammad heard about this practice, he tried to diminish its effects by restricting its application and in no way did he ever teach that it should be done. Female circumcision is absolutely not endorsed in Islam.

The final cultural oddity is also quite unfortunate and likewise has no precedent in traditional Islam. This is the strange belief in some rustic Muslim cultures that girls should not go to school or be educated. Muhammad himself said: "Acquiring knowledge is a duty on every Muslim male and female." Classical Islamic civilization is replete with examples of female students and scholars, and even in Muhammad's own time there were many highly educated females who had students of both sexes. Again, it is ignorance combined with poverty and a warped sense of *machismo* that developed in the last few centuries that brought such un-Islamic values to several traditionally Muslim lands. Muslim women in more developed countries are at the forefront of education, and it is hoped that with the rising standards of living across the world that more men could relax enough to allow women their Islamic-given right to be educated.

Women's Rights in Islam

The Qur'an says: "Women shall have rights similar to those of men." There are, however, some specific issues of difference that are often misinterpreted in the West. People have charged that in Islam a woman's testimony is only half of a man's, that women are cheated out of half of their inheritance, that the Qur'an allows wife-beating, that men can divorce on a whim and have four wives, and that Islam promotes unfair segregation.

These charges are usually bandied about to "prove" that Islam is an unfriendly and chauvinistic religion toward women. When each is looked at in context and with accuracy, not false hype, then even these objections melt away. Let's examine each of them separately.

Are Women "Half" of Men?

The charge that a woman's testimony is only half of a man's arises from a Qur'anic verse (2:282) that talks about business contracts. A woman is asked to have a friend come along when she negotiates a business contract. Later on, should the other party to the contract try to cheat her, her friend can remind her about the details in a court situation. Does this sound all that bad? (Note how the second woman does not need anyone to back her up. Her word is accepted as fact.) In seventh-century Arabia, aggressive men routinely cheated women and this Islamic rule leveled the playing field. Even today, such advice is still valid. A witness who will see to it that fairness is maintained is a good idea. In this and all other testimony, a woman's word is accepted as equal to that of a man. The second witness for business contracts is merely a safeguard for the woman. In any other court business, there is no requirement for a woman to have a second witness.

ASK THE IMAM

If a woman feels her husband is not providing enough financial resources for her use on the family, Islamic Law says she can secretly take money from him because she is only taking what is rightfully hers.

Why Only Half an Inheritance?

The Qur'an is very specific about who gets what after a person dies. In fact, the verses that deal with this topic (4:11–12) are so detailed that it takes a lawyer to apply the formulas for all of the heirs. One of the dictates is that a female will inherit a share that is only half that of the man's. This seems unfair on the face of it, but remember the role of men in an Islamic family. The man has to support the family as a matter of religious obligation while the woman is not obligated to spend a dime unless she wants to.

When a man marries, he must pay to the woman a dowry that can be as much as she wishes. The man is supposed to pay mandatory alimony and palimony, while no such requirement is upon women. A woman cannot be forced to share her fortune with her divorced husband. A man also must support his unmarried sisters and his mother if his father dies. So a woman gets half an inheritance to keep for herself but a man is obligated to spend on all those around him. Even the extra inheritance share may not always be enough!

Does Islam Allow Wife Abuse?

Domestic violence is one of the most important issues for women. In the West, this scourge has been called the invisible crime because of its widespread but under-reported nature. Men in every society and every culture can become abusers. It is not promoted in any religion on Earth, yet Islam is sometimes falsely charged with allowing it because of one misrepresented verse in the Qur'an:

> As to those women from whom you fear defiant conduct, first admonish them, then refuse to share your bed with them, and then, *daraba*. Then if they relent, then take no further action against them and do not look for excuses to hassle them. (Qur'an 4:34)

The Arabic word *daraba* in this verse is often translated as strike, hit, or beat them, yet as you will see, this has been a gross misinterpretation of the actual practice of Muhammad. To understand the import of this verse, we must examine the context in which this passage was revealed to the Prophet. The Arabs of the city of Mecca had a very macho culture in which women were quite subservient. After Muhammad and his followers escaped persecution at the hands of their fellow Meccans and migrated to the northern city of Yathrib (Medina), they encountered a more cosmopolitan city in which women had vastly more rights. The Meccan women quickly adopted the more outspoken nature of their hosts, and this irked many of the Meccan migrants who were unused to their wives talking back to them and defying them in public. Some men went to the Prophet to complain and they asked for advice about what to do. Muhammad told them that if their wives were behaving this way, that they could do "daraba." The next day, around 70 women went to the Prophet and complained that their husbands had beaten them. The Prophet was upset when he heard this and he angrily pronounced that any man who beats his wife, "is not the best of you," which in prophetic parlance meant that they were the worst. He then declared that any man who beats a woman is not a good man. He gathered his male followers and told them: "I cannot bear the thought of a man with the veins of his neck swollen in anger against his wife while he's fighting against her."

So this brings up two questions: 1) How does this verse from the Qur'an define conduct that is defiant? and, 2) What did the Prophet mean by the word *daraba*? To answer the first question, the Prophet defined defiance simply as one's spouse openly cavorting with a member of the opposite sex or revealing secrets about each other (and this offense can apply to either spouse). As a side note, defiance is not defined by traditional jurists to be merely talking back or a lack of domestic skill. As to the second question—the meaning of *daraba*—when Muhammad heard about the men beating their wives, he was angry about it, so he clearly did not mean what they did. To understand how he interpreted *daraba*, one need only look into how he himself applied the three steps listed in the verse quoted above. There was a period when he had problems with his own wives. They were sick of living a life of poverty (for Muhammad lived in self-imposed austerity). They began to treat him disrespectfully and did not hide their anger in public. Muhammad followed the first step in the verse quoted previously; namely, he tried to talk to them and reason with them for a time. When that didn't work, he began to boycott sleeping with them for several weeks, which is the second step. After that didn't improve things, he tried the third tactic: he moved into an apartment away from all of their apartments and offered them a divorce with a hefty payment. None of them wanted a divorce so they didn't accept his offer and they repented, bringing domestic harmony back into the Prophet's life. What was the name of this third strategy that the Prophet used? You guessed it! He did *daraba*, for another meaning of the word *daraba* is "to separate or go away from." In other words, this verse of the Qur'an has long been interpreted by (male) theologians to allow a man to hit his wife (though they add the caveat that it must be no more than a light tap). However, the Prophet seems to have understood *daraba* to mean an offer of divorce and separation, and that's just how he employed all three steps of the verse in question.

So actually, if you look at the verse in context, and use the mandatory interpretation of the Prophet, there is never any reason for a man to hit his wife in any way. Are there Muslim men who disregard the Prophet's interpretation and abuse their wives, and for no good reason? Yes, and the Prophet said of such men that it was awful for a man to beat his wife and then try to sleep with her later. The golden rule, aptly stated by Muhammad, is: "The best among you are those who are best to their families, and I am the best to my family." He never laid a hand on a woman in anger.

To restate, Islam does not allow a man to beat his wife; it simply provides a three-step process for the man to symbolically express his displeasure when his wife is committing open defiance that threatens the stability of the family. Have some Muslims not understood this or interpreted this verse according to their whims and engaged in abusive behavior? Undoubtedly; but this is again where the educated Muslim would say that Muslims need to be reacquainted with the actual teachings of their religion so they can create harmony both in the home and in society.

Polygamy in Islam

The Qur'an allows a man to marry up to four wives. Before Islam there was no limit in Arabia to the number of wives a man could have. The Qur'an restricted this to a maximum of four. But at the same time the Qur'an gives a rule to any man considering multiple marriages: "If you can't treat each wife fairly in all things, then marry only one, as it is more just." (Qur'an 4:4) This disqualifies most men immediately. In practice, 99 percent of the marriages in the Muslim world are with a single woman. What could be the reason for this seemingly licentious privilege for men, and why is it so rare?

Islam is a faith that boasts a solution to every problem. If one is not immediately recognized, then the scholars can do *Ijtehad* (independent reasoning) and come up with an Islamically inspired answer. *Polygyny*, which is commonly mislabeled as "polygamy," is the practice of having multiple wives or female partners. It is an often misunderstood solution to certain unique problems. (Both Judaism and Christianity allowed men to have multiple wives, though this practice has fallen out of favor since the Middle Ages.)

What do you do if there is a shortage of men, say, because of war? Only a limited number of women would find husbands. What about the rest? Multiple marriage is better than having unattached women become the secret mistresses of married men. What about women who for whatever reason cannot find a suitable match, especially if they suffer from a debilitating condition? What if a woman is barren? Should she be divorced and cast aside in favor of a fertile wife? What about those women who want careers and don't necessarily want a full-time man to look after?

ASK THE IMAM

A man with more than one wife is required to treat them equally in all respects. Each wife gets her own house or apartment, and the husband must divide his days equally between them. Any money or gifts he gives to one he must give to the other as well. If he is unfair, on the Day of Judgment God will cause half of his body to be paralyzed.

Polygyny is the answer to all of these problems. It actually works in women's favor by tying the man to each wife so much so that he is more aware of his responsibilities, trying to earn enough to support his extended family. Of course, polygyny is not for every woman, and there are those who will not have any part in it. (It is illegal in the United States and even some Muslim groups attempt to discourage the practice.) Islam says that's fine, too. For other women it is a way to get a part-time husband rather than having no husband at all. Is this allowance ever abused? Yes, but as I explained before, people have shortcomings that the religion should not be blamed for.

Divorce in Islam

Islam envisions marriage as the bedrock of a healthy society. But it also recognizes that two people may not be compatible. The Qur'an calls for men and women to make every effort to resolve their marital differences, and it even makes suggestions for mediators. However, if the discord is too great an obstacle, then divorce is the best option so that people can move on with their lives. Muhammad said, "The most hateful thing that God has created and allowed is divorce." It is not a step to be taken lightly because it affects children and the community in many negative ways. Both males and females have the right to ask for a divorce and a fair division of property, and it is also worth noting that children under the age of puberty automatically go to the mother under traditional Islamic Law.

Islam and the Dress Code

Images of veiled women and turbaned men in flowing robes permeate Western conceptions of Muslims. Fashions in the Islamic world actually vary from place to place. Arabs dress differently from Pakistanis, who in turn dress differently from Muslim Filipinos. There are certain requirements that Islam places on both men and women in dress, however, and I explore them here.

On Veils and Turbans

Men have the following dress requirements that can be expressed in a variety of fashionable ways:

- No tight clothes allowed.

- Men must allow a beard to grow if they can do it. (There is no sin or stigma on men who cannot grow a beard.)

- A turban or a kind of hat called a *kufi* is proper formal attire.

- The area from the knees to the navel must be covered in public at all times.

Women have a slightly different dress requirement. The idea is that women are so alluring to men that males may judge them only by their looks or may try to accost them sexually. To protect women from this type of abuse and degradation, and also to make them aware that God judges them by their hearts and not their looks, Islam asks them to cover their hair and wear loose-fitting clothes so that their full beauty is concealed. (Of course, the Qur'an tells men and women to lower their gaze and not to ogle each other.) By the way, Muslim women don't need to wear their veils at home or when only women or their close family members are present. Proper dress for Muslim females includes …

- A veil to cover their hair in public (called a *hijab or Khimar*).

- Loose-fitting clothes.

- Long pants or a dress to the ankles and a shirt, gown, or blouse that covers to the wrists.

DEFINITION

Hijab is the common name of the veil Muslim women wear over their hair. It literally means to screen off from view. Opinions vary among Muslims as to its necessity, though most Muslims believe it to be a requirement of the religion based on a direct saying of Muhammad to that effect and one verse of the Qur'an in which it is mentioned.

Some Muslim women follow dress customs that are not specifically required in Islam. These include wearing a veil over the face (*niqab*), wearing an all-enveloping robe called a *burqa*, and wearing socks and gloves in public. These women seek a greater level of piety and thus try to conceal from male view as much of their bodies as possible. Again, there is no requirement for all women to cover the face or wear a burqa, though some Muslim cultures promote these practices vigorously.

The hijab, *or head scarf, is a requirement for Muslim women to wear in the presence of men they are not married or related to.*

Purdah and Islam

Some Muslim cultures practice a form of female seclusion called *purdah*. This word originates from the Persian language and describes the system whereby women are not allowed to leave their homes except for the direst emergencies. This is not an Islamic custom but was picked up by some Muslims who settled in Iran and India where it was an established pre-Islamic tradition designed to showcase the wealth of a family (in other words, we're so rich our women don't have to leave the house and work in the fields). Many people in the West have the misconception that this practice is widespread. The fact is that most Muslim women in the world are not locked away in their homes. Purdah is practiced mostly in the Indian subcontinent and in Saudi Arabia.

The Least You Need to Know

- Islam views women as equal partners with men in life as well as in religion. Islam does not teach that women are inferior to men.

- Poverty and illiteracy in general, not religion, are the root cause for the plight of women in some developing nations.

- A Muslim man can marry up to four wives only if he can treat each equally. The norm is monogamy in the Muslim world.

- Islam does not allow wife beating. If abuse occurs in some Muslim homes, it is due to the same factors that cause some men to abuse their wives anywhere else in the world.

- Islamic Law relieves women of all financial responsibility for the family and instead places the entire burden on the man.

The History of Islam

History textbooks often mention the rise of Islam in a summarized fashion, as if it wasn't as important as the Vikings, the pharaohs, or the Reformation. Very little space is given for describing the land of Arabia before Muhammad's advent, for analyzing the events of his life, or for describing what happened after his passing. This oversight in our education is unfortunate and inexcusable, for Muhammad changed the course of human history in a dramatic way. Just who was he, and what did he accomplish and how?

After Muhammad's passing, Islam produced a world-class civilization that many scholars feel was more vibrant, long-lived, and vivacious than many of the civilizations that arose in the wider world. Great dynasties arose and fell in the Muslim heartlands, and the landscape from Morocco to China was dotted with fabulous cities containing many of the modern conveniences that we take for granted today. Although there were setbacks, Islam always seemed able to absorb any challenges that came before it. In this part, I provide a survey of Muslim history from the time just before Muhammad to the events that are affecting Islam to this very day.

Muhammad in Mecca

In This Chapter

- Learn more about ancient Arabia, the land where Islam began
- Discover Muhammad's early childhood influences and upbringing
- Meet the people who formed Muhammad's inner circle
- Find out what Muslims believe about Muhammad's ascension to heaven

Throughout the course of this book, I have made many references to the Prophet Muhammad and his role as the central personality in Islam. Who was he, and how did he come to have enough courage to complete a mission that oftentimes seemed doomed to failure? In this chapter, I finally take a thorough look at the life of Muhammad, from the conditions of the society he was born into until his migration from Mecca to Medina. It is interesting to note that this one man, who has done so much to change the course of human history, was actually a thrice-orphaned child from a poor clan who grew up tending sheep. As you learn more about his early life, you will gain a greater appreciation for both the man and the simple directness that Islam is famous for.

Arabia: The Birthplace of Islam

Arabia—the name conjures up images of sand dunes and desert oases. Bedouins on camels, groves of frankincense and myrrh, and the ruins of the Nabateans compete in our imagination with modern clichés about oil and mysterious princesses in forbidden desert palaces. This contrast of the rare and exotic, and the harsh and surreal, is not far from the reality that has permeated much of this peninsula's history. But while it is true that vast deserts fill most of the land between the Red Sea and the Indian

Ocean, there are also scattered fertile valleys, oases, and sleepy coastal cities. Arabia is by far a land of many contrasts. Think of Arizona or New Mexico, and you'll have a pretty good idea of the nature of the land there. In addition, the people are not as unknown to the West as one might think. Since before the Roman Empire the inhabitants of that strategic plot of land have been the middlemen in the trade of many of the spices and other goods that our modern world now takes for granted.

One Arabian city, in particular, that has been of great importance is Mecca. This dusty oasis town was a main stop on the East-West trade route and has always been considered one of the main centers of Arabian culture. It owed its financial existence to the spending habits of the frequent travelers who passed through its otherwise barren valleys. Religion, also, was a form of big business, with hundreds of idols from tribes all over central Arabia being housed and venerated inside the *Ka'bah.* In return for housing their gods in a place of honor, the tribes that inhabited western Arabia gave generous guarantees of protection to the caravans that issued forth from Mecca twice a year. To the Meccans, religion equaled money, so the more gods the merrier.

There was no king in Arabia nor a central government. Arabian civilization in the sixth century centered on the concept of the tribe as one's nation. A tribe was a collection of loosely related individuals living in a certain territory. The tribal leader was called a *shaykh,* and he was usually the oldest member of the most important family. Although subclans existed within the tribe, internal differences were usually suppressed for the greater good of the whole. Wherever you were, your tribe was your passport and status. A complex series of alliances maintained some semblance of order but petty tribal wars and a culture of raiding each other's property kept the land in a constant state of flux. Though a well-developed concept of bravery was in force, and guests were treated like the members of one's own family, beyond these two virtues it was in many respects a land gripped in the worst of security situations. Think of the Wild West in American history and double its severity and you'll get some idea about what life must have been like for those who lived there.

DEFINITION

Shaykh is the term for any leader or chief of a group or organization. It has both religious and secular connotations.

Meet Muhammad's Parents

Abdullah was a handsome young man of the Hashim clan, a subgroup of the dominant Quraish tribe of Mecca. He had been married to a young woman named Aminah for only about six months when he decided to join a caravan heading for Syria, where he hoped to make a quick fortune in the lucrative trade fairs of Damascus. By this time, his wife was pregnant and she tearfully bade her husband farewell. Little did she know that on his return journey, Abdullah would catch a fever and die in Yathrib, a city far to the north.

A few weeks after Abdullah had left, Aminah confided in her servant, an African girl named Barakah, that she had had a dream in which a voice told her to name her unborn child "Muhammad." This was an odd name and had never before been used among the Arabs. It meant "highly praised." The baby was born in about the year 570. News of the tragic death of the father reached Mecca just before the baby's birth, and the sorrowful grandfather, 'Abdel Muttalib, comforted the newly widowed young wife by saying, "He will be like a little Abdullah to us."

Thank God I'm a Country Boy!

The custom in those days was for city mothers to send their babies to foster mothers from the countryside for a few years so that the infants would grow up in a challenging environment. Every year women would come from the hinterlands and go door-to-door offering their services. No one went to Aminah's door because they knew she was a widow and couldn't pay much. At the same time, there was a frail-looking foster mother named Halima, who couldn't seem to find a baby to take. 'Abdel Muttalib brought the pair together, and the baby Muhammad was taken to be raised by the tribe of Sa'ad in the open desert.

Muhammad spent several years with the tribe—longer than was customary because of fears about a plague in Mecca—learning the life of a nomadic herder and picking up good manners from the rough but simple folk. His primary playmate was Halima's daughter, just a few years older than he, who helped Muhammad adapt to the harsh ways of Bedouin life. When he was five years old, he was finally returned to his grateful mother in Mecca. His manners, rugged constitution, and good grammar impressed many. His mother wanted to show him off to her distant relatives in Yathrib and to visit her husband's grave, so she took him and Barakah on the 10-day journey northward. She spent two weeks there in the oasis town, bunking with relatives in the night while weeping most of every day over her husband's grave. Muhammad, still quite young, spent his time playing with his cousins.

On the return trip, about halfway to Mecca, Aminah fell ill with fever and couldn't travel any further. Her condition continued to worsen, and as she lay dying in her tent by the side of the caravan trail, she made Barakah promise to always look after Muhammad. The tearful servant and child buried the departed lady soon afterward, and the pair returned to 'Abdel Muttalib's home in sorrow. A couple of years later, this loving grandfather would also reach the end of life. But before he died, he asked his son, Abu Talib, to look after Muhammad as if the boy were his own. Thus, Muhammad and Barakah went to live in his uncle's already poverty-stricken household. Muhammad had been orphaned three times before the age of 10.

War and Trade in Mecca

Abu Talib put Muhammad to work tending his small flock of sheep in the hills above the city. For most of his teen years this was Muhammad's only occupation. Thus he was not able to carouse with the other boys his age in the city, who spent their youth drinking, visiting prostitutes, and fighting or on raids. The only excitement in Muhammad's young life came when the Quraish tribe fought a battle against a rival tribe. Muhammad, along with the other teenage boys, had the dangerous job of retrieving any enemy arrows that fell on the battlefield. Muhammad didn't actually engage in any of the fighting himself.

Muhammad: Citizen of Mecca

Muhammad soon grew into a well-respected young man, and by his early twenties he had developed a reputation for honesty and integrity. He even had two nicknames: "the truthful" and "the trustworthy." Having been inadvertently sheltered for most of his youth from urban values, he was known to be more mature than other young men his age.

Muhammad remained a poor man, however, with limited opportunities until a lucky break came. A wealthy widowed woman named Khadijah was looking for someone to lead her caravan to Syria and conduct business on her behalf. Muhammad's uncle got him the job, and he was so successful and honest that when he returned, Khadijah soon fell in love with him and asked him to marry her. He was 25, and she was 40. He agreed to the match, which one of Khadija's friends arranged, and the couple would eventually have four daughters and two sons. (The sons would both die in infancy.)

After 15 years of blissful married life, however, Muhammad became restless. He never participated in idolatry because his established frame of reference (owing to his occupation as a shepherd) was the vastness and grandeur of nature. He saw right through the gods made of sticks, stones, and severed animal heads. He wanted to know where he could find the answer to the mystery of life. By his late thirties he began retreating to a lonely mountain cave that he had found earlier as a young man tending his uncle's flocks. There he could think without interruption.

A Prophet Is Chosen

In Chapter 18, I related the entire episode about the angel who came to Muhammad and revealed the first verses of the Qur'an. It was quite a spiritual experience, and as Muhammad ran home from the cave he looked up and saw the angel's face, filling the space between the earth and the sky. "Muhammad, you are the messenger of Allah," the angel said, "and I am Gabriel." When Muhammad burst in through the front door, he frantically called to his wife, "Cover me! Cover me!"

While her husband shivered feverishly through the night, Khadijah went to consult her old cousin, Waraqa, who was something of a gnostic Christian, though he was forced to keep his beliefs to himself because of an edict from Mecca's ruling council some years before that outlawed the open practice of that faith. When the frail blind man heard what had happened, he told her that if Muhammad's story was really true, then that was the same angel who had talked to Moses. Meanwhile, the angel came again to Muhammad, this time in his dreams: "You, who are wrapped up, get up and warn people! Glorify your Lord and keep your clothes pure! Avoid the idols. Don't give in charity expecting anything in return. For your Lord's sake be patient." (Qur'an 74:1–7)

When Khadijah returned home, she found her husband sitting up in bed. She asked him to rest further, but he replied, "Khadijah, the time for resting is over. Gabriel has asked me to warn people and to call them to Allah and His service. But whom shall I call, and who will listen?" Khadijah thought for a moment, and then told him she would be the first to listen. Thus, a woman became the first convert to Islam.

What Would Islam Ask of the Meccans?

The religion that the Meccans would soon learn about would be based on monotheism, which was a radical idea in a society that depended on idolatry for its financial health. Tourism, connected with the attraction of a *Ka'bah* filled with idols, fueled the local economy and gave a measure of authority to the dominant tribe of Quraish, which had custody of the holy sanctuary. But the many changes that Islam would be asking of people would run far deeper than mere theology.

The Arabs did not believe in an afterlife or in a Day of Judgment, and the Qur'anic revelation as it grew in scope and content would propose both. In addition, the concept of accountability for one's own actions before God would be unnerving in a society where literally anything was allowed. "What!" the Qur'an records the idolaters as later saying, "When we're dust and bones we're going to be raised up again? That would be a lousy re-creation." The Qur'an will answer, "Yes, indeed, your ancestors and everyone who came after!" (Qur'an 56:48–49)

The moral and ethical codes of Islam would also emphasize honesty, charity, mercy, respect for others' rights, and an elevated conception of the female gender. Muhammad would even pronounce that animals had rights and could not be beaten or overworked. Perhaps the straw that would break the camel's back, however, would be Islam's attack on blind tribal loyalty. The community of believers was a more important bond than who your relatives were. All of these ideas, as they would come to light, would soon begin to upset the Meccan leadership, especially as more and more people would start converting to this new way of thinking.

How Was Islam Received in Mecca?

When Muhammad began to preach his message publicly, (after about three years of private preaching to family members and friends) the Meccans didn't know how to respond at first. Muhammad was a member of the Hashimite clan, a poor but respected arm of the Quraish tribe. Many people from this clan were converting, and some of them were relatives of powerful people. After a few months of hoping the problem would go away by itself, however, the Meccan leaders decided to respond.

Their first tactic was to try to bribe Muhammad, offering him money, a beautiful girl of his choosing, a free visit to a witchdoctor to cure him of his "demonic visions," or even a prominent seat in the tribal council of Mecca, but he refused all offers. Next, they called upon the venerable Abu Talib to convince his nephew to stop his newfound occupation. Muhammad gave this famous reply in answer to his uncle's entreaties, "Uncle, by God, if they put the sun in my right hand and the moon in my left, and asked me to give up my mission, I wouldn't do it until either Allah made His way succeed or I died trying."

The angry Meccans began to harass any Muslims who came near the *Ka'bah* to pray. It was after a steady stream of converts from other clans began to join Islam that the real abuse started. Clan leaders, finding that they were losing control of some of their own members, began a policy of old-fashioned discipline to reinforce their authority. Thus sons and daughters who converted were subject to hazing, corporal punishment, and loss of livelihood. Soon thugs began to attack converts from the fringe elements of society, slaves, immigrants, and those who had few family connections, bullying and beating them in the streets while the citizenry turned a blind eye. The slaves, in particular, had it rough. Those who accepted Islam were tortured by their masters more mercilessly than ever before. One woman burned her slave's forehead with a hot poker, and another slave owner staked out his slave in the hot desert sand and rolled heavy stones on his chest.

The poets of the city began weaving slanderous prose and reciting it in the marketplace. When Muhammad went out of the city to greet incoming caravans to call them to Islam, these poets would follow behind, shouting, "Here is a madman. Don't listen to him." Because Muhammad and his followers were verbally abused wherever they went, many people who wanted to convert to Islam were forced to keep their choice a secret. (Three of Muhammad's own daughters were divorced by their idolatrous husbands and sent home in disgrace because they had converted as well.)

FROM THE SOURCE

Muhammad used to get depressed about the constant verbal and physical abuse he and his followers suffered. The Qur'an contains several passages in which God is basically telling him, "Hold on, things will get better." This focus on hope during hardship is a primary theme in Muslim mental health practice.

After two more years, the Meccans decided to expel Muhammad's entire clan to a barren valley a few miles outside the city. Hundreds of men, women, and children were rounded up by armed Meccan warriors and marched into a steep-walled valley with nothing but the clothes on their backs. This was the Muslim "Trail of Tears." Muhammad and the people of his clan were forced to live there for three long years with only limited food supplies that were smuggled in from sympathetic relatives and friends. The deprivation during the Boycott, as it was called, was so bad that Muhammad's beloved wife, Khadijah, fell ill and died. The virtual prisoners were released only after some visiting Arab delegations shamed the Meccans into lifting their cruel and unusual policy.

The African Migrations

Although they were able to return to their homes, the situation remained precarious. Muhammad forbade his followers to fight back, even though he himself had to endure people throwing garbage at him and putting thorns in front of his door. Any resistance on the part of the Muslims would have been seized upon by the Meccans as an excuse to wipe them out in one blow. Muhammad was, nevertheless, heartbroken to see such insane violence directed against his followers, so he prayed for guidance and made a plan of escape (at least for a few of his followers). He would send the most vulnerable members of his community across the Red Sea into the Christian kingdom of Abyssinia. One group of a dozen made it safely and without notice. Soon thereafter Muhammad sent a larger group of about 80 men and women. Such a large departure wasn't without notice, however; and the Meccans, concerned that Muhammad was trying to open up a new base of strength, sent two of their most skilled ambassadors to petition the Abyssinian king to return the refugees as criminals.

The wise king brought the representatives of the Muslims before him and asked to know more about Islam. The Muslim leader, Ja'far, explained the details of the faith. After a heated exchange with the Meccan ambassadors involving the Muslim concept of Jesus, the king decided to allow the Muslims to stay in his country.

Muhammad's Night Journey and Ascension

After 11 years in Mecca, the Muslims numbered over 200 men, women, and children. Daily, Muhammad and his followers endured violence at the hands of the Meccans, and it seemed that the situation would never improve. But one morning, Muhammad emerged from a relative's house in which he had spent the night, and made a public announcement so dramatic that some new converts to Islam threatened to renounce their faith. Muhammad said that he had been taken to Jerusalem, had ascended from there into Heaven, and then had returned to Mecca—all in the same night!

How did Muhammad explain all of this? He said that after he had finished his late-night prayer, the angel Gabriel came to him accompanied by a fantastic horse-like creature called the *Buraq*, whose every stride took it to the farthest extent of its eyesight. Muhammad mounted the *Buraq*, and they reached Jerusalem within a few minutes. The spirits of the past prophets appeared, and Muhammad led them all in prayer in the darkness of midnight. Then Muhammad remounted the *Buraq*, and Gabriel ascended with him into the next realm and through the seven layers of Heaven.

Muhammad was able to see Paradise and all of its delights, and he was greeted by some of the prophets who dwelled within. He was taken to the farthest edge of the seventh Heaven beyond which Allah manifests His power. They could go only as far as the edge, and Muhammad reported seeing lights and sounds and sweeping streams of energy that he couldn't describe in words. When the tour was over, Gabriel took Muhammad back to Jerusalem and then back to Mecca.

The Meccans, of course, took this as proof that Muhammad really was crazy. That morning, the streets were abuzz with what Muhammad was proclaiming. Some Muslims rushed to Abu Bakr, Muhammad's closest friend, to get his opinion on the matter. Without hearing anything from the Prophet yet, Abu Bakr exclaimed, "By God! If Muhammad himself said it, then it's true. He tells us that the Word of God comes to him any time of the day or night, and we believe him. Isn't that a greater miracle than what we're doubting here today?"

Abu Bakr then joined the throngs in front of Muhammad and asked him questions about Jerusalem, the kinds of buildings, the main features, and other peculiarities, because Abu Bakr had himself stayed there once. Muhammad answered the questions accurately, and this caused even more confusion because everyone knew he had never been there before. Then Muhammad told of a caravan he had passed on the road back to Mecca. He described it in detail, and a few hours later it arrived. The idolaters backed off their claims of insanity and resumed their old line of attack that Muhammad was gaining converts by means of sorcery.

This event is considered noteworthy by Muslims and is celebrated every year with religious speeches, parties, and gatherings. The journey to Mecca is called the *Isra'*, and the ascension to heaven is called the *Me'raj*. Today the famed Dome of the Rock stands over the place where Muhammad made his journey into the next realm. For this reason, Jerusalem is considered the third-holiest city in Islam, after Mecca and Medina.

DISPELLING THE MYTH

There is an apocryphal story that Muhammad was willing to compromise and accept three Meccan deities in exchange for religious liberty. Both Western and Muslim scholars have proven that this report is completely untrue and out of character with Muhammad's life and work. The novel penned by Salman Rushdie, *The Satanic Verses,* is a loose reference to this fallacious story.

A view of the rock in Jerusalem upon which Muhammad ascended to heaven.
(Courtesy of Aramco)

The Great Escape!

Meccan attacks continued unabated, and Muhammad himself was no longer safe from their brutality. His uncle and protector, Abu Talib, passed away just as the cruel boycott was being lifted, removing the last facade of family support. Muhammad had to do something to save his beleaguered followers and himself. After unsuccessfully petitioning the leaders of the nearby city of Ta'if to accept him and his people, Muhammad chanced to run into a group of people visiting from Yathrib. He explained Islam to them over a campfire outside the city, and they accepted it! Two years later a larger group of 70 people, representing the Auws and Khazraj tribes, pledged their belief in Islam, all in secrecy at night lest the Meccans find out. Before leaving, however, they invited Muhammad to move northward and rule their civil war–prone city. A way of escape had opened up and not a moment too soon!

By the year 622, the Meccans, after 13 years of enduring a movement that challenged every facet of their tribal way of life, decided to end Islam once and for all. They intended to murder Muhammad, and to cover their murder they wove a carefully contrived plot in which a group of young men, one from every major tribe, would sneak into his house at night and all would stab him (so that Muhammad's clan would be powerless to take revenge on anyone).

Muhammad got wind of this devious scheme and ordered his followers to pack their bags and leave for Yathrib in small groups over several days so as not to attract any undue attention. When nearly every one of the Muslims had left, Muhammad and Abu Bakr made their exit as well under the cover of darkness. Muhammad's cousin, a young man named Ali, was to stay behind and sleep in Muhammad's bed, making it look like he was home. The six assassins sent by the Quraish discovered the ruse and soon the alarm was sounded that Muhammad had escaped. The Quraish set a huge bounty on Muhammad's head, and soon Meccan warriors were combing the country-side. After eluding their pursuers through a circuitous route, first heading southward and then northward toward Yathrib, Muhammad finally made a triumphant entry into the city that would be his home for the rest of his life. In his honor the name Yathrib was quickly dropped in favor of *Medinat-un-Nabi, the City of the Prophet,* or Medina for short.

The Least You Need to Know

- Arabia was one of the many crossroads of civilization. Caravan routes linking Asia with Europe traversed much of that desert land.
- Muhammad had developed a reputation for honesty and trustworthiness in his youth and earned nicknames to that effect.
- The Arabs of Mecca opposed Muhammad's preaching and persecuted his followers.
- Muslims believe that Muhammad was given a tour of Heaven by the archangel Gabriel. This is the famous ascension of Muhammad from Jerusalem.

The Victory of Islam

In This Chapter

- Learn about the battles fought between the Muslims and the Idolaters
- Find out how Muhammad defeated the Meccans
- Discover why Muhammad was married 13 times
- Understand Muhammad's life in its totality

Islam was a persecuted religion in its earliest years. At any moment it could have been eliminated because the Muslims in Mecca were a scattered and vulnerable lot. Conditions became so unbearable that Muhammad had to send some of his followers to Africa to escape the wrath of the Meccans, and Muhammad himself had to flee for his life to Medina. But even as the Muslims regrouped in Medina, the Meccans initiated armed attacks against them to keep them under pressure.

Over the next several years, the Meccans would mount three invasions of the north that almost succeeded in vanquishing the fledgling religious movement. But the Muslims, though vastly outnumbered in every battle, had an unshakable faith in their cause. The Meccans had no such motivating factor, only blind, unfocused hatred. My focus in this chapter is to describe how Muhammad led his community through these and other crises and continued to organize his followers and train them in the ways of Islam and discuss more about his life. By the time he passed away, the movement he started was poised and ready to challenge the superpowers of the world.

The First Islamic State

Muhammad and Abu Bakr entered Medina to great fanfare. Everyone, Arab and Jew alike, lined the streets to see this man of Mecca who claimed to be a prophet. As he wound his way through the streets, shouts of "Come stay in my house!" echoed from many lips. Muhammad, however, knowing that to disappoint anyone on his first day would be unwise, dismounted his camel and announced he would stay wherever the camel stopped. It wandered for a few minutes, paused briefly in front of one man's house, and then moved on until it sat down in a vacant lot near the city center. Muhammad would lodge in the lucky man's home where the camel had paused while his quarters (along with the great mosque of Medina) would be built.

Before construction started, however, there was a serious problem to attend to. The Muslims who had fled Mecca came with little more than the clothes on their backs. Muhammad mobilized the good-natured converts in Medina to the benefit of the hundreds of destitute Meccan refugees. He asked the people of Medina to "adopt" their fellow believers from Mecca and share half their goods with them. Every family adopted one of the newcomers, and the immediate problem of poverty was alleviated.

It took seven months of hard labor to build the mosque and an attached apartment for the Prophet. But after it was finished, the simple brick building with a palm leaf roof provided a focal point for the Muslim community. It was there that Muhammad would conduct meetings and accept new converts from surrounding tribes. The mosque became a kind of community center, city hall, classroom, prayer area, and homeless shelter for the steady stream of destitute new Muslims who needed a place to sleep at night.

DEFINITION

Two terms were coined as a result of the Muslims' flight to Medina: *muhajirun*, meaning "immigrants" to signify those Muslims who fled Mecca; and *Ansar*, meaning "the helpers," to identify those Medinans who offered assistance to the refugees.

Muhammad wrote a city charter, guaranteeing the rights of all citizens, and he also had his secretaries draft treaties of friendship with the local Jewish tribes and with other communities in central Arabia. Within Medina, members of the two main Arab tribes were rapidly converting, and Muslims were preaching and teaching Islamic brotherhood on a constant basis. New verses of the Qur'an were continually being revealed, with new social rules, civil and criminal laws, and doctrines to live by. This was the first Islamic state, and it is to this time that Muslims today hearken when they talk of re-establishing Islam as a political system.

The Desperate Times

The Meccans greatly feared the growth of Muslim power in Medina. The main caravan route to Syria passed within range of that city, and they thought that Muhammad might try to interfere with their trade. (After all the Meccans had done to him, it was only natural to fear retaliation.) In the tradition of raiding one's neighbor, the Meccans began to carry out a sort of guerilla warfare against the Muslims. Small groups of Meccan warriors would frequently attack the outskirts of Medina, as well as any travelers and farmers in the area. This forced Muhammad to organize regular patrols, and frequent clashes in the hills became common.

The Battle of Badr

A particularly large caravan was returning to Mecca from Syria. It was laden with trade goods, and the people of Mecca anticipated it eagerly. The master of the caravan, Abu Sufyan, became afraid that the Muslims of Medina might try to intercept it in revenge for the raids that the Meccans had been making. He sent a message ahead with a fast rider telling his Meccan compatriots to come to his aid if need be.

The Meccans, who were looking for any opportunity to galvanize their populace against the Muslims, decided to raise an army and attack Medina. They recruited a thousand warriors who were well equipped with horses, camels, armor, and supplies. Abu Sufyan had said in his message that he was going to stop at an oasis called Badr, so that's where the Meccan army decided to march first.

Back in Medina, Muhammad found out about the caravan and the massive threat. He managed to cobble together a dedicated, though poorly equipped, force of 313 men. The Muslims, thinking that the Badr oasis would be the likely location for the caravan to go, made their way there in all haste. After a couple of days of hard marching, they arrived at the wells first. Muhammad ordered his men to fill in the wells with sand and to take up positions on a small ridge.

Abu Sufyan decided to avoid the wells altogether and was safely on his way back to Mecca, but the Meccan army disregarded his written pleas to retreat. The thirsty horde arrived at Badr only to find the water blocked and a force of men ahead of them standing under a black flag. The idolaters, seeing that they vastly outnumbered the

Muslims, engaged them in a fierce battle. The Muslim ranks never wavered, however, and they turned back the tide, forcing the Meccans to retreat in disarray.

The Muslims won a splendid victory and suffered only minimal losses, while the defeated Meccans returned home in shame. They lost several of their top leaders, and nearly 100 men were killed or taken prisoner. Later, after much discussion in Medina as to what to do with the many captives, Muhammad decreed that any captured soldiers who could teach 10 Muslims to read would be freed. Any detainees who were illiterate could be released upon payment of a fee from their families. The Qur'an explained that this tremendous victory was due to God's favor and the staunch determination of the true believers.

The Battle of Uhud

The Meccans were not at all content with their defeat. In Arabia personal and tribal honor were among the most sacred concepts, and to be defeated by a weaker foe was shameful indeed. The famed poets of the Arabs began to recite verses lamenting the Muslim victory and calling for revenge. A year later, the Meccans managed to organize an even larger army consisting of 3,000 men and set out to challenge the Muslims once again. Their destination was a small mountain called Uhud, which stood just outside of Medina.

When Muhammad was informed about the devastating force that was about to challenge his community, he called a council of war and asked for his companions' opinions about what to do. The consensus was to go out and meet them in battle, rather than fight them within the city. Accordingly, Muhammad organized a force of 1,000 men and marched them to the far side of Mount Uhud.

When the Meccan forces arrived on the field of battle, a treacherous commander on the Muslim side pulled out and took 300 of his men with him. He was what was known as a *hypocrite:* someone who pretended to accept Islam in Medina just to appear trendy but who secretly worked against it whenever possible. The disheartened Muslims now had only 700 troops to meet 3,000. Muhammad, thinking quickly, placed 50 archers on a side pass to prevent any Meccan cavalry from launching a rear assault and placed the main body of his forces into a frontal defensive position.

The onslaught of the Meccans was swift and fierce, but the Muslim lines held. At one point, Muhammad ordered a charge and the Meccans began to flee in confusion. It began to look as if the Muslims would achieve another stunning victory, but the archers on the hill, seeing their chance at participating in the war (and perhaps collecting the booty left on the battlefield) begin to diminish with every yard the Meccans retreated, left their posts and ran down into the battlefield to join the mad rush. This was the worst mistake they could have ever made.

The commander of the Meccan cavalry, Khalid ibn Walid, saw his chance, and he raced his mounted warriors behind Uhud and through the pass and attacked the surprised Muslims from behind. The Meccan infantry, seeing the new development, arrested their retreat and attacked anew; thus, the Muslim forces were caught in the middle. In the confusion, dozens of Muslims were killed and the Prophet was knocked down and slightly wounded.

> **DEFINITION**
>
> The **hypocrites** of Medina were people who pretended to be Muslims. They gave such trouble to Muhammad and the real Muslims that the Qur'an devotes dozens of verses to their description and their negative effects on the Muslim community.

The Muslims hastily retreated up toward the steep mountainside and took up positions there as the elated Meccans postured and then finally began to comb the battlefield, looking for dead and wounded Muslims to mutilate and torture. The Meccans withdrew later that day, and the Muslims returned to Medina, chastened that some of their number had disobeyed orders, causing the battle to be lost.

The Battle of the Ditch

As you learned in Chapter 16, the Muslims and Jews of Medina eventually engaged in civil war. The two Jewish tribes of Banu Qaynuqa and Banu Nadir both broke their treaties in turn and were consequently expelled from the city. The last Jewish tribe, the Banu Quraiza, still lived peacefully with the Muslims.

Representatives of the Banu Nadir tribe, which was now settled in a northern city named Khaibar, traveled to Mecca and roused them to end Islam once and for all. Under their guidance, the Meccans became allies with numerous tribes all throughout Arabia, and a force of over 10,000 warriors was assembled—the largest Arabia had ever seen! This massive horde converged upon Medina with the goal of destroying Islam and enslaving any Muslims who might survive its brutal assault.

The Muslims had precious little time to organize a proper defense or court allies. A Persian convert named Salman al Farsi suggested that a wide and deep trench could be dug all along the exposed front section of the city, while the walls in the rear of the city could be blocked and fortified. The Prophet and his companions agreed to this plan, and the trench was finished just before the enemy arrived. The Muslims who watched the approach of the horde were awestruck with terror. The Meccans, however, halted their advance when they espied the trench and were confused about what to do. It was a tactic unknown in Arabia, so their momentum was interrupted. After a few unsuccessful infantry assaults, a kind of stalemate ensued.

For almost a month the frustrated Meccans tried to breach the trench, but their men were beaten back every time under a furious rain of arrows. The cavalry was, of course, useless because the chasm was too wide to jump. The Muslims inside the city were running low on food, but their spirits were high. The Banu Nadir, however, succeeded in getting the Banu Quraiza to join the alliance. They held the rear flank of the city and could attack the Muslims from behind.

The Meccans' strategy was to initiate an all-out assault from the front and rear of the city, and it would have succeeded except for the fact that Muhammad used a double agent to sow doubts in the minds of the alliance's leaders. He was able to make the Banu Quraiza hesitate and to split the Meccans from their Bedouin allies with false rumors and reports. A fierce desert sandstorm blew over the plains the next night, and the alliance broke apart. The once proud coalition dissolved and quit the siege.

The Conquest of Mecca

The Muslim victory over the Meccans and their allies elevated their status among the tribes of Arabia. Numerous tribal chiefs were converting, and it seemed as if the Muslims would become strong enough to rival Mecca. But the following year, during the annual pilgrimage season in Arabia, Muhammad organized a group of 1,400 pilgrims to march to Mecca for religious rites. They were virtually unarmed!

When the Meccans found out about the Muslim pilgrims, they were alarmed. They sent their cavalry to prevent the Muslims from entering the city, but the Muslims took a different route and set up camp just outside Mecca. The stunned idolaters sent representatives to Muhammad, and the two sides hammered out a 10-year-long peace treaty called the *Treaty of Hudaibiyah*. Both sides agreed to halt any hostilities and to rein in their allies. Although the Meccans stipulated that the Muslims could only begin making pilgrimages the following year, the Muslims returned to Medina with a new sense of security.

But the peace treaty was to be short-lived. A tribe allied to the Meccans attacked a tribe allied to the Muslims and massacred a large number of their people. This violated the treaty, and when news reached Mecca of Muhammad's displeasure, the Meccans at first publicly repudiated the treaty. Abu Sufyan, however, who was the Meccans' most influential leader, saw that Muhammad's power had grown too great for them to handle. He rushed to Medina to plead for the reinstatement of the treaty, but Muhammad refused to see him. A couple of weeks later, a force of over 10,000 Muslims marched upon Mecca. They arrived at night and made camp all around the hills above the city. Muhammad ordered each group of soldiers to light several campfires so that it would look as if their already overwhelming numbers were much greater.

The Meccans sent Abu Sufyan to Muhammad's camp to surrender peacefully that night. Abu Sufyan even converted to Islam in an audience with the Prophet. As per the terms of capitulation, the next morning Muhammad led the victorious Muslims in a triumphal march into the city. After his soldiers took up positions throughout the town, he led a column toward the *Ka'bah* and found a large throng of Meccans standing there. These were the people who had tortured him and his followers for years. By any standard of justice he could have had them punished. They called out to him, "What are you going to do with us?" He replied, "You are all forgiven today. Go back to your homes. You are all free."

And so, Mecca was taken without a fight. Western scholars have long praised Muhammad for this act of wise clemency, calling it an example of both a humane and intelligent strategy, but for Muslims it is a sign of Muhammad's character: he was long-suffering and tolerant. Within days nearly the entire population of the city decided to convert under no coercion. The main task that Muhammad called for was to remove the idols from the Ka'bah, and the Muslims joyfully executed this duty, turning the venerated gods of the Arabs into a pile of rubble in the street. Muhammad spent the next few weeks in Mecca so he could organize its administration, after which he returned to Medina, the recognized seat of the Islamic State.

Confronting the Superpowers

The Byzantine Roman Empire and the Persian Empire were the two superpowers of the day. Muhammad had sent letters of introduction and invitation to the emperors of both countries; the Byzantines seemed undecided about Islam, but the Persians declared their hostile intentions. Nevertheless, it was the Byzantines who first threatened the Muslims. Their emperor, Heraclius, ordered his troops to menace the allies of the Muslims in northern Arabia. To counter this threat, Muhammad marched an army all the way to the borders of Syria. Mysteriously, the Byzantines backed down and withdrew their army. No battles took place, and Muhammad succeeded in cementing several important alliances with local tribes and political leaders. This expedition would mark the end of Muhammad's active participation in any defensive or military endeavors.

Taking Another Look at Muhammad's Marriages

Some Western scholars have charged that Muhammad was licentious on account of the many marriages he contracted. Popular myth has maligned the Prophet and cast a shadow over an otherwise universally accepted great leader. But what was the nature of these marriages, and do they demonstrate a weakness for pleasure? Let's examine this issue more closely.

When Muhammad married Khadijah in Mecca, he was 25 years old and she was 40. He lived with her monogamously for almost a quarter of a century (23 years). He didn't take another wife until after she died, and he was over 50 years old. If he was licentious, the time to have married multiple women would have been in his youth, not when he was an old man charged with the endless duties of being a prophet. (He spent most of his days in meetings and a portion of every night in the mosque praying.)

DISPELLING THE MYTH

How could Muhammad marry more than four wives when the Qur'an established a limit? The verse prohibiting more than four wives (4:3) was revealed after the last of Muhammad's marriages.

He remarried while still in Mecca only at the insistence of his companions, and his first new wife was an overweight widow whom none of Muhammad's other companions wanted to marry. His next marriage was to the daughter of his friend Abu Bakr. Muhammad had had a dream that he was supposed to marry her, and when he approached his friend, he found out that A'ishah was already engaged to someone else. Abu Bakr succeeded in getting that engagement cancelled and then engaged his daughter to the Prophet. The controversy surrounding this marriage is that A'ishah was very young. She was somewhere between the ages of 6 and 12 at the time of engagement. Although the actual marriage and consummation would not take place for at least three to five more years (after the Muslims migrated to Medina), looked at from today's standards the age difference is often deemed inappropriate. This has led to the baseless charge that Muhammad was, in the words of Pastor Jerry Vines (and defended by Jerry Falwell) "a demon-possessed pedophile."

Setting aside the insulting nature of the comment, what must be remembered is that in seventh-century Arabia there was no social stigma attached to marrying someone dramatically older or younger, even if the age difference was extreme. A'ishah was engaged to Muhammad while still a child, but she did not join the Prophet's household as his wife until after she attained puberty (somewhere between the ages of 9 and 12). Neither A'ishah nor her parents had any objection to the marriage, and she, herself, always expressed her love and affection for the Prophet even into the many decades that she outlived him. (A'ishah became one of the most important early scholars of Islam and was the teacher of many of the greatest leaders in the early Islamic Caliphate.) If Muhammad were a pedophile, he would not have waited for A'ishah to reach puberty before completing the marriage, nor would he have stopped at only one marriage to a young girl.

All the rest of Muhammad's marriages occurred in Medina and were spread out over 10 years. After the 3 wives already mentioned, he married 11 other women. With the exception of one divorcée, all of them were widows or freed captives of war (whose fathers were most often chiefs of tribes, thus allowing a political alliance to be cemented). Muhammad asked their consent before marrying each, and they readily agreed. Muhammad divided his time with each equally and helped with the housework in each wife's apartment. Again, if he was addicted to sex, he would have married all young women. Instead, they were mostly old and/or widowed and he rarely had time to spend with any member of his family, because of the strong demands on his time as both a temporal and spiritual leader.

Each wife had a special status in the community. They were known as the *Mothers of the Believers* and people deferred to them as respected members of the Prophet's family. After the Prophet passed away, his nine surviving wives took up the task of being teachers and social activists. Many Muslims today name their daughters after the Prophet's wives.

The Passing of a Prophet

Muhammad conducted one final pilgrimage to Mecca when he was nearing 63 years of age. He delivered a famous address, known as his Farewell Speech, and then retired to Medina where he tried to continue with his duties as best he could. By this time, however, he was frail and weak, owing to age (and possibly also due to an unsuccessful poisoning attempt directed against him years before by a woman belonging to the Banu Nadir). He became progressively reflective and introspective in the eyes of those around him and made more frequent visits to the graveyard to commune with his thoughts. When he became too ill to lead the congregational prayers in the mosque, he chose Abu Bakr to stand in for him. Finally, after suffering through several days of an intense fever, Muhammad raised his eyes to Heaven and called out, "Better the next world on high." With his head resting in his beloved A'ishah's lap, Muhammad passed away. The date was June 8, 632. He was buried in the place where he breathed his last. Today the famous green dome of the Prophet's Mosque in Medina marks the spot where his grave lies.

The Least You Need to Know

- The Muslims were attacked three times by the idolaters of Mecca, and each time they survived.
- Muhammad made a treaty with the Meccans, but they broke it. The Muslims then marched to Mecca in force, and the city surrendered without a fight.
- Muhammad forgave all the people who had persecuted him and let them go free after his conquest of Mecca.
- Muhammad had only one wife for over twenty years, and only married multiple wives later on to cement alliances and provide support to widows.
- Muhammad was born in the year 570 in Mecca and died in the year 632. He is buried in Medina.

The Rightly Guided Successors

In This Chapter

- Know what the ideal Islamic government is really like
- Learn about the men who ruled the Muslim community after Prophet Muhammad's passing
- Understand the challenges that Islam faced after the Prophet was gone
- Find out why the first generation after Muhammad experienced two civil wars and numerous political assassinations
- Retrace how the political system of Islam changed from a democratic tradition to a dynastic dictatorship

The Muslim community had to deal with a temporary crisis of faith after the death of Prophet Muhammad. For 23 years Muhammad had guided his followers, teaching them a completely new tradition and acting as their spiritual, legal, and moral focal point. What would become of Islam without him? Drawing upon the Qur'an, the answer became clear: "Muhammad is no more than a Messenger." "Many were the Messengers who passed away before him. If he dies or is killed, will you turn and run?" (Qur'an 3:144)

The Muslims not only didn't give up their faith, they quickly elected a leader and quelled several internal uprisings as well as confronted dangerous external threats. The first four rulers of the Muslim world were so faithful to Islamic precepts that the period of their rule is known affectionately as the *Khulafa ar Rashidah*, or the Period of the Rightly Guided Caliphs. However, within the space of 30 years the political structure came under such pressure that the egalitarian democratic system of elections gave way to a hereditary monarchy that forever changed the Islamic political tradition until the fall of the Ottomans in 1918. How did this happen and what were the major events that transpired?

Islam on Government

The government of the Prophet Muhammad was unique in that he was the sole authority because of his position as the spokesman of God's will. He appointed governors in many cities and territories throughout Arabia and gave them tremendous leeway in how they carried out their duties. His only stipulation was that they abide by the Qur'an and his *Sunnah*. If the people of any locality felt their governor was unjust or slack in his religious character, they could petition the Prophet, who would investigate and appoint a new governor if necessary.

Non-Muslims had the basic legal status of free citizens, and their religious liberties were respected. By the decree of the Prophet, further backed up by the Qur'an, forced conversion was forbidden, and any non-Muslim who felt wronged by a Muslim could be assured of a fair hearing. The most prominent companions of Muhammad formed the core of the informal administration, and their sincere belief in the truth of Islam emboldened them to work tirelessly at the many tasks at hand. No real structure of government existed beyond that, and as long as Muhammad was there, none was needed.

DISPELLING THE MYTH

The Qur'an promoted a political system highly suggestive of representative government in which the people should be consulted on all affairs not connected with clear religious dictates; in other words, representative democracy, of sorts.

One practice that Muhammad established early on was a regular schedule of public meetings with the community members to get their advice on political actions, alliances, governors, and other mundane affairs. These meetings were held in the Mosque of Medina for the most part, and they presented a chance for all members to speak their minds on the issues that faced the community. Muhammad never silenced anyone nor took action against those who expressed differing opinions. Moreover, he often concurred with the majority consensus. This process was called the *Shura*, or Tradition of Consultation, which forms the basis of the representative political structure in Islam.

After Muhammad passed away and was buried, one such Shura was called to determine what the Muslims should do next. The main issue on the table was, of course, who should lead the community now that the Prophet was gone. (It was understood that this new leader would not be a prophet and would assume only a political role.) Muhammad himself had given numerous instructions to his companions on the functions and responsibilities of the future head of state. The top position would be an elected post, and the tenure of that leader would last as long as he abided by the tenets of Islam. Thus, an Islamic government consists of a *khalifa*, or caliph, and a representative council that can override or remove the caliph if he oversteps his bounds.

The Caliphate of Abu Bakr As-Sadeeq (632–634)

The meeting to choose a caliph, or successor to the Prophet's political function, got underway quickly and was attended by all of the prominent companions of Muhammad, except for those in other cities who could not arrive in time. The Medinan converts proposed that one of their number should be elected as the leader, but after heated debate it was decided that Abu Bakr, who was from Mecca, was the most qualified to lead. He had been Muhammad's closest friend and had been given the job of leading the prayers in the main mosque when the Prophet lay ill. Abu Bakr stood before the citizens of Medina and gave an acceptance speech, which included the following:

> O people, I have been chosen to be your leader, even though I'm no better than any of you. If I do right, help me. If I do wrong, correct me. (Rafi Ahmed Fidai, *Concise History of Muslim World*, New Delphi, 2001)

The only real dissent to Abu Bakr's election came from the Prophet's cousin, Ali ibn Abi Talib, who voiced his opinion that he should have had a say in the meeting. (At the time he was busy making the funeral arrangements for the Prophet.) Ali withheld his pledge of support for some months but later relented. Some of Ali's more ardent supporters, however, became disenchanted from the start with the argument that Ali, being a close relative to the late Prophet, had more right to rule. As we shall see in Chapter 26, this nascent group of dissidents would eventually grow into the breakaway sect of the Shi'as.

Getting back to Abu Bakr's immediate challenges, it must be noted that not everyone who had become a Muslim in Arabia was sincere or particularly enthusiastic. Some Arab tribes, especially those far away from the area of Mecca and Medina, accepted Islam only because it seemed to be the trend. This fact became immediately clear when several of these tribes rebelled and declared that they would no longer pay their *zakah* and do other Islamic duties. To make matters worse, several claimants to prophethood arose seeking to create their own religions and political fortunes. Soon Arab Bedouins led by these false prophets began raiding Muslim outposts even as far as Medina and creating all sorts of trouble for the Muslims.

Abu Bakr had few troops left in Medina because he had just sent a large army to Syria to guard against the Byzantines and their allies, who were menacing some tribes allied to the Muslim state. That large army was under the command of a teenager named Usamah bin Zayd, whom the Prophet himself had appointed for that task. Even with most of the army deployed in Syria, Abu Bakr was still able to gather a small force to defend Medina against the increasing Bedouin attacks.

After securing the capital, he ordered his small but tough army to subdue the Arab rebellions in the hinterlands. Before beginning the battle, however, the Muslim generals invited the rebels to return to Islam, and many tribes gave in without a fight. Still, a few unruly groups were hungry for a war and engaged the Muslim forces. But in battle after battle, the Muslims were victorious over the rebellious Bedouins and made them sign treaties of peace. This series of minor wars was known as the Wars of the *Riddah* and lasted only about a year.

The two great empires of the day were the Byzantines and the Persians. As noted in Chapter 22, the Prophet had sent letters to the rulers of both lands inviting them to Islam, and they had both refused, even to the point of starting to fight against Muslim communities in northern Arabia. The Persians were supplying arms and money to the rebellious Bedouins in an attempt to bring about the defeat of Islam. In the interests of self-defense, the Muslims felt compelled to go on the offensive.

One Muslim leader, who lived near the border of Persian-controlled Iraq, came to Medina to ask for protection for his people from constant Persian threats and attacks. Abu Bakr sent an army of 8,000 men in the year 633 to engage the Persians in battle. With a series of stunning victories, the outnumbered Muslims captured huge areas of prime real estate. Within one year, most of the lands of southern Iraq were firmly in the control of the Muslims.

On another front, Muslims in southern Syria were under constant danger of attack from the Byzantines. Abu Bakr ordered the army to shift into Syria to meet the new threat. After a few important battles, the Muslims drove out the Byzantines and secured the entire northern frontier of Palestine. In one battle, a group of Muslim women, who were acting as the medical corps for the Muslim army, were surrounded and attacked by the Byzantines. The women picked up their tent poles and used them as spears to fight the raiding enemy soldiers. The short swords of the Byzantines proved worthless against the women's long poles. The women held the enemy away and killed many of them.

Umar ibn al Khattab and Persia's Defeat (634–644)

Two years and three months had passed with Abu Bakr as caliph, but he was very old and eventually fell ill. Just before he passed away, he called a council of the most important companions of the Prophet and discussed with them who should rule after him. He suggested that Umar ibn al Khattab should lead the *Ummah*, or community, and everyone agreed that he was the best choice. A few days later Umar was confirmed in a public vote as the new caliph.

DISPELLING THE MYTH

Most of the cities that the Muslims laid siege to in Palestine and Syria surrendered under the Muslim promise that no harm would come to the population or their property. Muslim soldiers did not engage in looting or plundering when they took a city. Tax rates from the new Muslim governors were also generally lower than what the people were used to paying.

Umar had no time to rest. Pressure from the Persian army on the Iraqi front was increasing, and action was called for. A new army was sent from Medina to a place near the Euphrates River called Qadisiyyah. The people who lived in the area threw in their lot with the Muslims and rebelled against their Persian overlords who had always treated them harshly. After a fierce battle, the badly outnumbered Muslims defeated the Persian army and took control of almost all of the land west of the Euphrates River.

Meanwhile, in the West, the Muslim forces facing the Byzantines in Syria were winning battle after battle. In almost every case, the Muslim army had only to surround a city, cut off its supplies, and ask the people to surrender, promising them that they would not be harmed. Nearly every city in Syria fell to the Muslims this way, and almost no actual fighting occurred.

After the Muslims captured the key city of Damascus, the Byzantine emperor, in far away Constantinople, decided to organize an army of 250,000 men to fight the Muslims. At a place called Yarmuk, in the year 636, an army of 40,000 Muslims defeated the Byzantines and forced them to retreat. In that same year the patriarch of Jerusalem agreed to hand over control of his city to the Muslims, and Umar himself came (at the patriarch's request) to accept the surrender of the city. The strategic regions that bordered northern Arabia were in Muslim hands for good.

DISPELLING THE MYTH

When Umar entered Jerusalem to accept the surrender of the city's leaders, he was asked to pray in a prominent church. He refused, saying he feared that people would turn it into a mosque after him.

Umar helped to further organize the national Muslim government. The expanding Muslim world was divided into eight provinces, each ruled by a governor appointed by the caliph. He also reorganized the system of tax collection and the treasury. The Muslim calendar was also fixed, tying the year zero to the Hijra, or migration, of the Prophet in the year 622 of the Western calendar. Other achievements are as follows:

- Egypt, Syria, Palestine, and a large part of present day Iraq were captured from the Byzantines and Persians.

- Umar garrisoned Muslim armies in separate camps and military towns, rather than quarter them in conquered cities. The major city of Basra in southern Iraq began as one such town.

- Umar reiterated Islam's tolerant nature toward Jews and Christians, assuring them of their rights and forbidding forced conversions. Many administrators in the lands taken from the Byzantines and Persians were, in fact, non-Muslims who were retained in their positions.

Umar ruled as caliph for 10 years until a Persian assassin stabbed and killed him. As he lay dying from his knife wound, he appointed a committee of important Muslims to choose a new caliph within three days of his death. After a few days of debate, the choice fell upon Uthman ibn Affan, who was a trusted companion of the Prophet.

Uthman ibn Affan and the Great Conspiracy (644–656)

Uthman became the leader at a time when Muslims were making strides on all fronts. To add to this progress, Uthman ordered the building of the first Muslim navy. He also made sure that an official copy of the authorized Qur'an was available in every main Muslim city to pre-empt any dispute about its contents in the expanding (and increasingly non-Arab) empire. Everything seemed to be going well for the Muslims, but some new problems began to arise. Uthman was not as strict in taking subordinates to task as Umar and was often hesitant about confronting corruption. People loved the gentle character of Uthman, but when it became known that some of the governors in the provinces were corrupt or incompetent, people began to complain that Uthman wasn't taking strong enough action against them.

Part of the problem was that the Muslim administrators in the new territories relied heavily on the system of local government that the Persians and Byzantines used. The Arabs were still not skilled at governing large cities and lands, so they often left in place whatever city workers and tax collectors they found there. Financial abuse and mismanagement were rampant, and oversight was lacking. Uthman removed some of the inept governors, but others, such as those in Syria and Egypt, became so powerful that they sometimes simply ignored the caliph's written orders. A third problem was that Uthman seemed to have appointed several of his relatives to governorships early on, and this fueled charges of nepotism. Opposition and dissatisfaction soon spread throughout the empire.

A group of people came to Medina from Iraq to complain about their own unjust governor. Uthman listened to them and promised that he would take some sort of action, and this seems to have mollified them. As they were returning to their own province by caravan, however, a non-Muslim saboteur planted a fake letter in the baggage ordering all the people who complained about their governor to be killed when they returned home. He signed the letter with a forged name reading: "Uthman." When the people in the caravan found this letter, they believed that Uthman intended to murder them.

Accordingly, they returned to Medina, surrounded Uthman's house, and demanded he come out. When they showed him the letter they had found, Uthman said the letter was a fake and that he didn't have anything to do with it. The mob refused to believe him and, later, some of their men killed him while he sat reading his Qur'an in private. To make matters worse, they wouldn't flee the city and instead stayed to publicly press their case. The Muslims in Medina were shocked and in grief. Uthman was loved by all for his gentleness and kindness, and now he had been cruelly murdered.

Ali ibn Abi Talib (656–661)

Ali was selected as the next caliph of the Muslims by a vote of the people in the main mosque in Medina. Soon, people from all over Arabia came to give him their pledge. But the immediate problem that faced him was the same one that had faced Uthman: what to do about the rebellious governors in Iraq, Egypt, and Syria. In addition to this, a large number of Muslims began demanding immediate punishment for the killers of Uthman.

Ali was in a difficult situation. He decided to delay his investigation into the murder until the situation could be better understood and addressed. This was in keeping with his cautious nature. He was always against hasty decisions made through enflamed emotions. But some people took this delay the wrong way and thought that Ali was refusing to bring the killers to justice. When A'ishah, the widow of the Prophet, heard about this, she joined with a group of like-minded people who decided to take drastic action against the caliph to force him to punish the killers.

Meanwhile, Ali was doing his best to address the political problems before him and decided to make a clean break from the scandal-tainted rule of the governors appointed by his predecessor. Consequently, he sent written messages to all the recalcitrant governors, asking them to step down from their posts. For the most part his orders were ignored, as the issue of Uthman's murder and the lack of justice meted out against the perpetrators galvanized the powerful elite to stall. Most important, Mu'awiya of Syria refused to even read the caliph's letters.

DISPELLING THE MYTH

The caliph, Ali, had to contend with two major civil wars during his rule. A rebel group known as the *Kharajites* (seceders) later assassinated him. Rule by elected caliphs gave way to dynastic succession in the world of Islam after his time.

The Battle of the Camel

A'ishah and a group of companions intent on taking revenge for Uthman's murder decided to travel to the new Muslim garrison city of Basrah to raise an army to confront Ali. They found some of the killers of Uthman along the way and executed them. Then they defeated Ali's supporters in the region. They soon gathered a huge army that was large enough to march against Medina itself. When news of this reached Ali, he organized an army of his own and marched to Basrah to stop A'ishah and her supporters. He didn't want A'ishah, or anyone else, to take the law into their own hands. Accompanying Ali's army was Abdullah ibn Sabah, a treacherous man who may have been behind the forged letter that resulted in Uthman's death. When Ali asked Abdullah and his men to leave, knowing that they were suspicious characters, the provocateur thought of a daring plan. As you will see, it would be the cause of a great disaster.

The two armies met outside of Basrah in the year 656. Ali and A'ishah met face-to-face between the two armies and negotiated a peace agreement. After they returned to their camps, Abdullah ibn Sabah made his move. Before anyone could stop them, a few of his men, who were hiding behind the front lines of both armies, charged out, swinging their swords and pretending that the battle had begun. In the confusion, the men of both armies rushed to fight each other, thinking that they had been ordered to do so.

Thousands of Muslims were engaged in battle against each other, and the slaughter was fierce. Upon seeing the fighting begin, however, A'ishah became alarmed and tried to stop it. She mounted her camel and rode out into the melee trying to tell her men to hold, but her own army thought she had come to encourage them to fight even harder, so the battle went on for hours.

When Ali saw that A'ishah's presence was making the situation even hotter, he ordered some of his soldiers to rush her position and cut down her camel so that none of her men would be able to see her. After Ali's men had carried out the order, they escorted her off the battlefield. Ali's army defeated the rebels and peace was restored. The affair was known as the Battle of the Camel, after A'ishah's daring ride into the battlefield. She returned to Medina in sorrow and resumed her activities as a teacher.

The Struggle for Power

To save Medina from any more political trouble, Ali moved the capital of the Islamic empire to the new Muslim city of Kufah, near the border with Iraq. With the immediate trouble solved, Ali again turned his attention to the rebellious governors. He decided to replace every governor ever appointed by Uthman, thinking that they were weak and untrustworthy. But Mu'awiya of Syria again refused to step down and instead gathered an army to defend his position. He also launched a propaganda campaign against his rival.

In the year 658, Ali marched his army to a place in Syria named *Siffin*. There he found Mu'awiya's army ready to face him. Ali tried to start peace talks with Mu'awiya, but his foe refused, saying that he would never negotiate until the issue of Uthman's killers was settled once and for all. A three-day battle followed, and Ali's army made steady progress against Mu'awiya's forces. When it looked like he was going to lose, Mu'awiya ordered his cavalry to hang pages from the Qur'an on the ends of their spears to make Ali pause. The trick worked, and Mu'awiya and Ali began negotiations.

A radical group of Ali's men were angry that their leader didn't pursue total victory against the rebels. Known as the *Khawarij*, or Kharajites, they deserted and returned to Kufah to prepare an army to attack Ali's forces. Meanwhile, Ali and Mu'awiya pulled back their armies and returned to their own lands while the negotiations went on. Ali put down the revolt of the Kharajite fighters when he returned and then worked to strengthen his position in Kufah.

A Compromise with Syria

After several months of sending messages and proposals back and forth, both Ali and Mu'awiya agreed that they would each step down, pending arbitration by a three-man committee, and that neither one of them would campaign for the office. But this was a trick on Mu'awiya's part. In a large public gathering, after Ali's representative declared that Ali would step down as caliph, one of Mu'awiya's supporters then stood up and said that Mu'awiya would now be the new caliph! Confusion and turmoil engulfed the meeting.

This blatant double-cross and political brinkmanship angered many, and the angriest people of all were the few remaining Kharajite men who had gone into hiding or who had pretended to make peace. They decided to kill both Mu'awiya and Ali and then find a new caliph. While they wove their schemes, Mu'awiya and Ali's armies began moving against each other from Egypt to the Hijaz region of Arabia. Mu'awiya's forces even briefly attacked and occupied both Mecca and Medina!

Finally, one lone Kharajite assassin was able to sneak up on Ali and stab him. He died in the year 661, just after his morning prayers. The last of the true caliphs who had lived by Muhammad's precepts was gone. (The Kharajite agent sent to kill Mu'awiya failed to assassinate his target.) Under Mu'awiya's undisputed rule from Damascus, the Islamic Empire would become a monarchy. Although the religious aspects of Islam would still continue to be promoted vigorously, the political system enshrined in the Qur'an would never again function the way it did in Medina. The first Islamic dynasty, centered on the tribe of Umayyah, was thus born. Known as the Umayyad Dynasty, it would last for less than 100 years but would soon itself give way to a more vigorous dynasty which would oversee the true flowering of Islamic civilization.

The Least You Need to Know

- The first four caliphs, or leaders, after Muhammad are considered by Muslims to have been "rightly guided," or sincere to their religion in their governance style.
- The Muslim community was forced to fight the Byzantines and the Persians in Palestine, Syria, and Iraq; they won many stunning victories.
- Islam was not spread by the sword. This is a popular myth that was cultivated by propagandists in the Middle Ages. Forced conversion is forbidden in the Qur'an.
- The Islamic political structure began as something akin to a representative democracy but was transformed into a hereditary monarchy by ambitious men 30 years after Muhammad passed away.

Islamic Civilization: The Dynastic Period

In This Chapter

- Learn about the Umayyads, the first Muslim dynasty
- Discover the wonders of Baghdad and its Abbasid flavor
- Step into the world of Muslim culture, art, literature, and architecture
- Find out why the Muslim world fragmented into several competing states

Islam produced a civilization that in many ways far surpassed Rome at its height. From the time of Muhammad's famed Hijrah, or migration, to Medina in 622 until the year of the fateful destruction of Baghdad in 1258, a single Muslim government ruled over most of the ever-expanding world of Islam. Although civil wars and dynastic feuding would engulf the political tier, life for the average Muslim citizen was far better than in Europe, which was a land of mud huts and illiteracy. In the Muslim world, vibrant cities teeming with artists, scholars, merchants, and rogues provided endless opportunities for enrichment and intellectual advancement.

Muslim rulers were patrons of the arts and learning, and they set up such public services as hospitals, primary schools, colleges, and even rest stops on the caravan trails. Any Europeans who could afford to do so made their way to the great universities in the Muslim world; there they could study and learn what no Christian school could offer. But this upward growth was rudely interrupted by invasions that left much of the Muslim world occupied by either heathen Mongols or fanatic Crusaders. Rising out of the ashes, the unitary Muslim state that had disappeared in the year 1258 was supplanted by a fragmented jigsaw puzzle of competing kingdoms and sultanates. In this chapter, I take you on a grand tour through this period in Muslim history.

The Umayyads

After the death of the fourth caliph, Ali, in 661, his son, Hassan, declared himself eligible to be the next caliph. As the grandson of Muhammad and the son of Ali, Hassan had a lot of support in Arabia and Iraq. (Many people around the area of Kufah had developed a kind of hero-worship toward Ali that would later result in the formation of the distinctive *Shi'a* sect of Islam.) But Mu'awiya, the governor of Syria, also laid claim to the title of caliph. Another protracted civil war might have ensued except for the fact that the pious Hassan quickly retracted his claim and retired to private life before the situation spiraled out of control. Mu'awiya was then able to anoint himself the caliph of the entire Muslim world.

The *Umayyads,* as this dynasty was called, would rule for the next 90 years from Damascus. During their tenure, the borders of the empire expanded in all directions, from China to France. Islamic learning flourished, and the major traditions of Islamic Law began to be established. Hundreds of books were written every year on every subject imaginable, from gardening to politics. Free public hospitals and schools were set up in every city and town, and Muslim scientists and philosophers were busy making new discoveries and organizing the knowledge they had acquired from their subject nations.

DEFINITION

The name **Umayyad** comes from *Banu Umayyah,* a clan that falls under the umbrella of the Quraish tribe of Mecca.

How the Caliphate Became Hereditary

Mu'awiya broke an important Islamic rule about choosing new leaders. Instead of letting the Muslims form a committee to elect a new caliph after his death, Mu'awiya decreed that his own son, Yazid, would be the caliph after him. This outraged many Muslims because Yazid was known to drink wine and to live a wasteful lifestyle—two indulgences that were forbidden in Islam. The hereditary question also was a problem because the Prophet was very clear about choosing people on merit and not on birth.

Mu'awiya died suddenly in the year 680, and Yazid promptly declared himself the caliph. Many religious scholars and the few surviving companions of the Prophet openly opposed him, including Ali's other son, Hussain, who refused to accept the worldly minded Yazid as the new sovereign and instead assumed the title himself.

Hussain was able to gather a small group of supporters and began to set up his government in Kufah. Yazid meanwhile sent an army of 4,000 to crush this challenger, and when word of the approaching invasion reached Iraq, most of Hussain's men deserted him. At a place named Karbala, the Syrian army surrounded Hussain's forces, which now numbered less than a hundred, and killed them all to the last man and woman. It is this episode of cruelty that Shi'as commemorate every year in the first month of the Islamic year.

ASK THE IMAM

Every year, Muslims from the Shi'a sect of Islam hold passion plays to commemorate the martyrdom of Hussain at Karbala. Some go to extremes and cut their foreheads or beat themselves with whips to express their sorrow at his cruel murder. Sunni Islam rejects the validity of this practice.

After Yazid's death, many caliphs of his line came and went. Some were effective administrators, while others were lackluster. One of the most famous of the later Umayyad rulers was Umar ibn Abdul Aziz, who ruled from 717 to 719 C.E. He was known as an excellent Muslim and earned the nickname "the Second Umar," after the famed early head of the Islamic state. He ruled with justice and fairness. He even sent Muslim missionaries as far away as Tibet and China. Umayyad rule would last until 750, when internal dissent brought the second and last great dynastic house in the unified world of Islam to power: the Abbasids.

The Abbasids and the Mongol Invasions

A group known as the Abbasids overthrew the Umayyads after a series of wars and internal rebellions. The caliphs of this line, who claimed to be descendants of the Prophet's uncle, Abbas, were to rule for the next five centuries, and it was under their auspices that the greatest progress was made in the arts, sciences, literature, and medicine. In Abbasid cities, libraries, and schools jostled for space with bazaars and the mansions of the wealthy. The city of Baghdad, known as the jewel of the world, was founded by the second Abbasid caliph as a unique fortress city built in the shape of a wheel, with all roads leading to the palace in the center.

The Abbasid Empire gradually declined, however, in its later years, owing to bad government practices and a weakness for foolish spending among many of the nobles and leaders. Some of the caliphs were more interested in constructing palaces, holding expensive pageants, and drinking alcohol than in upholding the banner of the

Islamic way of life. One notable exception was the famed Harun ar-Rashid, who is the caliph mentioned often in the famous collection of stories entitled *The Thousand and One Nights.*

An inside view of Jerusalem's famous Dome of the Rock, built during Umayyad rule. Muslims call it Al Quds, or the Holy Place.
(Courtesy of Aramco)

In the dynasty's waning years, local warlords and charismatic leaders carved several semi-independent states out of the empire, actions that further weakened the central authority. By the year 1000, North Africa was completely lost to a Shi'a dynasty known as the Fatamids, named after the Prophet's youngest daughter. The most important new force to weaken Abbasid power, however, was that of the Seljuk Turks. They were recent converts to Islam whose military prowess came to be a vital support to Abbasid authority. Eventually they got smart and realized they could usurp power for themselves, and they succeeded in reducing the power of the caliph to that of a ceremonial head. The last Abbasid ruler spent all of his time in vain ceremonies and refused to act when word of an impending invasion reached him. As history would show, the invaders would not spare his beloved city, as he had hoped, and the Muslim world was soon going to find itself on the verge of annihilation.

Abbasid rule and the city of Baghdad were wiped out in 1258, when vicious invaders called the Mongols swept into Muslim lands like a tidal wave. They conquered all of Muslim Persia and Iraq and unleashed a reign of terror against the populace that is eclipsed only by Adolph Hitler's Nazi war machine. It is estimated that over 16 million people were massacred in Persia and Iraq alone. (It took the Mongols 40 days to execute the entire population of Baghdad.) Libraries were burnt, cities were razed, and the practice of Islam was forbidden under Mongol decree.

Eventually, however, after several generations of life off the harsh Central Asian steppe, the grandchildren and great-grandchildren of the original Mongols converted to Islam. It took nearly 100 years but they were finally able to appreciate and learn about the teachings of the faith and the civilization it bore. Soon the Mongol rulers were restoring mosques, reopening schools, and adopting the cultures of the lands they lived in. They even went on to conquer nearly all of Hindu India and a large part of southern Russia and Eastern Europe for Islam. But the power and might of the Abbasids would never again be achieved by any other Muslim empire.

The Golden Age of Islamic Civilization

Islam as a religion promotes study and learning. Contrary to popular opinion, Islam is not against modernity or scholarship. In fact, for most of the last 1,000 years it was the Muslim world that was advancing on all fronts and the Christian world that was lagging behind in the arts and sciences. During the Abbasid caliphate, Muslim cities were the largest in the world, with well-established social services and a cultural vibrancy that caused Europeans to marvel. Free public hospitals, universities, local public health inspectors, even paved roads were everyday parts of life for citizens in Muslim lands.

The Islamic world was a cosmopolitan mix of people of all races and colors who spoke dozens of different languages (Arabic was the *lingua franca*, being the religiously sanctioned tongue). The mighty caravan routes were much like superhighways are today and were filled with traffic and congestion. International business was booming, and for the first time, merchants could rely on writing checks that would be honored at banks throughout the Muslim world. Travel was easier than at any time in human history, and the practice of medicine was no longer a quack's profession, with aspiring doctors required to pass exams. The Islamic world, in short, was much like modern America with the exception of the technology available today.

Islamic Art Forms

Muslim artists often quote a maxim attributed to the Prophet: God is beautiful, and He loves beauty. The Muslim world produced many different art forms, even as Muslim artists continue to ply their trade today. But there is a prohibition in Islam against painting or drawing people or animals that appear *too* lifelike. This is in keeping with the anti-idolatry trend in the faith. But beyond this there are few other curbs on free artistic expression. The following list presents the main art forms that the world of Islam produces:

Calligraphy   Writing the Arabic script in a fancy and artistic manner. Primarily, Muslim calligraphers have used verses of the Qur'an as their subject matter. There are several styles of writing the Arabic script, much like the different fonts on today's word processors; and the flourishing strokes of a good calligrapher are highly prized in the Muslim world.

Geometric design   Tessellations, as they are called, are repeating geometric designs. Muslim mathematicians made this type of artwork possible with the development of algebra and trigonometry. Most mosques in the traditional Muslim world have some element of this art form in their construction.

Arabesque   A distinctive combination of floral design and artistic patterns. Europeans copied many of these motifs during the Renaissance, and Muslim influences can be seen in cathedrals throughout France, Germany, and Italy.

Persian miniatures   Small paintings by Muslim artists of scenes that depict a variety of subjects from kings to peasants. This style of painting spread over several regions of the Islamic world.

Architecture

Public buildings have always had a special place in Islam. The mosque, which has to hold large crowds every day, was often the largest and most beautifully constructed edifice in any Muslim city. Architectural monuments such as the Taj Mahal and the Blue Mosque in Istanbul stand out as stunning achievements. Palaces, colleges, and libraries also received grand treatment and rival the great castles and palaces of Europe in their beauty and complexity.

Literature

Every civilization is judged by the knowledge it leaves behind. Although the world of Islam is by no means gone from world affairs, its greatest period of intellectual and cultural achievement occurred during the Abbasid caliphate, with later contributions by the various Muslim states that broke away. It was during this time that papermaking was adopted from China, enabling the publication of books on a large scale.

For the first time, authors writing in Arabic, Farsi, and other languages were actually able to make money from their efforts. Because of the religious commandment in Islam that Muslims must learn to read and write, the tremendously large literate populations of the teeming Muslim cities were fertile ground for a steady stream of books, manuals, and letters. The main library in Baghdad had thousands of titles that people could borrow, and bookstores made an appearance for the first time as well. Some of the best-known authors from this period were the satirist Al Jahiz, the philosopher Al Ghazali, and the adventurer Ibn Batutta. A fictional practical joker named *Goha* who stars in a collection of stories was also quite popular.

Famous works of literature include …

The Arabian Nights   A collection of stories, from Sinbad and Ali Baba to Aladdin and Ma'ruf the Cobbler, that have entertained people for centuries.

The Mathnawi   Poetry from Jalaluddin Rumi. Currently, his poems about faith and life sell more books in America than any other poet's.

Layla and Majnun   The classic Romeo and Juliet tale by Nizami that predates Shakespeare by centuries.

The Conference of Birds   Farid ud-Din Attar's story of the quest to find the king of the birds and what the weary travelers really find.

The Musings of Rabi'a al-Adawiya   Passionate, intense, and moving verse from Islam's most famous female mystic.

The Adventures of Seyf bin Dhi Yazan   Sort of like a Muslim Robin Hood and Prince Charming rolled up into one.

The Island of Animals   A fable about the animals of the world taking man to court for mistreating them.

The Rubbaiyat   Poetry of Omar Khayyam. Irreverent and often philosophical verse that begs the reader to love life.

The Beginnings of Rival Muslim States

As I mentioned earlier, the strength of the Abbasid caliphate weakened to such an extent that entire regions were able to break away and achieve de facto independence. After the Mongol invasions, the permanent dismemberment of the unitary Muslim state was complete. Even though the Mongols eventually converted, they merely remained the lords of their own nations. From the thirteenth century onward, several large Muslim empires competed amongst themselves. These included the Persian Empire, the various Turkish states, the Mamlukes of Egypt and Syria, and the Mughals of India. (In those territories where Islam was spreading through missionary efforts, these areas developed political realities of their own, such as in western Africa and Southeast Asia.)

Although the Ottoman Turks would eventually unify much of the Muslim heartland in a state that would last until the twentieth century, they were never able to extend their sway over the eastern half of the Muslim world. Thus, a distinctive western and eastern Islamic flavor could be seen for the first time. Ironically, even though the Muslim world became so fragmented, it survived, albeit in truncated form. By contrast, when the Roman Empire collapsed in the fifth century, its civilization disappeared. Islam did not suffer the same fate because it is more than a culture and a civilization; it is also a religion offering spiritual guidance.

Islam and Spain: A Unique Blend

When the Abbasids seized power from the Umayyads in 750, they ordered the execution of every member of the Umayyad ruling elite. (They didn't want some prince to pop up and rally the people against them in the future.) But one member of the Umayyad household managed to escape, and he made his way across North Africa and into Spain, where he founded a new branch of the Umayyad house. Muslims had already conquered Spain, as early as the year 711, when Tariq bin Ziyad, the famous Muslim general, crossed the Strait of *Gibraltar* at the invitation of a Spanish Christian chief.

DEFINITION

Gibraltar comes from the term *Jabal Tariq,* or the Mountain of Tariq, after the place where General Tariq bin Ziyad landed in Spain.

Spain was quite easy for the Muslims to take, given that the populace was in a constant state of dissatisfaction with their king, Roderick the Visigoth. During the first major battle, two flanks of his army, which were commanded by his rivals, actually switched allegiances and joined the Muslim side, resulting in the defeat of the despised ruler. By 718 the Muslims were in possession of nearly the entire peninsula.

For the next 800 years, the Islamic government in Spain worked to build a civilization so advanced that its influence helped to bring Europe out of the Dark Ages and resulted in the Enlightenment. The fabulous Muslim cities of Cordoba, Seville, Toledo, and Granada boasted paved streets lit by oil lamps, hospitals, universities, endless bazaars, libraries, and public gardens. Europeans flocked to these great cities and returned home with new ideas and a burning zeal to make backward Europe as advanced as Muslim Spain.

Unfortunately, the unity of the Umayyad state in Spain was to be short-lived. Eventually it broke up into competing fiefdoms—more than 20 at one point—which became easy prey for the Christians in northern Spain who began reasserting their power. By the year 1492, the Spanish Catholics had conquered the last Muslim stronghold of Granada. They turned thousands of mosques into churches, burned mountains of books written in Arabic, and initiated the infamous Inquisition in which hundreds of thousands of Muslim civilians were rounded up and tortured to death by the Church. The legacy of Islamic Spain can be seen even today in the thousands of buildings that still stand and in the flavor of the Spanish language and the Spanish culture, which were heavily influenced by Muslims during their rule.

DISPELLING THE MYTH

Jews in Islamic Spain had more rights than Jews anywhere else in the world at that time. They lived generally in safety and prosperity alongside their Muslim and Christian neighbors. This period of intense Jewish cultural growth is often called the Golden Age of Judaism.

The Mughals

Muslim rule in India began in the year 712. Hindu pirates, acting under the authority of a local lord, attacked a ship carrying Muslim civilians. When the pirates refused to release them, the Umayyad governor of Iraq ordered an army to attack what is today Pakistan. But it wouldn't be until the sixteenth century that Muslim rule over nearly the entire subcontinent would be complete.

The famed Mughal dynasty, which ruled India from 1526 to 1857, produced many great works of art and architecture, most notably the Taj Mahal. However, the insidious designs of the encroaching British spelled the doom of Muslim rule in India. After a final major battle to drive the British out of his domain, the last Mughal emperor was captured and sent into exile. The British chopped off the heads of all of his sons and sent them to him on a tray as a "present."

The Crusades

No other event has defined Muslim-Christian relations to such a great degree as the Crusades. These were a series of European invasions, lasting from 1095 to 1270, into the Middle East to capture the Holy Land for Christendom. The first of the eight expeditions was wildly successful from the Christian standpoint, but the rest were ill-organized and doomed to failure. The Muslim world was weak and divided, and the Abbasids held no influence in the region.

Europe's First Colonies

Although the Holy Land was under Muslim administration for over five centuries, Christian pilgrims were still allowed to visit and perform their religious rites. In addition, a large Christian and Jewish population lived in peaceful coexistence with their Muslim neighbors. Owing to the general lack of education among European Christians, however, pilgrims from that continent would often enter Jerusalem and create public spectacles with loud singing, dancing, and rowdy musical bands. When the Muslim authorities attempted to curtail the unseemly activities, Christian monks began spreading wild rumors and increasingly inflamed propaganda that the Muslims were interfering with their religious rights.

At the same time the emperor of the ever-shrinking Byzantine Empire was sending a passionate plea to the pope in Rome to save his kingdom from the Seljuk Turks. This event combined with the already tense situation in the Holy Land provided a rallying point. Pope Urban II called upon the petty kings of Europe to march to the Holy Land and capture it for their religion. He promised to forgive their sins and admit them to Heaven for their trouble. The kings of France, England, the German fiefdoms, and Hungary were the first to respond, though they just promised loot and fiefdoms to their noblemen.

> **DISPELLING THE MYTH**
>
> Saladin was known for his great self-restraint, chivalry, and manners. He exemplified the Qur'anic ideal of the warrior-scholar. When Richard the Lion-Hearted lost his horse during the course of one battle, Saladin sent him a new one with the message, "It is not right that so brave a warrior should fight on foot."

The unprepared Muslims withered under the massive invasion force; on June 15, 1095, the victorious Europeans entered Jerusalem. They promptly got down to business and slaughtered the entire population of the city. A contemporary Christian writer reported that so much blood was spilled that the streets were filled with streams of it. (The phrase "Kill them all, God knows His own" was coined by a representative of the pope who was asked what to do about the Christian Arabs who looked just like the Muslims.) One by one, other Muslim cities fell, and the butchering of civilians went on. When the Crusaders ran out of steam, they established effective rule over a territory stretching from southern Turkey to the border of Egypt.

The End of a Dream

The Crusaders were disunited and constantly quarrelling amongst themselves. The fossilized feudal system they had carried with them from Europe made it nearly impossible for them to work together or to improve the lives of their subjects. Their demise was assured after a Muslim sultan named Saladin rose to power in Syria. He united several Muslim regions under his command and fought a furious campaign to liberate the conquered territories. The most decisive battle occurred in 1187 at Hattin in Syria. Saladin completely defeated the Frankish army, and nothing stood between him and Jerusalem.

In 1192, Saladin forced the surrender of the city and entered it under a peace agreement. In contrast to what the Christians had done, he did not punish the civilians or soldiers of the city but only took over the administration. This story was repeated throughout the rest of Palestine. Although the Europeans made many other attempts to retake the Holy Land, they failed. By 1270, the Christians had resigned themselves to Muslim control over Jerusalem and had resumed their pilgrimage customs under guarantee of safe passage from the Muslim authorities.

The Least You Need to Know

- The political structure of the Islamic state became a family dynasty 30 years after Muhammad's passing.
- The first dynasty, which lasted 90 years, was called the Umayyad dynasty.
- The second Muslim dynasty, the Abbasid, came to power in a violent uprising and further expanded the borders of the Islamic state. The Abbasids founded the city of Baghdad as their capital.
- Muslim civilization produced great painters, authors, architects, and calligraphers whose works are on a par with the artistic achievements of any other civilization.
- The Mongols practically wiped out Islamic civilization in their destruction of over half of the Muslim world.
- The Crusades were a series of European invasions into the Middle East. Muslim forces eventually drove them out but not until Muslims united under a determined leader named Saladin.

The Legacy of Islam

Great civilizations have often passed on a considerable legacy before being extinguished. Although Islam is far from extinct, its greatest influences occurred at the same time that Europe was sunk in the Dark Ages. Greek learning and the discoveries of other nations were rapidly assimilated into the growing Muslim scientific community, where they were refined and added to. Indeed, Islam produced some of the finest scientists that humanity has ever seen, and they made discoveries that laid the groundwork for many modern technological achievements.

Islam as a phenomenon continues to evolve in our world. Through its many forms and sects and trends, the influence of Muslims upon the economic, political, and moral life of the world is considerable. In this part, I discuss who the Muslims are and how they differ across regions, sects, and cultural traditions.

Discover the Influences of Islam

In This Chapter

- Learn how the knowledge of the ancient Greeks was saved by Islamic civilization
- Discover the Muslims' involvement in the European Renaissance
- Meet some influential Muslim philosophers and scientists
- Find out how the legacy of Muslim civilization has shaped the modern world

The rapid expansion of the Muslim world in its first 1,000 years encompassed more than just the acquisition of territory and converts. Islamic civilization absorbed the learning, ideas, books, and philosophies of the Greeks, Romans, Indians, and Persians, thus making a new synthesis of knowledge possible. But Muslims went even further; they built upon this knowledge with new discoveries of their own, inventing algebra, ophthalmology, trigonometry, historiography, and many other sciences.

Islam created a multicultural, vibrant transnational society more diverse and productive than Rome ever was. Europeans, whose feudal nations were backward and undeveloped until five centuries ago, fed off of Muslim achievements and found their desire for advancement was ignited in the translated books they acquired from the universities and libraries of Islam. Nearly every aspect of modern society, whether something as mundane as writing a check or as lofty as astronomy, has been influenced by Islamic discoveries, refined and honed in the great civilization brought about by the Qur'an. As I take you on a tour through the legacy of Islam, think of how Muslim achievements have made life easier for all of us today.

Charting the Muslim Influence on Europe

Muslim rulers took it as an act of piety to construct mosques, hospitals, schools, and universities. Consequently, in every major Muslim city there are numerous examples of each. Perhaps the greatest era of advancement in education took place during the Abbasid caliphate (750–1258). As a multiethnic society, the Abbasid rulers enjoyed wide access to the ideas and discoveries of many previous civilizations. This in turn led to the widespread availability of manuscripts for use by both scholars and students.

ASK THE IMAM

The oldest continuously functioning college in the world is Al-Azhar University in Cairo, Egypt. It was founded in the year 970 and has achieved the status of the most authoritative school of Islamic sciences in the Sunni Muslim world.

The expansion of knowledge in Muslim civilization can be divided into three phases. The first phase was inheritance. Ancient writings from the Greeks and others were collected and translated into Arabic. The availability of paper made duplication of these manuscripts possible, so universities as far away as Spain or Timbuktu could have their own copies on hand.

The most famous institution for the collection and translation of ancient books was known as the *Baytul Hikmah*, or House of Wisdom. Established by the Caliph, al-Ma'mun, in 830, this think tank was staffed by Muslims, Christians, Jews, Hindus, and Buddhists, and was given the task of making all the knowledge of the world available in the Arabic language. The works of Plato, Socrates, Aristotle, and Ptolemy were preserved for future generations through the medium of the Arabic language. (These were later translated from Arabic into Latin for Europe's consumption.)

In the second phase, Muslim scholars and scientists synthesized the diverse areas of knowledge into organized bodies of thought whose premises could be tested and proved or disproved. Muslims developed the scientific method of formulating a hypothesis and testing it to see whether it is correct. Visiting European students marveled over this process, which was unknown in dogma-plagued Europe. Adelard of Bath, a prominent Christian scholar of the Middle Ages, wrote: "Indeed, I have learned from my Arab masters to follow reason as a guide."

In the last stage, Muslims began adding to this store of knowledge with new discoveries of their own from the ninth century onward. The list of sciences either refined or invented by Muslims is dizzying: algebra, chemistry, astronomy, medicine, cartography, botany, and navigation, to list just a few. (The term Greco-Arab science was coined to label this synthesis of learning styles.) Given the religious impetus to learn to read and write, Muslim populations were generally literate enough to provide a steady stream of students, both male and female, to the great lecture halls of Islamic universities. By way of contrast, during this same period in Europe few could read beyond a scattering of priests and nobles.

The major conduit for Muslim learning into Europe was through the great colleges of Muslim Spain. Christians flocked to Cordoba, Toledo, Seville, and Granada to study subjects that were unknown in the rest of Europe. One contemporary Christian priest lamented, "All our young men are vying with each other to learn Arabic." This is no small statement. As much as English today is the international language of science, art, and technology, if you can imagine it, Arabic was that language from the ninth to the fifteenth centuries. New words such as *astrolabe*, *algorithm*, *soda*, *syrup*, and *zenith* were adopted into European languages, and Christians read the voluminous writings of Muslim scholars with enthusiasm.

DISPELLING THE MYTH

The main library in Muslim-ruled Cordoba had 400,000 books. The ninth-century rulers of Cairo maintained a public library with two planetariums, numerous reading rooms, and a collection of 1,600,000 different manuscripts.

Illuminating the Science Hall of Fame

Throughout the height of Muslim civilization, great Muslim thinkers represented every field of learning. Many of them were religious authorities, poets, and novelists in addition to being top scientists. Omar Khayyam, for example, who is best known for his risqué collection of poetry, *the Rubbaiyat*, was also an accomplished astronomer who produced a solar calendar far more accurate than the Gregorian calendar used in Europe. The following list summarizes some of the most famous Islamic thinkers and scientists:

Mohammad al-Khawarizmi (d. 840)   He is the founder of algebra, and he also laid the foundation for trigonometry.

Hasan ibn al-Haitham (d. 1040)   He established the science of optics and linked algebra with geometry.

Abu Raihan al-Biruni (d. 1048) He correctly established the circumference of the earth and studied the difference between the speed of sound and the speed of light.

Ibn Sina (d. 1037) Known as Avicenna in the West, this one man produced a textbook on the practice of medicine (known as the *Canon*) that was so comprehensive it was the main medical guide in Europe for more than five centuries. In another book, he classified all known pharmaceuticals and their uses. He also determined that the speed of light was constant.

Ali Ibn Rabban at-Tabari (d. 870) He wrote the first encyclopedia of medicine that collected together all known medical knowledge. This work spanned seven volumes.

Jabir Ibn Haiyan (d. 803) He is considered the father of modern chemistry through his work in classifying the elements and experimenting with their properties.

Abu Abdullah Al-Battani (d. 929) Like many other scientists in the Muslim world, Al-Battani knew the world was round. He was the first to correctly identify the length of the solar year to the second. He also made many discoveries in astronomy and mathematics.

Mohammad al-Razi (d. 930) His accomplishments in medicine were enormous. His 10-volume encyclopedia dealt exhaustively with Greco-Arab medicine. He correctly identified the source for smallpox and was the first to classify substances into organic and inorganic compounds.

FROM THE SOURCE

Muhammad said, "Acquire knowledge. It enables its possessor to distinguish right from wrong. It lights the way to heaven. It is our friend in the desert, our society in solitude, our compassion when friendless. It guides us to happiness. It sustains us in misery. It is an ornament among friends and an armor against enemies."

These are just a few of the great minds who revolutionized their areas of expertise. Visiting Europeans learned voraciously and returned to their lands to found colleges and universities such as the famous academies in Chartres, France.

Sadly, all of this vitality and progress in the sciences came to an end by the close of the fourteenth century. In the East, the Mongol devastation, the Crusades, and civil wars among the surviving rulers effectively ended the influence of the *'ulema*—the Muslim scholars and scientists—over the elites. The result was a decline in support for institutes of higher learning. Although important colleges remained opened, never again would there be that high level of intellectual activity.

In the West, the Catholic reconquest of Spain from Muslim rule resulted in massive mountains of Arabic-language books being burned by the Church, under the suspicion that they might be Qur'ans and were thus a threat to the state. The universities were closed, the scholars dispersed throughout the rest of the Muslim world, and the torch of Islamic inquiry was put out permanently—though not before Europe had been dragged out of its Dark Ages and into a new era of enlightenment. This was the legacy and the gift of Islam to our modern world today: the preservation of Greek knowledge and the great discoveries that made modern science possible.

Speaking in a Familiar Tongue

Islamic colleges in Spain were the most advanced in the world all throughout the Middle Ages. Every year hundreds of Europeans, eager to learn, enrolled and then later took their knowledge back to their home countries. They also eagerly translated books into the Latin language and circulated them widely. As they worked, they encountered many new terms and, having no other word for them, simply modified them for use in their own languages. Through this process, several European languages adopted thousands of words of Arabic origin, much like foreign languages today incorporate many English words, such as *computer, jeans,* and *okay.* Spanish has an estimated 6,500 Arabic words. English has nearly 10,000!

Uncovering the Unique Features of Islamic Civilization

What was life like in Cordoba, Cairo, or Baghdad during the height of Islamic civilization? Whether you were a commoner or a noble, chances are you would have been able to go to school and have a comparable level of education. Free schools for the less fortunate were established as early as the Umayyad caliphate, in accordance with religious dictates that Muslims must learn to read the Qur'an.

Every society needs a police force and other government officials to keep order and look out for the welfare of the population. In the Muslim world, this job was allotted to the *Muhtasib,* or Inspector General of Weights and Measures. These men and women were given wide powers to act on behalf of the public welfare. They regulated food production, fined polluters of rivers and streams, oversaw the sale and transport of milk, inspected restaurants and bathhouses, and strictly enforced a series of medical exams before any prospective doctor could begin to practice. One of the many surviving *Muhtasib* manuals included the following regulations:

- **#109** No seller of fruit or vegetables is to weigh his own merchandise by picking up his scales himself; on the contrary, they are to be hung at a fixed point.

- **#139** No one should be allowed to claim mastery over an art which he does not possess, above all in the practice of medicine, since this can lead to the loss of human lives: in truth it is the earth covering the tombs of dead men which hides the mistakes of the physician ... Each artisan's activities should be limited to the exercise of his own trade; only those whose experience is recognized may claim to have mastered a skill.

- **#195** A beast of burden should not be left standing in the bazaar, because it blocks the road and hinders people from passing and it might ... kick someone walking by.

- **#213** Metal workers and brass beaters must be made to stop the noisy part of their work during the required prayer times.

In addition to a reasonable amount of regulation in society for both hygiene and business, citizens of a typical Islamic city enjoyed paved streets lit by oil lamps at night. Spacious homes competed for space with apartment flats, and jobs were plentiful. The poor or homeless could count on public welfare from the *Zakat* officer in the town hall, and those who felt wronged could hire a lawyer, called a *hakeem*, and bring suit in court. Even the ruler could be sued. A man claiming that his animals were unlawfully sold to him once sued Saladin, the Muslim hero of the Crusades. Saladin sat in court with his lawyer and argued his case and was cross-examined at length. (The plaintiff later dropped his case after evidence was presented to prove him wrong.)

Muslim judges, called *Qadis*, could be male or female and were either appointed by the government or chosen by local communities. Following the dictates of the Qur'an to judge in all fairness, the Qadis also had to be masters of the Islamic legal sciences and honest individuals as well. Detailed records of actual court cases spanning the last 1,000 years of Islam have survived to this day.

Another benefit people enjoyed was the safety of depositing their money in institutions called *al bank*, which is the forerunner of the modern banking system. Venture capitalists could borrow money from the banks with an agreement to share a percentage of their profits with the lending institution. (Charging interest on loans is forbidden in Islam, so banks were picky about whom they loaned money to.) The much-publicized Islamic banking system today operates in much the same way.

DISPELLING THE MYTH

Muslims are allowed to live in non-Muslim lands provided they promote their religion to those around them. They must also respect the local laws of their adopted countries as long as the laws don't contradict the laws of Islam.

Travelers could count on safe roads, patrolled by the caliph or sultan's troops; and frequent rest areas, called *khans* (caravansaries), dotted all major roads. If travelers were short on cash, government offices would make non-interest loans to the truly needy ones or give a gift of funds outright. Checks could be written that would be honored by banks in other cities. Hotels, butlers, and the ever-present shopping mall known as the bazaar made shopping a snap.

The features of Islamic civilization sound suspiciously similar to many of the facets of modern life in the West. Now can you understand what the world of Islam lost? Muslims want that back, but they are saddled with fragmented states, outside interference, poverty and illiteracy, and bad governments. If American civilization were to come to an end and be replaced with something like that, wouldn't the descendants of today's citizens dream of what we have now?

The Least You Need to Know

- Muslim civilization preserved the knowledge of the ancient Greeks and others and passed it on to Europe.
- While Europe was in the Dark Ages, the Islamic world was the center for learning, inquiry, and science.
- The foundations for modern science and the scientific method were laid by Muslim researchers from the ninth to the thirteenth century.
- Muslim scholars invented algebra, made astounding astronomical discoveries, systematized chemistry, developed the practice of medicine to the highest standards in the world at that time, and made great strides in many other fields.
- Islamic civilization left a legacy upon which modern civilization is built. The western Europeans who studied in Muslim universities took what they had learned and built upon it.

Meet the Islamic Sectarian Movements

In This Chapter

- Learn about the different sects that existed in the early centuries of the Islamic Empire
- Understand the position of the Qur'an regarding religious diversity within the Muslim community
- Investigate the main differences between the majority Sunni sect and the minority Shi'a groups
- Discover the Sufi path and how it relates to Islam

Diversity is often praised as an essential component of the human experience. This diversity extends through all aspects of life, and many people would assert that pluralism in religion, both within and outside of a particular faith, is desirable and indicative of the overall health of the belief system. In this regard, all religions are divided into sects; whether they coexist in harmony is another matter. Christianity, Judaism, Hinduism, and Buddhism each contain myriad diverse branches that all took root from the same tree. The same is true of Islam. There are currently about two dozen different sects in the Muslim world. Some have ancient roots, whereas others are really quite recent.

The two largest sects that have survived to this day are the Sunnis and Shi'as. Together they account for more than 95 percent of the world's Muslims, with the Sunnis being in the vast majority. Other smaller groups continually compete for breathing space around the periphery of these two monoliths. What does Islam say about sectarianism? While the Prophet Muhammad did tolerate and even praise some differences of opinion, he did not approve of outright division. This sentiment is echoed in the Qur'an, which expressly forbids ideological conflict within the same religion to the point where overall unity is endangered. Why did the unity of the Muslim religion become compromised, and what are the reasons for each major split? This is the issue I explore in this chapter.

Sectarianism and Islam

The Qur'an accepts that preceding religious communities have broken up into sects. Although Islam calls upon its followers to be tolerant of people of other religions, it does not mention favorably the existence of sects within them. The Prophet Muhammad is quoted as saying, "The Jews have broken up into seventy-one sects. The Christians have broken up into seventy-two sects and my community will break up into seventy-three, and all of them will be in hellfire except one." When he made this pronouncement, the Muslim community was a single entity, centered on Medina, and no one could have conceived that Muslims would become so divided. One man asked, "Which sect will go to paradise?" Muhammad answered, "The one which I and my companions belong to."

This prediction contains the caveat that only one Muslim sect will be correct, and as a consequence, every different Muslim party, from Sunnis and Shi'as to Sufis and Salafis, vehemently claims that it is following the *authentic* tradition of the Prophet and his immediate followers. So which Islamic sect is the true one? As in the case of Christianity and Judaism, it depends on whom you ask. What I can say is that Islam is very explicit when it calls sectarianism a fault. The Qur'an warns Muslims, "And don't be like those … who split up their religion and became mere sects, each rejoicing in what it claims it has." (Qur'an 30:31–32)

DEFINITION

The term *Shi'a* literally means partisan of something, and thus is a descriptive name for Islam's second-largest sect, whose founders were ardent supporters of the Prophet's cousin, Ali, in the struggles for power in early Islamic history.

Without attempting to discuss the merits or drawbacks of any particular sect, I explore some of the most important ones and show how they have influenced the Muslim community through the years until the present time. For the record, the beliefs and practices of Islam, as outlined in this book thus far, are from the majority Sunni position, unless otherwise noted.

The Kharajites: An Early Sect

How did sectarianism begin in Islam, and what were the first sects? To answer this question we need to look at events during the period of the first four caliphs (632–661), for the decisions made within that time frame resulted in most of the sects we have today. The first two groups to break off from the mainstream majority were the *Kharajites*, which you read about in Chapter 23, and the *Shi'a* (sometimes spelled as *Shiite*). The *Shi'as* are discussed later in this chapter. A third group arising a few centuries later attempted to blend Islam with Greek philosophy. Although each of these early sects resulted from complicated political feuding, only the Shi'a have survived as a viable force to the present day.

The Kharajites were originally just a political faction in the army of the fourth caliph, Ali (d. 661), who was struggling for control of the empire with a rival named Mu'awiya. When Ali entered peace talks with his foe, the Kharajites took it as a sign of weakness and *seceded* in their loyalty to him (thus the meaning of their name). The members of this group, however, soon began looking beyond politics and started delving into theology. Being outside the mainstream effectively meant there was no check on their activities.

The Kharajites focused almost exclusively on issues related to fate and the nature of sin. They had the uncompromising belief that if a Muslim committed a major sin, he was no longer a believer. Another issue they tackled was entry into Islam. Was a child born automatically into the fold of Islam, or did each individual have to choose Islam after attaining the age of puberty? The Kharajites opted for the latter. (Think of the Protestant/Catholic debate on when a person should be baptized and you'll understand the significance such questions had in early Islam.) Their main contribution, however, was in calling attention to the practice of unfairly assigning new converts to the role of junior members in existing Arab tribes. This sect, which never gained a large following, is now relegated primarily to the country of Oman where it is called *'Ibadiism*.

DEFINITION

The Qur'an and the sayings of Muhammad are the main sources from which Islam is derived. The controversy caused by the early sects lay in interpreting what that data actually meant and how it applied to religious ideology.

The Sunnis and Shi'as

It has been estimated that Sunnis make up approximately 85 percent of the world's Muslim population, with Shi'as accounting for much of the rest. When people talk of sectarianism in Islam, these two names, which are rooted in the earliest days of the Islamic caliphate, are mentioned the most. It may be tempting to make a passing comparison here with the great Protestant-Catholic divide in Christianity. However, whereas that division didn't occur until well over a thousand years into the life of the Church, the great Sunni-Shi'a break came within the lifetime of the surviving companions of the Prophet Muhammad and was not originally centered on doctrinal disputes, but on politics and succession.

The main reason for the existence of the Shi'a sect is directly related to the election of Abu Bakr as the first caliph of the Muslim community in the year 632. The Prophet had just passed away, and the leaders of Medina gathered to choose a political successor to keep the fledgling Muslim nation united. There was no question about doing this because the Prophet had spoken about it so often. After a heated debate, Abu Bakr was chosen to lead. Ali, the cousin and son-in-law of Muhammad (he was married to Muhammad's favorite daughter, Fatimah), was not present at that meeting, and he later protested that he should have been given a fair shot at being selected the caliph.

Although Ali refused to swear allegiance to Abu Bakr for a few months, eventually he caved in and both he and his supporters took the oath. The stage was set for bad blood, however; and as each new caliph was elected, Ali's friends stood by in anger, watching other men being given the nod while their beloved leader was passed over (hence the name Shia't Ali, or Party of Ali). Finally, in 656 when Ali was finally elected the fourth caliph, his group felt vindicated. Ali's rule was short-lived, though; and the Shi'as (as his followers came to be known), who were still just a political faction at that time, felt that the clan of Banu Umayyah had unfairly snatched away the caliphate through war and deception. That the victorious Mu'awiya would decree his own son to be the caliph after him was an especially impious affront.

The die was soon cast for permanent division as the sons of Mu'awiya and Ali carried on their fathers' rivalry for the caliphate. Hussain, the son of Ali, gathered a small number of supporters to oppose the rule of Yazid, the son of Mu'awiya, who, in turn, raised his own army to crush this impetuous challenge to his widely unpopular elevation as caliph. In the year 680, Yazid's army was able to intercept Hussein near the city of Kufa in Iraq, and his men completely decimated Hussein's badly outnumbered quarry. Hussain's head was sent to Damascus in a bag as a trophy, much to the consternation even of many of Yazid's followers. Another son of Ali, known as Ali Zayn al Abideen, who was not present at the battle, was allowed to live unmolested until his death in Medina in 713. It is from this child of Ali that the line of Shi'a authority would descend through the generations.

The Shi'a Under Umayyad Rule

During Umayyad rule there were occasional uprisings of Shi'as, mostly in Iraq and Iran, but they met with little success. The Shi'as became more aware of themselves as a separate reality, however, and allegiance to their leader, or Imam, became much more strict. Thus by the waning years of Umayyad rule, Shi'as became an identifiable political party of sorts whose ultimate authority rested in a descendant of Ali. By the fifth generation, however, there was a split in loyalty between two half-brothers named Zayd and Al Baqir. Those who followed Zayd's leadership halted the direct line of spiritual succession with him and thus became known as the "Fivers." They believe any descendant of Ali from that point forward can be the Imam regardless of the directness of his family tree. Today the Zaydis, as they are called, reside mostly in Yemen where they make up over 40 percent of the population. Their rituals and beliefs differ little from the majority Sunni population, and they even accept the caliphate of both Abu Bakr and Umar, though they are divided as to the legitimacy of the third Caliph, Uthman.

Al Baqir, however, engendered the lion's share of support. His son (and subsequently the sixth Imam), Ja'far as-Sadiq (699–765), is credited with formulating the basis of Shi'a legal and religious concepts. Being of such prestigious lineage, he was able to wield a great amount of influence over his flock, and he chose to concentrate his time on organizing and systematizing what had, up until that point, been a movement focused on the narrow issue of succession. He crafted a School of Islamic Law, or *madh-hab*, that differs little from the four major Sunni schools and is generally accepted as legitimate by them. Today the Ja'fari Madh-hab, as it is called, is the official legal reference for the majority of Shi'as worldwide.

 DEFINITION

The **Shi'a Imams** are a line of men whose ultimate ancestor was Ali. Different groups of Shi'as stop at different Imams in the line of the family tree and consider their chosen man to be the last and most authentic final guide. There are *Fiver, Sevener,* and *Twelver* Shi'as. Each group has diverse religious doctrines.

After Ja'far's death in 765, the Shi'a divided into two separate sects, each following one of his two descendants, Musa and Isma'il. The Isma'ili sect, as it is called today, stopped the line with the latter and went on to develop its own doctrines further. This group held that the Imams were part of a grand cycle of history. In place of a ruling Imam, however, temporal leaders who could speak for a future-awaited savior would govern. (The Aga Khan is currently considered the worldwide head of one of the two existing Isma'ili branches of Shi'aism.) This group was active in missionary work and converted many peasants and people on the frontiers to its cause. They even succeeded in establishing several Isma'ili dynasties at different points in Muslim history.

From Political Movement to a Separate Sect

Near the end of Umayyad rule in 750, when the Abbasids (who were descendants of the Prophet Muhammad's uncle, Abbas) were gathering their supporters to stage a coup, the Shi'as joined the cause, thinking that the new rulers would hearken to their call and choose a descendant of Ali to be the caliph. When the Abbasids chose one of their own instead, the Shi'as withdrew their support and began looking inward. Periodic persecution followed by periods of neglect by the central authorities defined much of their early evolution into a distinct religious sect. Indeed, by the end of the eighth century, they had started to develop doctrines of their own that were quite specific and unique.

Accordingly, the Shi'as began to compile their own books of prophetic traditions and Qur'anic interpretation centering on what they considered to be the correct view of Islam. Many of the traditions they recorded were different from the ones assembled by the majority community during and shortly after Muhammad's passing. A major text was also prepared called the *Nahjul Balagha* (Path of Eloquence), in which the attributed sayings and sermons of Ali are collected. Variations in how the Five Pillars of Islam were practiced crept in also. For example, many Shi'as today combine certain prayers so that they actually pray at only three points during the day, not five. The Shi'a call to prayer adds lines in which Ali is praised, and extra holidays commemorating events in the life of Ali and his descendants have been added, such as the Eid ul Ghadir and the passion plays surrounding Hussain's martyrdom. In addition, a kind of historical revision took place in which most of the Prophet's companions were vilified and considered unfaithful to Islam.

Another area of difference with the majority Sunni community occurred in the province of leadership. While Sunnis have always taken a more relaxed view toward the selection of a leader (the most qualified adult male), Shi'a doctrine came to teach that Ali and his male descendants have a secret, almost prophetic, knowledge that is passed on from father to son. They are sinless and infallible and are therefore the only choice to rule over the community of believers. The first Shi'as followed Ali as their leader based on his association with Muhammad, though he sometimes disapproved of their excessive emphasis of his role. Succeeding generations rallied around his descendants, whom they called their *Imams* (leaders).

The main group of Shi'as, whom we now know as the "Twelvers" went on to follow four more descendants of Ali and were united as a group in Baghdad all throughout the Abbasid caliphate. The Abbasid caliphs generally tolerated their existence (barring a few periods of suppression) so long as the Shi'a never involved themselves in politics. Consequently, the community again turned inward and began refining its doctrines and unique perspective on Islam even further. Five important Shi'a concepts and doctrines (which are not shared by Sunnis) are summarized as follows:

- **Imamate**   Only a descendant of Ali can legitimately guide the Muslim community. Imams are sinless and suffer persecution willingly on behalf of all sincere believers. On Judgment Day, they, along with the Prophet's daughter, Fatima, will have the power to intercede on behalf of the sincere. Their knowledge and power to govern on Earth comes from God.

- **Taqiyya**   Given that the Shi'a community has often been the target of persecution, individual Shi'as are allowed to hide their true beliefs when among those who would harm them. By extension, those Imams who compromised or submitted to the authority of the Umayyads or Abbasids are absolved of their acquiescence.

- **Taqlid**   This is a concept that developed among both Sunnis and Shi'as, and it means to imitate or model oneself on the example of a pious scholar. But whereas it is much maligned in Sunni thought today, in Shi'aism it is considered essential that every believer choose a scholar whose legal rulings, practice of daily rituals, and understanding of the faith they will imitate.

- **Khums**   Shi'as are required to pay one fifth of their yearly earnings to their local mullah or religious authority above and beyond the annual *zakat* payment. This control over funds has enabled Shi'a clerics to remain independent of governmental control throughout their history.

- **Mutah**   The practice of *mutah*, or temporary marriage, was initially allowed in Islam's earliest years as a concession to soldiers who may have had to travel for weeks or months from home. Before he passed away, Muhammad outlawed the practice, according to Sunnis, though Shi'as dispute this and allow its practice. A man who enters into a *mutah* marriage pays an agreed amount of money to a woman with a marriage contract that has a set expiration date after which the marriage is no longer valid.

With the death of the eleventh Imam in 874, who apparently left no heirs, the Shi'a developed the concept of a twelfth *Hidden Imam,* who was taken as a baby into another realm of existence. A prominent Shi'a family of Baghdad, the Banu Nawbakht, called themselves the agents of the Hidden Imam and claimed they had contact with him and spoke his will. After 941, this contact was declared closed. The next phase of leadership for the Shi'a community then passed into the hands of men who were charged with speaking on behalf of the twelfth Imam, who communicated his will through dreams. This arrangement was to go on indefinitely until some future date when the Hidden Imam would return as a Messiah to liberate the Shi'a from the oppression heaped upon them by the usurpers of Ali's rightful office. He would also usher in a period of righteous rule over the earth.

The Twelver Shi'as gradually developed a new hierarchy of leadership consisting of an infallible pope-like figure to lead the community. This person would rule the masses through a temporal priesthood consisting of men with such titles as *Ayatullah, Mullah,* and *Hojatulislam.* (The late Ayatullah Khomeini, who participated in the Iranian Revolution in 1978, achieved the highest rank in the eyes of many of the worldwide Shi'a community and was considered infallible.) After the United States conquered Iraq in 2003, it soon found out how much allegiance ordinary Shi'as gave to their religious leaders, with the top Shi'a cleric in the country, Grand Ayatullah Sistani, playing the role of deal maker and breaker on a variety of issues ranging from elections and security to influencing the contents of the country's new constitution. (By way of contrast, Sunnis have no similar priesthood or identifiable religious structure.)

 DEFINITION

Ayatullah, the Shi'a term for a top-level cleric, means Sign of God.

The Shi'a differ with the majority Sunnis on many issues related to leadership, doctrine, practice, and scriptural selection. Competing Shi'a and Sunni political factions have struggled for power all throughout Muslim history. While some Shi'a dynasties were formed, most notably the Fatimid dynasty of Egypt (910–1171), it has pretty much been a Sunni party for most of Muslim history.

In recent times there has been a resurgence of Shi'a identity, especially in Lebanon, Iraq, Iran, Pakistan, and elsewhere. Iran, in particular, is governed as a Shi'a theocracy with democratic overtones. Sunni movements ranging from the benign to the puritanical have also enjoyed a renewed period of growth, and this has sometimes led to tensions in various parts of the Muslim world. One small puritanical movement in particular, known as Wahhabism, which began in Saudi Arabia in the late eighteenth century, has declared its opposition to Shi'aism in no uncertain terms, labeling Shi'as as apostates and unbelievers. (They also label most traditional Sunnis as unbelievers as well!) Unnoticed by many in the West, there has been something of a low-level war ongoing between the more radical followers of each group in such diverse places as Pakistan and Iraq, often consisting of small-scale attacks on each other's mosques and leaders.

With tensions high throughout the world, considering the ongoing fight against global terrorism, the situation may get worse before it gets better. What must be realized is that Islam, as taught by Prophet Muhammad and lived by his companions, cannot be blamed for passions and extraordinary events any more than Jesus can be blamed for the long list of unfortunate events that have happened in Christian history. One positive thing that has occurred recently in the Muslim world is that many have begun to question the illogical and un-Islamic teachings that have been put forward by oddball extremist groups for years. One would hope that something of a reformation back to authentic original Islam would soon make its appearance, giving hope once more to those who dream of a world based on justice and sincere devotion to the best in humankind. This describes the goal of the majority of all people of faith everywhere.

The Sufi Path

Sufis are perhaps the most well-known Muslims in the world. *Gentle, introspective,* and *highly spiritual* are the words that come to mind when Sufis are mentioned. However, *Sufism* is not really a sect of Islam; rather it is the name of a spiritually oriented trend that is promoted within any given existing sect. For example, you can have Sunni or Shi'a Sufis. Sufism implies a very esoteric, spiritual emphasis in one's practice of Islam (*tasawwuf*). The Sufis seek to bring the experience of faith deep within their hearts to attain a state of inner ecstasy. The famous poet Jalaluddin Rumi expressed it best when he wrote: "What God said to the rose and caused it to laugh in full-blown beauty, He said to my heart and made it a hundred times more beautiful." (*The Mathnawi*, vol. III, couplet 4129)

The Sufi movement didn't begin with a single founder, nor are all Sufis united in one organization. It was the culmination of many social trends that first arose in the Umayyad dynasty. With the rapid growth of the empire, wealth began pouring in from all corners of the world, and a lot of otherwise faithful Muslims began to over-indulge in worldly pleasures. (Islam, on a very basic level, is against overindulgence, and Muhammad's personal example was one of frugality and self-denial of most of life's pleasures.) In addition, as the legal schools of thought, or *madh-habs*, were being formulated by the scholars of Islamic Law, some people felt there was too much emphasis on the rules and not enough on the spirit behind them.

Conscientious individuals began to see the rise of opulence, legalism, and pageantry among the Muslim community as a kind of deception. The dangerous life of the world was about to engulf the pure message of Islam and leave nothing but an empty shell in its wake. These spiritually minded people started to renounce the world and live very simple lives to promote an example for others to follow. The very name *Sufi* comes from the Arabic word for wool, which became the preferred clothing of these people (who shunned silk and other fineries). This train of thought was not some-thing invented out of thin air, however, for the Qur'an often spoke of the deception inherent in the life of the world. It also emphasized God's love and the importance of making His remembrance the focal point of one's life.

In time, as the dynastic struggles of the Umayyads and Abbasids wore on, intellectual and spiritual geniuses arose throughout the Middle East who attracted followers and students seeking to emulate the Sufi state of self-enlightenment. This ever-increasing association of individuals eventually gave rise to Sufi orders, or *tariqas*, from the twelfth century onward, which maintained headquarters and missions in many Muslim and non-Muslim lands. A *shaykh* would act as a kind of chief abbot and had absolute authority over his or her disciples. The basic foundation that Sufi shaykhs used to legitimize their power was the life of the Prophet Muhammad himself. They called him the exemplar of the God-oriented lifestyle and suggested they were merely continuing the tradition with their followers. The primary ideas of Sufism can be summarized as follows:

- Faith in God can be experienced by the devoted believer through a program consisting of meditation, chanting, selfless love for others, and self-denial.

- Worldly possessions, if not kept to a minimum, can corrupt a person's soul. Frugality is the key to spiritual wealth.

- The path of Sufism requires its followers to develop patience, thankfulness to God, and a complete reliance on God's knowledge of the future.

- In addition to the Qur'an and hadiths, another body of wisdom is contained in the teachings of the great Sufi masters. These consist of poems and wis-dom stories that have hidden meanings.

DEFINITION

The Whirling Dervishes are Sufis who follow the teachings of Jalaluddin Rumi (d. 1273). They spin rhythmically while chanting the 99 names of God in elaborate ceremonies called *semas*.

A new generation of Sufi literature soon arose that attempted to explain, often through allegory, the path of the sincere seeker and what pitfalls one may expect to find. Two of the most famous works from the twelfth century were *The Story of Layla and Majnun* and *The Conference of Birds.* The first is basically a Romeo and Juliet story whose subtext is meant to show how lost we are from God and what a hellish life we will have to endure until our ultimate reunion is achieved, while the second book is a Muslim-style *Canterbury Tales* in which a group of seekers are ushered on the path to their Lord and encounter a series of obstacles, each resolved with a story or allegory, until they ultimately learn that the path to God starts within themselves.

While most Sufis have generally remained within the pale of Islamic Law, starting during the Abbasid caliphate and beyond, some have gone to extremes. Bizarre rituals involving *jinns*, sword swallowing, numerology, and other stunts have become common fare in folk Sufism; and a few Sufis have even come to deny some very basic Islamic dictates, such as the prohibition against drinking wine, praying at the tombs of the dead, and self-flagellation. Many Sufis have also engaged in music and singing, much to the chagrin of the religious purists. This behavior has resulted in Sufism getting a bad reputation among the traditional *'ulema* (scholars), and many modern Muslim leaders look upon Sufism as suspect even to this day, despite the popular support of the masses in much of the Islamic world.

There were attempts to reconcile Sufism and orthodoxy in the Middle Ages. Several prominent theologians, especially Imam Abu Hamid Al Ghazali (1058–1128), worked tirelessly to formulate a grand synthesis of law and spirit. While schooled in the prevailing legal approach to Islam, he adopted Sufism into his own personal practice of Islam later in life, after realizing that legalism was not very spiritually satisfying. While the gaps were closed significantly through the efforts of him and others, and Sufis came to enjoy a renewed wide acceptance in the Muslim world, there are still notable exceptions. For instance, the Salafis, an ultraconservative Sunni movement, consider Sufis to be misguided at best and outside the fold of Islam at worst.

The Sufi movement has actually benefited the Muslim world in many ways. During the centuries of political and economic decline (1500–1900), Sufi orders took up the task of teaching Islam to the general masses. While traditional scholars largely were absent from Muslim society, preferring to study and debate within closed walls, it was the Sufis who traveled as missionaries, operated charities, and provided spiritual guidance in the countryside. Islam was introduced to places such as Indonesia and central Asia almost wholly in this way.

Sufi poetry, which tackles major religious and philosophical questions, is the source for inspiration for millions of Muslims—and now non-Muslims. In fact, poetry, storytelling, and verse have been the primary teaching tools for passing on Sufi knowledge. Perhaps the best-known poet in the world at this time is Rumi, whose anthologies of poetry now sell more copies than any other poet in North America.

Common Sufi practices for achieving enlightenment consist of the following:

- Chanting God's names and praises in unison (*zikr*) while seated in a circle or standing and turning slowly. This ritual can be done singly or in great performances with dozens, or even hundreds, of others. Music often accompanies such large gatherings.

- Fasting, Qur'an reading, and meditation in remote, natural places, especially in the early morning.

- Prolonged prayer at night and frequent supplications for knowledge and forgiveness.

- Sitting at the feet of a shaykh, listening to his or her teachings and stories, and then contemplating their meaning. Combined with spiritual rituals, over time the initiate can rise in the ranks to become a member of the inner circle.

- Pilgrimage to the shrines of past Sufi masters (who are known as *saints*).

- The use of aromatherapy to heighten awareness.

- Selfless devotion to the poor and needy to emphasize the true intent of religion.

Some of the main traditional Sufi *tariqas* (orders) that have established branches in the West are the *Naqshabandi*, the *Chisti*, the *Tijaniyya*, and the *Qadiriyyah*.

Sufism has enjoyed rapid growth in the West since the 1960s. Sufi orders are being established by Muslims and even by non-Muslims who don't necessarily want to convert to Islam, but who desire to participate in the spiritual discipline. The most organized order in the United States and Europe seems to be the Naqshabandis, whose activities can be perused on the web at www.sunnah.org. Although there is a vast difference in each Sufi group's adherence to basic Islamic teachings, there is no doubt that this spiritual trend found in Islam has found a new home and is now a part of the American religious tradition.

The Least You Need to Know

- Islam is officially against sectarianism, though Muhammad foretold its appearance among Muslims.
- The earliest sects of Islam were formed over political and doctrinal issues. The main areas of conflict concerned who should rule and what was the extent of humankind's free will.
- The Sunni sect is the largest single body of Muslims, consisting of approximately 85 percent of all the world's followers of Islam.
- The Shi'a sect of Islam began because Ali was not elected the first caliph. It would later develop its own unique doctrines.
- Sufism emphasizes spirituality and self-discipline as a way to achieve enlightenment. Sufis often chant and meditate on God and live lives devoted to frugality and charity.

Glossary

Allahu Akbar   An incomplete Arabic sentence which literally means, "God is greater than …" The implication of leaving it as an unfinished sentence is that no matter how you complete it, God is greater than that, too.

Ahl al Kitab   "People of the Book." Jews and Christians who received revelations (books) from God in the past.

alim   A scholar in Islam. Plural: *'ulema*. This office is open to both males and females.

Allah   "The One God before Whom there are no others." It is linguistically related to the Old Testament Hebrew name for God, *Eloh* (pl. *Elohim*), and the Aramaic word, *Elah*.

Ansar   "Helpers." Converts to Islam who lived in Medina and assisted the Prophet and the Meccan refugees who came with him.

aqiqah   The ritual for welcoming a baby into the world.

Asma' ul Husna   "The Most Beautiful Names." A list of the 99 names of God through which Muslims understand what God's nature is like.

assalamu alaykum   "Peace be upon you." The Muslim greeting of peace. The reply is, *"Wa alaykum assalam,"* "And upon you be peace."

ayah   "A sign." The term for a verse of the Qur'an.

Ayatullah   "Sign of God." The generic title for a major Shi'a cleric.

azan   The Muslim call to prayer consisting of several religious statements.

Bani Isra'il   The Children of Israel.

Barzakh   "The partition." The time between death and the resurrection. The
___ ___ ___ dead are in a stored state and are either dreaming pleasantly or being
___ ___ ___ d upon their faith and deeds while in the world.

___ ___ ___ ___ anti-Christ. It literally means *the Liar*.

dhikr (*ziker*)   Remembering God through repeating religious phrases. This is the
Muslim version of the rosary.

du'a   Supplication, personal requests to God.

'Eid ul adha   The Islamic holiday at the end of the *Hajj*.

'Eid ul Fitr   The Islamic holiday at the end of the fast of *Ramadan*.

Esa   The Islamic name for Jesus.

fatwa   A legal ruling by a competent Islamic legal scholar. Fatwas can be challenged
or overruled and are not automatically binding on the community.

fiqh   Understanding the application of the Islamic Law and how to formulate new
rulings.

fitrah   The inner moral compass that all humans are born with. People can become
influenced by it to seek God, or they can consciously bury it under a load of sin and
denial.

hadith   "An account." Any saying by, or action attributed to, the Prophet
Muhammad.

hafiz   "Guardian." A person who has memorized the entire Qur'an by heart.

Hajj   "Pilgrimage." The annual pilgrimage to Mecca, which takes place in the
twelfth month of the Islamic lunar calendar. All Muslims must make this journey
once in a lifetime if they are physically able and can afford to do so.

Hajji   "Pilgrim." The honorific title given to the person who has completed the
Islamic pilgrimage ritual.

halal   Allowed food to eat or activity to engage in.

haram   Forbidden food to consume or activity to engage in.

hijab   The head scarf worn over the hair.

Hijrah   The migration of Muhammad and his followers from hostile Mecca to
friendly Medina in 622. The Muslim calendar was later given this year as its start.

Iblis   "Frustrated." The proper name of Satan before he turned to evil.

Ibrahim   The Islamic name for Abraham.

ijtihad   Using independent thought to create a new Islamic legal opinion for an issue that has no clear answer in the two main sources of Islam.

Imam   "Leader." In Sunni Islam, it denotes primarily the person who leads the congregational prayers. In Shi'a Islam, it is the title of the supreme guides from God who were direct descendants of the Prophet through the marriage of his cousin, Ali, and his daughter, Fatimah.

Iman (Ee maan)   The term for faith or belief. English spelling is *Eman* or *Eemaan*.

Injeel   The Arabic name for the Gospel or *Evangel* of Jesus.

Islam (Iss laam)   "Surrendering to God and attaining peace." The Arabic name for the religion taught by Muhammad.

Jahannum   The name for Hell.

Janazah   Funeral rites in Islam.

Jannah   "Garden." Heaven or Paradise.

jihad   "To struggle, strive, or exert." Often mistranslated as holy war, this term can apply to any exertion in God's cause. Examples range from going to school or a woman making the *Hajj* to fighting a just war or even giving up a bad habit.

jinn   "Hidden ones." The term used for a class of invisible spirits that inhabit another dimension. They can communicate with us only through our minds. There are good and evil jinn. The caricature of the genie is based on this creature.

Jum'uah   "Gathering." Friday, the day for the congregational prayer.

Ka'bah   The cube-shape shrine in Mecca built originally by the Prophet Abraham. All Muslims pray in the direction of this shrine out of respect for Abraham and to affirm monotheistic unity.

kafir   "One who hides or covers the truth." Often mistranslated as unbeliever. Plural: *Kuffar*.

Khalifa   "Caretaker." The term for the supreme leader of the Muslim community after the passing of the Prophet. Spelled as *caliph* in English.

Kharajites   "The seceders." The ultra-purist faction that rebelled against the fourth Caliph, Ali ibn Ali Talib. Plural: *Khawarij*.

Khatmi Qur'an The name of the ceremony celebrating a child's first completion of reading the entire Qur'an. Also called an *Ameen* ceremony.

khul' A wife-initiated divorce.

Kiswah The embroidered black cloth that covers the Ka'bah in Mecca. It is replaced with a new one each year.

Mahdi The awaited hero who will rally the oppressed Muslims of the Earth to victory in the end-of-time. For Shi'a Muslims, he is the savior who will make Shi'aism transcendent.

Masih The Messiah. A term attributed to Jesus in the Qur'an. He was meant to be the Messiah for the Jewish people.

masjid "Place of prostration." The proper name for a Muslim house of worship in the Arabic language.

Masjid al Haram "The Restricted Mosque." Another name for the Ka'bah and the mosque that surrounds it. Many restrictions apply to a person who enters this mosque, such as the person must not kill any living thing, even a bug; and the person must be in a purified state.

Masjid an Nabawi The Prophet's mosque in Medina.

Maulid un-Nabi The birthday of the Prophet Muhammad. This widely celebrated holiday is controversial in some Islamic circles because it has no sanction from the main Islamic sources.

Mecca (Makkah) A city in southwestern Arabia founded by Abraham's wife Hagar and their son Ishmael. An important religious shrine is located there, and it is the birthplace of Muhammad.

Medina (*Madeena*) "City." Formerly known as *Yathrib*, this city became the first capital of Islam in 622, when Muhammad and his persecuted followers fled Mecca. Also spelled *Madinah*.

mosque The English term for an Islamic house of worship.

muazzin The person who gives the Muslim call to prayer five times daily from the minaret of a mosque.

Muhajirun The Meccan Muslims who fled to Medina during the Hijrah. Literally means *the immigrants*.

Muhammadanism   The name Europeans gave to the religion of Islam in the seventeenth century, thinking that Muslims worshipped Muhammad as God.

mujahid   A person who engages in *jihad*. Plural: *mujahideen*.

munafiq   A hypocrite.

mushrik   An idolater.

Muslim   "A person who is surrendering to God and finding peace." A follower of the religion of Islam.

nafs   The Islamic term for the *id*, or self. The real you; your personality and character.

nikah   The Islamic marriage ceremony.

Qur'an (Kuur an)   "The Reading or Recital." It is the name of the Islamic Holy Book. Muslims believe it is the direct word of God, delivered to Muhammad by an angel in small portions from the years 610 to 623 c.e. Also spelled *Koran*.

Ramadan (Rama Dan)   The ninth month of the Islamic lunar calendar. Muslims observe a dawn-to-dusk fast for the 29 or 30 days of this month.

sadaqa   Charity that is done for extra merit from God.

Sahaba   Companions of the Prophet. The people who accepted Islam and saw or heard the Prophet directly. They are our "primary sources."

salat   "Red-hot connection." The ritual Islamic prayers performed five times daily. Also spelled *Salah*.

Saum   Fasting. Also spelled *Siyam*.

Shahadah   "To witness or testify." The Muslim statement of belief: I declare that there is no god but Allah, and I declare that Muhammad is the Messenger of Allah.

shaheed   A martyr.

Shari'ah (*Shareeya*)   "The path." The term for Islamic Law.

Shaykh   "Respected elder or chief." Among Sunnis, it is commonly used as the title for a religious scholar. Also spelled *sheikh* or *sheik*.

Shaytan   "To pull away from." Satan in Arabic.

Shi'a   The second-largest sect of Islam. Shi'as claim that Muhammad's son-in-law, Ali, and his descendants are the only rightful rulers of the community.

shirk "Associating." Making others equal to God. The only unforgivable sin if a person dies while doing it.

Sufi The mystics of Islam.

Suhuf (*Soo hoof*) The Islamic name for the revealed scrolls of the Prophet Abraham. Literal meaning: scrolls or sheaf of leaves.

Sunnah The example of the Prophet Muhammad as contained in his *hadiths*, or sayings, including his actions and silent approval of actions done in his presence.

Sunni The largest sect of Islam that claims to follow the example of Muhammad and his companions.

surah (*Soo ra*) "A step-up or gate." The name for a chapter of the Qur'an.

talaq A husband-initiated divorce.

taqwa The conscious awareness that God is watching you.

Tariqa A Sufi lodge.

Taurah (*Taw rah*) The Arabic name for the Torah of Moses.

'ulema *See* alim.

Ummah The Muslim community or motherland.

wali The woman's representative during the courtship period. His or her job is to make sure the prospective groom is legitimate and will not take advantage of the woman.

walima The wedding reception after a marriage ceremony.

wudu The Islamic practice of washing the face, hands, and feet with water to achieve a ritually pure state.

Yathrib The former name of the city of Medina.

Zabur (*Za boor*) The Arabic name for the Psalms of David.

Zakah "Purification." The annual required charity from all Muslim adults in the amount of 2½ percent of one's yearly average savings after any debts have been discharged.

Further Reading

Now that you have taken your first look into the world of Islam, you might want to know more about a particular area or delve deeper into the philosophy, culture, or history of Islam. As you may have noticed, Islamic beliefs and teachings are not so complicated that it is impossible to gain a great amount of understanding. In fact, Islam has often been praised for its simplicity, directness, and explicability.

These qualities don't mean, however, that Islam is a lightweight subject or that there isn't a lot more to know and discover. On the contrary, within the pages of the Qur'an and Hadith books are myriad ideas, concepts, and meanings that invite further study. The history of Islamic civilization down to our present day is filled with hard-earned treasures of knowledge that make the Islamic experience even more rewarding and satisfying. In addition, Muslim folklore, fiction, philosophical essays, and religious commentary present a fascinating journey for the traveler thirsty for adventure, reflection, and challenge.

The Holy Qur'an (in English)

The best place to continue your journey, of course, is with the Holy Qur'an. While many translations of the Arabic text into English are available, some are more clearly translated than others. The most commonly accepted translations in the English world today are these:

The Meaning of the Holy Qur'an, translated by Abdullah Yusuf Ali. Beltsville: Amana Publications, 1995.

The Holy Qur'an in Today's English, translated by Yahiya Emerick. Charleston: Createspace, 2010.

The Message of the Qur'an, translated by Muhammad Asad. Chicago: Kazi Publications, 1980.

The Hadiths

For books of the Prophet's sayings, or *Hadiths*, I recommend any of these:

An-Nawawi, Imam Yahya. *Riyadh us Saliheen.* Translated by S. M. Madni Abbasi. Karachi: International Islamic Publishers, 1986.

Bukhari, Muhammad. *Imam Bukhari's Book of Muslim Morals and Manners.* Translated by Yusuf Talal DeLorenzo. Alexandria: Al-Saadawi Publications, 1997.

Khan, Maulana Wahiduddin. *An Islamic Treasury of Virtues.* New Delphi: Goodword Books, 1999.

Books About Islam

For excellent books about Islam, the Prophet Muhammad, and related topics, I recommend the following sources:

Abdul-Mateen, Ibrahim. *Green Deen: What Islam Teaches about Protecting the Planet.* San Francisco: Berret-Koehler Publishers, 2010.

Ali, Tariq. *The Clash of Fundamentalisms: Crusades, Jihads and Modernity.* New York: Verso Books, 2003.

Al-Ghazali, Abu Hamid Muhammad. *Remembrance of Death and the Afterlife.* Translated by T. J. Winter. Cambridge, U.K.: The Islamic Texts Society, 1995.

Al-Qaradawi, Yusuf. *The Lawful and Prohibited in Islam.* Indianapolis: American Trust Publications, 1999.

Anway, Carol. *Daughters of Another Path.* Lee's Summit: Yawna Publications, 1995.

Bendinar, Elmer. *The Rise and Fall of Paradise: When Arabs and Jews Built a Kingdom in Spain.* New York City: Barnes & Noble Books, 1983.

Bucaille, Maurice. *The Bible, the Qur'an and Science.* Indianapolis: North American Trust Publication, 1978.

Dirks, Debra. *Our Choice: Portraits of Modern American Muslim Women.* Beltsville: Amana Publications, 2003.

Dirks, Jerald. *The Cross & the Crescent.* Beltsville: Amana Publications, 2001.

Doi, Abdur Rahman I. *Shari'ah: The Islamic Law.* London: Ta Ha Publishers, 1984.

Dunn, Ross E. *The Adventures of Ibn Battuta.* Berkeley: University of California Press, 1986.

Ebrahim, Abul Fadl Mohsin. *Abortion, Birth Control & Surrogate Parenting: An Islamic Perspective.* Indianapolis: American Trust Publications, 1989.

Emerick, Yahiya. *Muhammad.* Indianapolis: Alpha Books, 2002.

Feldman, Noah. *After Jihad: America and the Struggle for Islamic Democracy.* New York City: Farrar Straus & Giroux, 2003.

Fernea, Elizabeth W. *In Search of Islamic Feminism.* New York City: Doubleday, 1998.

Green, Joey. *Jesus and Muhammad: The Parallel Sayings.* Berkeley: Ulysses Press, 2002.

Haddad, Yvonne, and Jane I. Smith. *Muslim Communities in North America.* New York City: State University of New York Press, 1994.

Hariri-Wendel, Tanja. *Symbols of Islam.* New York City: Sterling Publishing Co., 1999.

Khalidi, Tarif. *The Muslim Jesus: Sayings and Stories in Islamic Literature.* Cambridge: Harvard University Press, 2003.

Lang, Jeffrey. *Struggling to Surrender.* Beltsville: Amana Publications, 1994.

———. *Even Angels Ask.* Beltsville: Amana Publications, 1997.

Lings, Martin. *Muhammad: His Life Based on the Earliest Sources.* Rochester: Inner Traditions International, Ltd., 1983.

Maqsood, Ruqaiyyah Waris. *A Basic Dictionary of Islam.* New Delphi: Goodword Books, 1998.

———. *After Death, Life.* New Delphi: Goodword Books, 1998.

———. *The Muslim Marriage Guide.* New Delphi: Goodword Books, 1999.

Mattson, Ingrid. *The Story of the Qur'an.* Hoboken: Wiley-Blackwell, 2007.

Moore, Keith L. *The Qur'an and Modern Science: Correlation Studies.* Makkah: WAMY, 1990.

Omid, Safi. *Progressive Muslims: On Justice, Gender, and Pluralism.* Oxford: Oneworld Publications, 2003.

Qadhi, Abu Ammaar Yasir. *An Introduction to the Sciences of the Qur'aan.* Birmingham: Al-Hidaayah Publishing and Distribution, 1999.

Rauf, Feisal Abdul. *Islam: A Sacred Law.* Putney: Qiblah Books, 2000.

Sarwar, Shaykh Muhammad. *The Complete Idiot's Guide to the Koran.* Indianapolis: Alpha Books, 2003.

Schimmel, Annemarie. *My Soul Is a Woman: the Feminine in Islam.* New York City: Continuum, 1997.

Sells, Michael. *Approaching the Qur'an.* Ashland: White Cloud Press, 1999.

Sells, Michael, and Emran Qureshi. *The New Crusades: Constructing the Muslim Enemy.* New York City: Columbia University Press, 2003.

Stowasser, Barbara Freyer. *Women in the Qur'an, Traditions, and Interpretation.* New York City: Oxford University Press, 1994.

Wintle, Justin. *The Rough Guide History of Islam.* London: Rough Guides Ltd, 2003.

Islamic Non-Fiction, Fiction, and Poetry

Leisure reading from the world of Islam is a not-to-be-missed experience! Here are some very enjoyable books, both classic and modern, to feast your mind on:

Ali, Tariq. *Shadows of the Pomegranate Tree.* New York City: Verso Books, 1996.

———. *The Book of Saladin: A Novel.* New York City: Verso Books, 1999.

Al-Ghazali, Abu Hamid Muhammad. *The Alchemy of Happiness.* London: The Octagon Press, 1983.

Asad, Muhammad. *The Road to Mecca.* Gibraltar: Dar Al-Andalus, 1980.

Attar, Fariduddin. *The Conference of Birds.* New York City: Penguin, 1995.

Baig, Reshma. *The Memory of Hands.* New York City: International Books and Tapes Supply, 1999.

Burton, Sir Richard. *The Arabian Nights.* New York City: The Modern Library, 1932.

Emerick, Yahiya. *The Complete Idiot's Guide to Rumi Meditations.* Indianapolis: Alpha Books, 2008.

Hafiz, Shamsuddin Muhammad. *The Gift: Poems by Hafiz*. Translated by Daniel Ladinsky. New York City: Penguin, 1999.

Haley, Alex. *The Autobiography of Malcolm X*. New York City: Ballantine Books, 1978.

Helminski, Kabir and Camille. *Jewels of Remembrance, Poems of Rumi*. Putney: Threshold Books, 1996.

Irwin, Robert. *Night & Horses & the Desert: An Anthology of Classical Arabic Literature*. New York City: Anchor, 2002.

Shah, Idris. *The Exploits of the Incomparable Mulla Nasrudin*. London: The Octagon Press, 1993.

Wolfe, Michael. *One Thousand Roads to Mecca*. New York City: Grove Press, 1997.

Index

B

end of the world, 94
   false prophets, 97-99
   final day, 100-101
   Gog/Magog invasion, 99
   Jesus, 99
   prophecies, 95-96
   signs, 96-97
enlightenment, 298
equality of people, 91
equality of women
   improving, 216
   protection laws, 216
   struggle, 215-216
   teachings, 214-215
European colonialism, 174, 274-275
European languages, 283
expectations of normal lives, 51

F

Faith Listed in Detail. *See* Emanul Mufassil
Fajr, 114
false prophets, 97-99
family
   births, 206
   community ties, 201
   fathers' roles, 201
   marriages, 205
   men as caretakers, 200
   Muhammad's experiences, 200
   Qur'an's description, 200
   raising children, 202
   women's roles, 200-201
fard, 106
Farewell Speech of Muhammad, 252
fasting, 125-128
fears, 12
Festival of Fast Breaking, 128, 207
fighting, 142
Fiqh, 195
first Islamic state, 244

fitrah, 20-22
Five Pillars of Islam, 106-107
  Hajj, 132
    animal sacrifice, 138-139
    beginning, 136
    cutting of hair, 139
    encircling, 136
    ending, 139
    Ka'bah, 132
    male garments, 135
    Mina plain, 138
    Muzdalifah, 138
    origins of Mecca, 132-133
    Plain of Arafah, 138
    purpose, 134
    rewards, 134
    Station of Abraham, 137
    stoning Shaytan, 138
    'Umrah, 135
    walking the hills, 137
    Well of Zam Zam, 137
  salat, 114
    bowing, 116
    calling people to prayer, 115-116
    congregrational, 119
    differences, 117
    exceptions, 114
    humbleness, 117
    morning Salatul-Fajr procedure, 117-119
    prayer times, 114
    purpose, 116
    separating men and women, 119
  Saum, 125-128
  Shahadah, 107
    affirmation, 109-110
    benefits, 107
    conversions to Islam, 111
    monotheism, 108
    negation, 108
  zakat
    collecting, 125
    greed, 124

L

M

N-O

P

CHECK OUT
THESE BEST-SELLERS

More than 450 titles available at booksellers and online retailers everywhere!

978-1-59257-115-4

978-1-59257-900-6

978-1-59257-855-9

978-1-59257-222-9

978-1-59257-957-0

978-1-59257-785-9

978-1-59257-471-1

978-1-59257-483-4

978-1-59257-883-2

978-1-59257-966-2

978-1-59257-908-2

978-1-59257-786-6

978-1-59257-954-9

978-1-59257-437-7

978-1-59257-888-7

ALPHA   idiotsguides.com